B. P. Pratten

Proceedings of the Fifth Annual Meeting of the United Typothetae of America

Held on October 20th, 21st and 22nd, 1891, in the Scottish Rite Cathedral,

Cincinnati, O.

B. P. Pratten

Proceedings of the Fifth Annual Meeting of the United Typothetae of America
Held on October 20th, 21st and 22nd, 1891, in the Scottish Rite Cathedral, Cincinnati, O.

ISBN/EAN: 9783337241391

Printed in Europe, USA, Canada, Australia, Japan

Cover: Foto ©Lupo / pixelio.de

More available books at **www.hansebooks.com**

PROCEEDINGS

OF THE

FIFTH ANNUAL MEETING

OF THE

United Typothetæ of America

HELD ON

October 20th, 21st and 22d, 1891,

IN THE

SCOTTISH RITE CATHEDRAL,

CINCINNATI, O.

EVERETT WADDEY CO., PRINTERS, RICHMOND, VA.

UNITED TYPOTHETÆ OF AMERICA.

OFFICERS FOR 1891-'92.

PRESIDENT,

W. A. SHEPARD, Toronto, Ont.

SECRETARY,

EVERETT WADDEY, Richmond, Va.

TREASURER,

CHAS. BUSS, Cincinnati, O.

VICE-PRESIDENTS:

E. R. ANDREWS, *First Vice-President*,
Rochester, N. Y.

J. S. CUSHING, *Second Vice-President*,
Boston, Mass.

L. D. MYERS, *Third Vice-President*,
Columbus, O.

GEO. M. COURTS, *Fourth Vice-President*,
Galveston, Tex.

AI ROLLINS, *Fifth Vice-President*,
San Francisco, Cal.

E. G. O'CONNOR, *Sixth Vice-President*,
Montreal, Quebec.

EXECUTIVE COMMITTEE:

AMOS PETTIBONE, *Chairman*,
Chicago, Ill.

THEO. L. DEVINNE,
New York.

C. S. MOREHOUSE,
New Haven, Conn.

W. H. WOODWARD,
St. Louis, Mo.

WM. H. BATES,
Memphis, Tenn.

A. M. GEESAMAN,
Minneapolis, Minn.

WM. S. FISH,
Indianapolis, Ind.

UNITED TYPOTHETÆ OF AMERICA.

FIFTH ANNUAL MEETING.

FIRST DAY'S PROCEEDINGS.

The Fifth Annual Meeting of the United Typothetæ of America began in the Scottish Rite Cathedral, Cincinnati, Ohio, on Tuesday, October 20, 1891, at 10 o'clock A. M., being called to order by the President, A. H. Pugh, Esq., of Cincinnati.

The PRESIDENT. Gentlemen, I will now call to order the Fifth Annual Session of the Typothetæ of America, and I would be very much pleased, indeed, if the gentlemen who are vice-presidents and who are present would take their seats on the stage, and also Messrs. DeVinne, Rockwell and McNally, our former presidents. The President of the Cincinnati Typothetæ, Mr. C. J. Krehbiel, will now address you in a few words of welcome at the opening of this Convention.

Address of Welcome of President Krehbiel.

Mr. President and Gentlemen of the United Typothetæ of America:

You are familiar no doubt with the beautiful German salutation, "Gott grüsze Dich"—God greet you—and with that other and equally beautiful salutation of the German printer, "Gott grüsze die Kunst"—God greet the art. These greetings, so beautiful in significance, so cordial in sentiment and feeling, so reverential, Cincinnati would extend to you, most worthy exemplars of the art preservative, to-day. We greet you, and bid you welcome to our city, to our work-shops, to our hearts, and our homes. Words of mine can convey to you but faintly how highly we appreciate the honor which your presence here to-day implies; for in greeting you we feel that we meet the master minds, the embodied and concentrated experience, and the highest wisdom and business capacity of our craft; men familiar with the management of large enterprises, and into whose keeping may safely be intrusted the welfare of their associates and of the thousands in their employ.

In the treatment of the very important questions which will come before you, we feel that you will be calm, deliberate and wise—without passion, prejudice or fear—and that you will accord the same rights and privileges to others that you would demand for yourselves.

Our association was formed for the avowed purpose of "developing a community of interests and a fraternal spirit, and of exchanging information and assisting each other when necessary." These are lofty sentiments and purposes, and the meeting of a body bound by such aims as these is a wholesome and desirable influence in any community. So long as we maintain the standard we have set in our declaration of principles, so long shall we be able to rejoice in an organization perfect in adaptation and grand in its aims and purposes.

Last year Mr. Houghton gave you with a poetic touch the picture of two horsemen, one ascending and the other descending the globe, with the legend "You must increase and we must decrease." You have come to the section that has been and still is on the increase—for the past two decades the very centre of population of the country—the land which, in the mind of the people of a century ago, was a veritable Arcadia, over which shone refulgent the Star of Hope; the land so rich in soil and salubrious in clime, that red raspberries and strawberries grew so thick in the wilderness that they dyed the legs of the surveyors' horses crimson. It is the land where Boone and Wetzel hunted the fat red deer and outwitted their wily red foes—the land surveyed by Ludlow, and Filson the pedagogue, whose prophecy—

"Ere three score years have run
Our town shall be a city vast,"

has been fulfilled, despite the doubts and jeers of his companions, Denman and Patterson. We are proud of our city and believe in her great future. We are proud of her magnificent public institutions, and particularly of our public-spirited, high-minded, liberal citizens, the founders of the Music Hall, McMicken University, Art Museum, Exposition buildings, Young Men's Christian Association, and the various charitable institutions, and of our public schools. We are proud of our Chamber of Commerce, of our new city buildings, of our Armory, of our parks, and of our beautiful suburbs and Zoological Garden—all of which we hope to show you tomorrow, weather permitting—and of our Southern Railroad, which is owned entirely by Cincinnati, and which bids fair, under careful management, to make the city a municipality the equal in point of wealth of any other in the country. We are proud, also, of our magnificent business enterprises and institutions, especially those belonging to our own craft, two or three of which at least are not surpassed in amount of business by any others in the country.

There are some things we are not proud of, but of those we don't wish to speak.

Like ancient Rome, our city sits upon her seven hills, and in some measure at least,

> "From her throne of beauty rules the world,"

for is she not in her regal beauty indeed the—

> "Queen of the West
> In garlands dressed
> On the banks of the beautiful river"?

Our worthy President has admonished me to be brief, and has intimated rather broadly that we are here for work. And so we are. But Cincinnati, appreciating the courtesies that have been extended to her representatives in Chicago, New York, St. Louis and Boston in former years, and desiring to redeem the obligation which you have thus placed upon her as far as is in her power by every act of courteous, attentive and affectionate hospitality, has arranged a programme for your entertainment, which we hope you will enter into as heartily as you have always done. When we were all boys at school we had our hours of play sandwiched in between hours of study. And how heartily did we enjoy those play hours! With what *abandon* did we give ourselves over to healthful sport and rollicking mirth, till the blood went bounding through the veins, instilling new life and energy, and making lighter the tasks that were to follow. We are but children of larger growth, and amenable to the same influences. Let us, then, after our hours of work enjoy our recess heartily. We promise to lead you into no wrong-doings, for having had you in our hearts and on our minds for several months, we do not wish to have you on our consciences after you are gone.

Gentlemen, Cincinnati welcomes you and wishes you a harmonious session, in every respect pleasurable and profitable to yourselves, and fruitful in good results to the craft.

The President then delivered his address as follows:

GENTLEMEN : I desire to congratulate you upon meeting once more, and that we do not have to face an extraordinary exigency like that which confronted us when our organization was formed in Chicago; and though there seemed as large a cloud in the horizon as in the fall of 1887, there was no strike called in any city east of the Pacific coast where there was a Typothetæ organization.

Our immunity was due, I think, to the fact that our local organizations have been so well constituted, and managed so conservatively during the past year. At a meeting of the International Typographical Union in June, at Boston, a resolution was passed putting it to a vote of the various Typographical Unions throughout the country, that on and after the 1st of October, nine hours should constitute a day's work, and it seemed as if we would be called upon again to face the troubles that many of us had to undergo during the nine hour strike in 1887.

From a correspondence with the various members of the Executive Committee, it was thought advisable to call a meeting of the Executive Committee in the early part of July; and on the 17th of that month the entire committee met at the Gibson House in this city to take up, amongst other subjects, the question as to what would be the most desirable course to pursue to combat this effort to shorten the hours of labor. In various sections of the country resolutions were passed by our local Typothetæ to the purport that it would be advisable for the national body to meet at some early date in September, and it was with much concern that this matter was carefully discussed at that meeting. The result of their deliberations will be presented to you in the very comprehensive report of the chairman of that committee.

Instead of the overwhelming majority that the Typographical Unions anticipated would be voted in favor of this resolution, there were not enough votes cast in favor of it to carry it. By reference to the *Typographical Journal*, the official paper of the Typographical Union, of September 15th, 1891, I note that in twenty Unions, comprising the leading cities of the country, there was a total vote of 3,985 in favor, and 1,257 opposed to this question; yet, when we analyze this vote it will be seen that its influence lessens considerably, as these votes were cast out of a total membership in these twenty Unions of 13,483, being less than thirty per cent.; and of a total membership of 33,074, the total number of votes in favor are 9,340, or twenty-eight per cent., and 148 Unions did not cast a vote either way. In the language of a correspondent of this *Journal:* "We ought to feel thankful that we did not enter into a Waterloo." That the organizations of the local Typothetæ had something to do with this, I will quote what this writer further says: "And then there is the Typothetæ, stronger by far than it was four years ago, and united in its opposition to the nine-hour day. Of this fact, very little was thought in the action last June. Evidently it did not strike the late Convention that it takes two parties to make a bargain, but it is time that recognition were made that we have employers, and that there must be employers to carry on any business. There are rights on both sides to be respected, and with us, the one-sided business should come to an end, if we expect to gain anything in the nine-hour move."

On principle, I believe printers are very strongly in favor of nine hours as a working day. I believe the proprietors recognize that opinion, and were they assured that it would be generally carried out, and in the jurisdiction of our organization nine hours was the rule in practice, much of their opposition would vanish, but it is because they do not see the way to that realization that united opposition is now taken. And the Typothetæ, through its Executive Committee at its late meeting, presented this, as I call it, fair proposition:

"While we recommend opposition to this nine-hour rule, which has been made exclusively by the employed, without a proper knowledge of the conditions of the trade, we are ready to unite with the employees of our respective offices in any feasible attempt to secure a common advantage by means of mutual concession."

I think that this correspondence fairly represents the feeling of those craftsmen who are a credit to their trade. I think the results of the meeting of the Executive Committee, and the advertisements which they caused to be inserted in the newspapers throughout the country, had much to do with this action of the various Typographical Unions throughout the country, and the defeat of the effort to reduce the number of hours of labor at the present time. Still, I think the subject of shorter hours for a working day is one, which, like Banquo's ghost, "will not down," and in some form or other will come up until by mutual concession the employer and employee will come to an agreement. If our organization carries out that spirit of progress and conservation upon which it was founded, and would take this matter up and declare as one of its principles that it was not opposed to the shorter day, provided a concession would be made by the employee, and that at some future day the various members of this organization throughout the country would put a shorter day into effect, it would disarm a class of people who are continually agitating this subject. I trust that no sense of delicacy will prevent there being a free discussion of this subject, as it certainly is one of the greatest importance.

In connection with other information sought for, there has been sent to your President a general summary of the value of the printing plants of members of our organization, and it is with a feeling of pride that I point to the fact that there is invested over $50,000,000 in the plants owned by members of your association. Now the question arises, what is the best manner to protect this property so as to insure a fair return on the investment, as well as a fair compensation for the employee? What method of instruction is the best to fill our offices with a class of labor that will add to their advantage, both financially and artistically, in the art preservative? Each year, in the addresses of your able Presidents, the subject of a form of apprenticeship has been presented and referred to a committee to report upon, and no doubt in each local organization the same subject has formed an important subject for discussion, and some form or other of apprenticeship has been introduced or adopted; and yet we reach no nearer the point of the best method of educating this labor. Neither the employer nor the employee is willing to sign it—the employer to obligate himself to educate the apprentice, and take care of him for a certain number of years, and when this education is completed, fondly imagine that he will have a better class of labor than he has had; that this has not been carried into effect must be due to the fact that experience teaches the employer that this will not be the result, and the cost of manufacturing this labor is more than he realizes from it.

Now the question arises in my mind, whether labor should not be placed upon the same plane as paper, ink, machinery, and other articles of merchandise we buy. Would it not pay to buy good labor? Would there not be a supply of good labor when it was understood that labor could find a market? Would it not be more profitable for local Typothetæ to guarantee in a measure the cost of maintaining teachers of typography and press-work in a technical school? Or if it is not practicable to support a school devoted exclusively to that end with complete outfit of type, presses, etc., would it not be more economical to teach the boy this labor there than to pay the expense of educating it in a narrow sort of a way in one's own office, and after the term of apprenticeship was completed, to find that, on account of the associations formed in the course of that education, it has pledged itself to some society to go out on a strike whenever that society may see fit? Would not a higher class of labor be more self-reliant? Would it attach itself to associations in which the majority were ignorant and uneducated, and would it be willing to sacrifice a part of its wages in order to even up some tramp? I do not think there is an employer in our organization but would be willing to pay the very highest market value for the best class of labor, provided he did not have to pay an unwarranted amount for poor labor.

Of course, if labor itself would take this matter in charge and grade itself, giving a higher certificate to a man of a higher class, it would be much better. But in labor matters as in politics, the men who make a business of agitating comprise the majority, and the good man does not appear to be "in it," except when a vote is wanted.

I present this idea, which has not met, I am well aware, with the unqualified approval of my friends with whom I have discussed it, as a subject worthy your consideration.

One of the greatest difficulties we have to contend with in our business is that of ignorant competition. It is not so much the fact that the man is willing to cut his own throat by doing work for less than the work is worth, but it is because he is not fully educated to consider the various items which compose the bill of cost of the estimate he is about to give. He leaves out sometimes the cost of the paper, sometimes cost of press-work; he rarely, if ever, figures in the cost of rent, taxes, insurance, general office expenses, etc. He thinks if the composition costs 30 cents per hour, and he gets 50 cents, that his net return will be 20 cents per hour, or if Mr. Jones, who employs a foreman and book-keeper, charges $100, he can save these expenses and do it for $90. And yet it has been fully demonstrated, by a careful examination of the cost of doing business in the larger cities of the country, that the lowest rate per hour which gives any profit is 100 per cent. more than the man's time, and even at this rate, it is only by a very economical management and careful attention to detail that a profit can be shown. And would not a better educated class of labor prove to be a better class of competitors when they become managers and employers?

At the meeting in Boston last year a resolution was passed that the Chair appoint delegates to meet with such fraternal bodies as might send invitations, and I desire here to express the thanks of our organization to the American Newspaper Publishers' Association, which met in New York city in February, and to the National Editorial Association, which met in St. Paul in July last, for the very courteous treatment paid our representatives who met with them, and whose reports will be received at the proper time.

There is a subject which has been a matter of much concern and discouragement to those of your officers who have had occasion to seek information from the secretaries of the various local Typothetæ, and that is the difficulty they have had in securing replies to their correspondence. It would make the duties which devolve upon these officers much pleasanter and much more agreeable if the local organizations would appreciate the fact that this is a labor of love on their part, and that any repetitions in the matter of correspondence are very irksome.

There is still another very important subject which I think demands the attention of our Convention, and that is the meeting of the Executive Committee. Some plan should be formulated by this body at this meeting whereby the Executive Committee can be called together at such time or place as your President or the Chairman of the Executive Committee might find expedient. At present this works severe hardships upon that committee, as they are expected to meet all the expenses that they may be put to. By an examination of the residences of the members of the present Executive Committee, it will be observed that the average time taken for them to reach Cincinnati, which was the most central point at which the meeting could be called, was twenty-four hours. They were in session two days, continually at work, and with their railroad fares, sleeping-car fares and hotel bills, their average expenses were not less than $50 each. It will be necessary for some provision to be made for meetings of the Executive Committee in the future, providing for the necessary expenses the members of this committee are put to, such as railroad fare and hotel bills. It goes without saying that this body, representing as it does an industry of over $50,000,000, does not expect its Executive Committee to travel 600 or 700 miles and give five or six days of individual time for the benefit of individual members of the association, and pay their own expenses. As no provisions have been made in the Constitution for the payment of the expenses of any officer excepting the Secretary, a resolution was passed by the Cincinnati Typothetæ amending that section of the Constitution increasing the dues, in order to have a larger fund at the disposal of the national organization, so that the question as to funds to meet this expense would be answered.

It should be the aim of this organization to teach the employees that they have common interest with them, and the employee should understand that if the employer does not succeed, he cannot, and the employer should understand that if his workmen are not well taken care of, that he cannot succeed; that this is a conservative body, and not an organization for the purpose of making outrageous demands on the employee. It is not an organization for the purpose of resisting strikes, but for the purpose of softening as much as possible the asperities of competition, and discussing those subjects which best develop the trade.

In the words of welcome of the able president of the Boston Master Printers' Club, "let us act on this high basis; let us seek to elevate our own profession; let us seek to elevate and look after the interests of every one connected with us, and then we cannot fail, but prosper, and we cannot fail to enjoy one of the greatest professions God has ever given mankind."

Before I close, there is one matter I yet wish to touch upon; it is with feelings of the deepest respect I refer to those of our delegates who have met with us in the past; I refer to the deaths I have been apprised of during the past year: H. G. Schepker, of Cincinnati, who was a delegate at the last convention in Boston; R. P. Studley, of St. Louis, one of our oldest and best known members, and last, but not least, our dear friend, Wm. C. Martin, of New York, whom we have met from year to year since our first meeting in Chicago. We will all call to mind with the greatest kindness and pleasure that tall form, that kindly air, ever beaming with goodwill and good advice. The impression he left upon us was clear cut, well made ready, and every line and shade brought out. I understand that the Typothetæ to whom these gentlemen belonged have passed resolutions of respect, and will have them presented at the proper time.

I trust you have borne patiently with me, and that you will not criticise too harshly what I have had to say. The gentlemen who have preceded me in the chair have been so able, so strong and so efficient that I fear you will judge me by too high a standard, and I crave your kind indulgence while occupying the chair.

The PRESIDENT. The first business before the meeting will be the matter of credentials of the members. It has been the custom, I believe, in former conventions, to take the book of register as the authorized list of delegates. If there is any delegate who has not registered, the book is here, and I would like to have the member register. What is your will in regard to the list of members?

Mr. BLAKELY, of Chicago. I presume that list or that register will be read for the information of the delegates, will it not?

The PRESIDENT. Yes, sir. The Secretary will read the register, subject to such amendments as the chairman of the delegation shall decide upon.

The Secretary then read the register, as follows:

Albany, N. Y.
C. F. Williams.   Jas. Taylor.

Boston, Mass.
Horace T. Rockwell.   W. S. Best.   F. H. Mudge.
J. Stearns Cushing.

Chattanooga, Tenn.
Frank McGowen.   E. W. Matson.

Chicago, Ill.
A. McNally.   Amos Pettibone.   Wm. Johnston.
Chas. E. Leonard.   Geo. E. Cole.   C. H. Blakely.
R. R. Donnelly.   P. F. Pettibone.   W. P. Dunn.
Thos. Knapp.   B. B. Herbert.

Cincinnati, O.
W. B. Carpenter.   Fred'k Spencer.   C. J. Krehbiel.
Chas. Buss.   J. F. Earhart.   Wm. A. Webb.
R. J. Morgan.   J. B. Davidson.

Dayton, O.
J. W. Johnson.   G. C. Wise.   Lewis G. Walker.
L. G. Reynolds.   L. D. Reynolds.   H. R. Groneweg.
                        Jno. Blum.

FIFTH ANNUAL MEETING.

Detroit, Mich.

Chas. M. Rousseau.	Jno. Boonman.	T. J. Williamson.
Jno. F. Eby.	Harry Winn.	

Indianapolis, Ind.

Wm. S. Fish.	H. O. Thudeum.	Sam'l J. Murray.
	W. B. Burfurd.	

Kansas City, Mo.

F. D. Crabb.		W. A. Lawton.

Louisville, Ky.

F. B. Converse.	Jas. Davidson.	S. H. Thomson.
	H. C. Wedekemper.	

Memphis, Tenn.

W. H. Bates.	Peter Tracy.	Thomas D. Taylor.
	Geo. S. Landis.	

Milwaukee, Wis.

N. L. Burdick.		H. H. Zahn.

Minneapolis, Minn.

A. M. Geesaman.	A. C. Bausman.	M. N. Price.
F. W. Nevins.	L. Kimball.	

Montreal.

E. G. O'Connor.		Joseph Fortier.

Nashville, Tenn.

J. H. Bruce.	Geo. B. Staddan.	C. H. Brandon.
	A. S. Ambrose.	

New Haven, Conn.

C. S. Morehouse.	Wm. H. Lee.	J. B. Carrington.
L. L. Morgan.	R. S. Peck.	

New York.

John Polhemus.	T. B. DeVinne.	Theo. L. DeVinne.
Howard Lockwood.	Rich'd R. Ridge.	Louis D. Gallison.
Francis E. Fitch.	Benj. H. Tyrrel.	Henry Bessey.
A. V. Haight.	Jno. C. Rankin.	Wm. J. Pell.
E. Parke Coby.	W. W. Pasko.	A. R. Hart.

Omaha, Neb.

Henry Gibson.	Julius Festner.	Samuel Rees.

Philadelphia, Pa.

Wm. B. MacKellar.	Chas. Eneu Johnson.	John W. Wallace.
C. R. Carver.	W. M. Patton.	

Providence, R. I.

E. A. Johnson.	Chas. C. Gray.	Benj. F. Briggs.

Richmond, Va.

Robert Whittet.	James E. Goode.

Troy, N. Y.

Charles C. Giles. *	E. H. Foster.	E. H. Lisk.

Rochester, N. Y.

E. R. Andrews.	Ernest Hart.	W. F. Balkam.

Galveston, Texas.

Geo. M. Courts.

St. Louis, Mo.

C. M. Skinner.	Edwin Freegard.	W. H. Woodward.
Sam Slawson.	W. J. Gilbert.	Richard Ennis.
Stewart Scott.	N. T. Gray.	W. B. Becktold.
	A. H. Witte.	

ALTERNATES.

Al. Lindsay.	Wm. Holtz.	C. B. Woodward.
C. A. Draeh.	Carl Schraubstadter.	John Tirrell.
C. W. Crutsinger.	F. O. Sawyer.	W. L. Becker.

St. Paul, Minn.

Geo. M. Stanchfield.	David Ramaley.	H. D. Brown.

Toronto, Canada.

W. A. Shepard.	Bruce Brough.	Jas. Murray.

Columbus, O.

L. D. Myers.	Geo. B. Hische.

Pittsburg, Pa.

Jos. Eichbaum.	Chas. A. Smith.	Theophilus Sproull.
P. F. Smith.	H. J. Murdoch.	Jno. I. Shaw.
	H. P. Pears.	

Washington, D. C.

Wm. F. Roberts.

Lafayette, Ind.
M. M. Mayerstein.

National Editorial Association.
A. S. Ochs, Chattanooga, Tenn.   B. J. Price, Hudson, Wis.
J. O. Ames, Sidney, Ohio.

Mr. REES, of Omaha. I move that the list as read be approved as the delegates, and that the officers be authorized to place on it the names of any delegates who present their credentials.

Seconded and carried.

Mr. BLAKELY. In the list from Chicago, I notice the name of Mr. Parker, which was read. Mr. Parker is here, and will present his credentials as representative of the Chicago Beneficial Association.

The PRESIDENT. Mr. Parker is here as a visitor, by courtesy, on the floor.

Mr. WADDEY, of Richmond. Richmond is only entitled to two delegates. I am not a delegate.

The PRESIDENT. Gentlemen, the next thing in order will be the report of the Corresponding Secretary, Mr. Waddey, of Richmond, Va.

Report of the Corresponding Secretary.

To the Officers and Members of the United Typothetæ of America:

As that clause in our Constitution which provides for the office of Corresponding Secretary makes it his duty to "give special attention to the organization of additional local societies, by furnishing information to persons and firms interested in the movement," it is, very properly, from his report that we should hope to hear encouraging tidings of the growth of our organization, of increased interest in those already established, and of the great hopes which we should entertain of the good to be accomplished in the future; and when I find, each year, that my report as Corresponding Secretary falls so far short of what it has been my hope that it would be, I feel that a mistake has, perhaps, been made by this association in the selection of the incumbent of that office.

It was very happily said on the floor of the Boston Convention last year, by one whose genial smile and kindly greeting are now drawn and hushed in the cold embrace of death, and whose vacant place creates a void in our hearts that no substitute can fill: "It never appeared to me to be a dignified position for us to take to urge those who know what the objects of the body are, or who do not know what the objects of the United Typothetæ or what the principles of the local organizations of it are, to enter into any of our schemes for the advancement of the interests of the trade. It seems to me what we propose to effect, or wish to effect, is to be done in a more dignified manner, by sending to their different cities, to the leading members of our profession, such documents, such reports and such papers as may be likely to affect them in regard to organizing for themselves." Acting upon this sentiment, and under the instructions of the Executive Committee to use my best judgment in forwarding the work of the organization of new branches of the United Typothetæ of America, I sent out nearly 2,800 copies of the Proceedings of the Fourth Annual Convention. Of these, 990 were sent to the secretaries of the various local Typothetæ for distribution to their members and those employing printers in their cities who were not members also, and 1,616 copies were mailed addressed individually to all employing printers rated as having $3,000 or more in ninety-four of the larger cities of the Union in which we have no organization. But the result was not such as to lead me to change my opinion that the majority of printers are fully convinced that they "know it all," or else that they are so afraid of each other as to be every one unwilling to take the first step, and hence the movement has never gotten started in the active, energetic manner hoped for.

In the cities of Dallas, Texas; Denver, Col.; Newark and Paterson, N. J.; Savannah, Ga., and St. Joseph, Mo., one or two members of the trade were awakened to an active interest in the subject, but their efforts have never yet materialized. In each and every case, after my earnest and best efforts had been expended and an offer made of a personal visit from the member of the Executive Committee residing nearest to the point from which the inquiry was made, there came back the sad refrain that the employing printers were so greedy in their competition and so anxious to "get even" that harmonious action was almost an impossibility.

Through the personal efforts of the President and Chairman of the Executive Committee the Indianapolis Typothetæ was organized with fourteen members. By correspondence from this office the Typothetæ at Lafayette, Ind., was organized with five members, and through the exigencies of a strike at Pittsburgh, Pa., the "Typothetæ of Pittsburgh, Alleghany and vicinity" has been organized with thirty members.

I am glad to be able to report that in nearly every instance in which a Typothetæ has been organized and once gotten in good working shape that, though the interest has sometimes flagged for a season, there is no case in which it has disbanded and in which it has not been productive of good results; and, while there are some seven or eight whose names are upon the list as having been organized in 1889, the correspondence of this office reveals the fact that they were never gotten thoroughly under way and should, therefore, by no means be counted as failures except in the perfecting of their organization.

One of the most encouraging reports that has reached this office comes from the Typothetæ of Chattanooga, Tenn., where, I am advised, a very excellent work has been done by the organization; a scale of prices has been adopted by the Typothetæ there which, while not obligatory on its members to adhere to, is recommended as the minimum at which the classes of work enumerated in it should be done. It occurs to me that this is a step in the right direction which is rather in advance of any that has come under my notice, inasmuch as, although no one can be accused of bad faith by a competitor who loses in the effort for work upon which several are bidders, the whole moral force of the organization is thrown in favor of a fair price; and he must be hard-grained indeed who would continuously violate an implied promise.

The circulars attached, received from the Typothetæ of St. Paul, Minn., and Troy, N. Y., upon the printing of envelopes by the United States Government, bring up anew the custom which has been condemned by every Annual Convention of the United Typothetæ of America since its organization, and leads me to make bold to suggest the appointment of a committee to appear before the Committee on Printing of the next Congress, or other proper authority, and urge, in the name of this association, the repeal of the law which authorizes the Post Office Department to do the work in question:

ST. PAUL, MINN., February 12, 1891.

At a regular meeting of the St. Paul Typothetæ, held this day, the following preamble and resolutions were unanimously adopted:

Gentlemen of the St. Paul Typothetæ:

Your committee to whom was referred the matter of the United States Government printing without charge, and delivering free to our customers, upwards of 200,000,000 envelopes yearly, the printing of which amounts to hundreds of thousands of dollars, and properly belongs to the job printers of the country, beg to report the following:

Whereas, Through the effects of this intermeddling the prices for printing envelopes have been brought down below the cost of labor, thereby closing the channels to which such work belongs—the job printers of the United States, and

Whereas, We have every reason to believe that this detriment to our business is growing, and that we are constantly losing work that properly belongs to us by this continued action of the Government, with which it is beyond our power to compete, and

Whereas, Believing the citizens of the United States are willing and desire to return an adequate compensation to the printers of the United States for such work properly executed; therefore be it

Resolved, By the Typothetæ of the city of St. Paul, an organization embracing all the employing printers (and a branch of the national organization), that a great injustice is done to a large body of workmen, by reason of Government interference in labor which properly belongs to the citizen; that the efforts of the employing printers are confronted by the ponderous power of the general Government in the furnishing of printed envelopes, making no charge for the printing, and forwarding the same in any quantity from Washington, free of expense to the consumer, thus rendering competition on the part of printers impracticable.

Resolved, That we earnestly appeal to the proper authorities to remedy this great and increasing evil.

Resolved, That a copy of these resolutions be sent to all the Typothetæ organizations, the Postmaster-General and to our Representatives in Congress assembled.

GEO. M. STANCHFIELD, *President.*

W. T. RICH, *Secretary.*

TROY, N. Y., March 9, 1891.

At a regular meeting of the Typothetæ of Troy, N. Y., held this day, the following preamble and resolutions were adopted:

Whereas, For years past the United States Government has furnished printed envelopes to any one desiring same at price only of envelopes—no charge whatever being made for printing—and the goods are also delivered freight free to any point in the United States; and

Whereas, Upward of two hundred million envelopes are yearly so furnished, the cost of printing which amounts to hundreds of thousands of dollars, which sum is a loss to the printers of the nation and a tax on the public, while only a small percentage of our citizens reap any benefit from such action of the authorities; and

Whereas, As the effect of this unbusiness-like policy on the part of the Government, the price for printing envelopes has been brought below the cost of labor, thereby working an injury to the job printers of the United States; and

Whereas, Believing that it is as unfair for the Government to do job printing for its citizens as it would be to engage in any mercantile or manufacturing enterprise, we protest against such a policy—it being an injustice to both printer and public; and

Whereas, We believe this detriment to our business is growing, and also believe that the citizens of the United States are willing to return an adequate compensation to the printers of the country for such work properly executed; therefore be it

Resolved, By the Typothetæ of Troy, N. Y., an organization embracing the employing printers of Troy, Cohoes, Lansingburgh and Waterford, that a foul injustice is done to a large body of workmen, as well as employing printers, by reason of the National Government printing envelopes and forwarding same from Washington to any part of the country free of charge, thus rendering competition impossible on the part of the printers of the country.

Resolved, That we earnestly appeal to the proper authorities to remedy this great and increasing evil.

Resolved, That a copy of these resolutions be sent to all Typothetæ organizations, to the Postmaster-General and to our Representatives in Congress.

HENRY STOWELL, *President.*

E. H. LISK, *Secretary.*

I also append a letter received from a committee appointed by the "Baltimore Yearly Meeting of Women Friends" asking its aid in securing the omission from the public press of "detail in the report of crimes, including murder, suicides, breaches of faith and honor," etc., which will have your hearty endorsement, although it may be beyond the power of this organization to lend more than its God-speed to the efforts which these noble women are making in behalf of the youth of the land in their endeavors to shield them from a debasing familiarity with vice as chronicled in the daily and weekly press all over the country.

To the United Typothetæ of America:

The members of the Baltimore Yearly Meeting of Women Friends, composed of representatives from Maryland, Virginia and Pennsylvania, realizing the power of the public press, and believing that this power possesses greater influence for the elevation of our people in virtue and morality than has yet been exerted, appeal to you to give your earnest attention to this matter and to devise some method by which this influence may be used most effectively. The omission of detail in reports of crime, including in these, suicides, scandals and breaches of faith and honor, appears to us the first step in this direction; and giving greater prominence to "whatsoever things are honest, just, pure, lovely and of good report" the second step.

As mothers and as guardians of youth, we are desirous of availing ourselves of the assistance of your publications in the home education of our children, but too often find the lessons for good they contain over-balanced by the lessons in evil. We ask also your earnest co-operation in arousing public sentiment to the demoralizing influence of many of the pictorial advertisements that defile the streets of our cities, and to our responsibility as citizens in this matter.

With heartfelt thanks for the aid you have given in works of philanthropy and reform, we are your sincere friends.

ISABELLA TYSON,
ESTHER LAMB,
MARY C. BLACKBURN,
ALICE C. ROBINSON,
Committee.

I cannot refrain from calling attention to the difficulties which attach to the satisfactory execution of the duties of this office, on account of the inattention of the officers of the local Typothetæ to inquiries and requests sent them from this office for information that we are compelled to have if our work is to be productive of results. The attempt to secure a list of the members of each Typothetæ in order that they might be published as an Appendix to the Proceedings of our last Annual Convention was a failure. Not more than one-half of your members responded, although repeatedly urged to do so. So too, an effort made by me in the last sixty days to secure a report of even the number of members of each Typothetæ has been responded to by only eighteen out of the fifty-six members of the national organization.

It may be interesting for you to know that since the last Annual Convention about 275 letters have been received and 385 letters written by this office, not including circular letters.

Respectfully submitted,
EVERETT WADDEY, *Cor. Sec'y.*

Mr. Gray, of St. Louis, moved that the report be received and accepted.

Mr. REES, of Omaha. I move that the report be referred to a committee of three to consider the recommendations that he makes.

The PRESIDENT. I think your resolution will be covered by the previous resolution, that all reports of officers be referred to a committee.

The motion of Mr. Gray was then put and carried.

The Recording Secretary, Mr. Becker, then read his report as follows:.

Report of Recording Secretary.

TO THE OFFICERS AND MEMBERS OF THE UNITED TYPOTHETÆ OF AMERICA:

Gentlemen—In accordance with instructions from your body, the following circular was mailed to all the membership of the United Typothetæ of America:

OFFICE RECORDING SECRETARY,
ST. LOUIS, August 28, 1891.

Dear Sir—At a meeting of the United Typothetæ of America, held in Boston in September last, Mr. Andrews offered the following resolution, which was adopted:

Resolved, That the several local Typothetæ be requested to furnish to the United Typothetæ of America a full list of their members, and that the Recording Secretary be directed to keep a record of such membership, and furnish copies to subordinate societies.

That I may be enabled to make this list complete, I request of you to send to me, as early as you can, a correct list of your entire membership. This does not contemplate each individual member of a firm, but only the firms or individuals comprising your society.

Your early attention to this request will be appreciated by,

Yours truly,
WM. L. BECKER, *Recording Sec'y*,
314 North Third street.

P. S.—It might be well to designate your officers.

This circular met with but very little response, and subsequently a second, and later a third notice was sent; these, together with a few personal letters, have resulted in my being able to present you with a list complete, with the exception of eight Typothetæ. These lists have been mailed to each member as far as list is completed. In this connection, I would like to say that too little attention is paid to communications by the different secretaries, as is evidenced by my circular dated June 15th, 1891, receiving its last response after the list had been printed, which necessitated an insert sheet as late as October 15, 1891.

On June 29, 1891, by notice from the Richmond Typothetæ, I issued the following circular:

OFFICE RECORDING SECRETARY,
ST. LOUIS, June 29, 1891.

Dear Sir—In accordance with Article IX. of the Constitution, notice is hereby given that the Typothetæ of Richmond, Va., will move the adoption of the report of the Committee on Revision of the Constitution of the United Typothetæ of America, at its next annual session, to be held in Cincinnati, October, 1891.

A copy of the report is herewith enclosed.

Yours truly,
WM. L. BECKER,
Recording Secretary.

Also, September 18th, by notice from the Typothetæ of Cincinnati, the following:

OFFICE RECORDING SECRETARY,
ST. LOUIS, September 18, 1891.

Dear Sir—In accordance with Article IX. of the Constitution, notice is hereby given that the Typothetæ of Cincinnati, Ohio, will move the adoption of the following resolution at the next annual session of the United Typothetæ of America, to be held in Cincinnati, October, 1891.

Resolved, That so much of Article VII. as refers to revenue, which reads: "as annual dues, a sum equal to one dollar for every one of its members," be changed to read, "as annual dues a sum equal to two dollars for every one of its members," that the revenues derived by the United Typothetæ of America be sufficient to cover such necessary expenses as should be incurred by the national organization.

Yours truly,
WM. L. BECKER,
Recording Secretary.

In conclusion, your Secretary would suggest that more attention be paid to communications from the United Typothetæ of America officers, thus very materially lessening their labors.

Respectfully submitted,
WM. L. BECKER.

On motion, the report was received and accepted.

The report of the Treasurer, Mr. A. O. Russell, was then read as follows:

Fourth Annual Report of the Treasurer of the United Typothetæ of America.

CINCINNATI, O., October 20, 1891.

Balance of cash on hand in general fund August 27, 1890, $206 05
Received since then the following initiation fees:

Sept. 26, 1890, Worcester Typothetæ	$10 00
" 26, " Montreal "	10 00
" 26, " Mobile "	10 00
" 26, " Toledo "	10 00
" 26, " Columbus, O., "	10 00
July 18, 1891, Indianapolis, "	10 00
Sept. 26, " Lafayette "	10 00
Oct. 16, " Pittsburg "	10 00
Total amount of initiation fees paid in	80 00

Regular annual dues were received during the current year as follows:

Sept. 26, 1890, Boston Master Printers' Club	$ 56 00
" 26, " Chicago Typothetæ	56 00
" 26, " Dayton "	11 00
Oct. 16, " Nashville "	10 00
Mch. 16, 1891, New Haven "	17 00
" 16, " Memphis "	14 00
" 20, " Dayton "	10 00
" 21, " St. Louis "	47 00
" 23, " Worcester, Mass., "	15 00
" 23, " New York "	62 00
April 4, " Troy "	17 00
" 4, " New Orleans "	16 00
" 15, " Toledo "	15 00
" 15, " Providence "	15 00
" 25, " Topeka "	5 00
" 25, " Albany "	14 00
Carry forward	$380 00 $286 05

UNITED TYPOTHETÆ OF AMERICA.

			Brought forward	$380	00	$286	05
April	25,	1890.	Washington, D. C., Typothetæ . .	7	00		
"	25,	"	Galveston " . .	5	00		
"	25,	"	Kansas City " . .	12	00		
"	25,	"	Detroit " . .	12	00		
May	2,	"	Rochester " . .	12	00		
"	8,	"	Omaha " . .	20	00		
"	21,	"	Boston " .	60	00		
"	22,	"	Minneapolis " . .	13	00		
June	11,	"	Portland, Ore., " . .	6	00		
"	15,	"	Philadelphia " . .	50	00		
"	25,	"	New Haven " . .	5	00		
July	6,	"	Toronto " . .	21	00		
"	6,	"	San Francisco " . .	25	00		
"	18,	"	Indianapolis " . .	14	00		
"	18,	"	St. Paul " . .	14	00		
"	23,	"	Cincinnati " .	31	00		
Sept.	4,	"	Chicago " . .	56	00		
"	4,	"	Nashville " . .	11	00		
"	4,	"	Milwaukee " . .	16	00		
"	21,	"	Louisville " . .	17	00		
"	26,	"	Richmond, Va., " . .	10	00		
Oct.	8,	"	Chattanooga " . .	10	00		
"	8,	"	Montreal (two years) " . .	20	00		
			Total amount of annual dues received . . .			827	00

Total am't cash (including above balance) rec'd to date, $1,113 05
Total amount of disbursements made from general fund
  during the current year, as per vouchers herewith..   918 36

Balance of cash on hand in general fund this date . $194 69

Am't of cash on hand in organization fund Aug. 27, 1890, $712 82
Oct. 31, 1890, received from Richmond Typothetæ . . .   89 00
" 20, 1891,   "   " New York "   . . .   95 00

   $896 82

Total amount of disbursements from organization fund
  during the current year, as per vouchers herewith . .   460 59

Balance on hand in organization fund this date . . . $436 23
Total amount of cash on hand in both organization and
  general funds $630 92

The following Typothetæ are in arrears for dues:
Little Rock Typothetæ owe for 1891.
Scranton Typothetæ owe for 1890 and 1891.
Fort Wayne Typothetæ paid their initiation fee May 24, 1889, but never paid any dues.
Seattle Typothetæ paid initiation July 5, 1890, but have paid no dues yet.
Mobile Typothetæ paid initiation fee September 26, 1890, but are in arrears for dues.
Columbus, O., Typothetæ also paid initiation fee September 26, 1890, but paid no dues.
All bills audited to date are paid.
The following bills are not yet audited:

  The United States Printing Company $6 00
  Howard Lockwood & Co 8 25

  Respectfully submitted,
     A. O. RUSSELL, *Treasurer*.

On motion, the report was received and accepted.

The PRESIDENT. It is necessary to have an Auditing Committee to examine this report and have it properly audited. I will appoint upon that committee, Messrs. C. B. Woodward, of St. Louis; W. S. Best, of Boston, and A. M. Geesaman, of Minneapolis. The next order of business is the report of the Executive Committee, Mr. Amos Pettibone, chairman.

Report of the Executive Committee.

MR. PRESIDENT AND GENTLEMEN:

Your Executive Committee respectfully beg to report that immediately after the close of the last annual meeting they held a session in the city of Boston, and fully discussed a general plan of action that would seemingly harmonize with the expressed wishes of the Convention regarding the organization of new societies as well as to stimulate into more activity others that were dormant, or whose final organization has not been made complete. It was our unanimous opinion that these objects would be best attained through the office of our Corresponding Secretary, who, upon publication of the Proceedings of 1890, was directed to give personal attention to the distribution of liberal quantities to such cities and individual printing establishments throughout the country as would be most likely to awaken an interest. In many instances they were accompanied or followed by letters urging an effort in the direction suggested. But the returns for this labor were so meagre that it was seemingly but little appreciated. The entire country being at peace, so far as any questions between labor and capital were concerned, the desirability of organization was not apparent. In one section, distrust and fear of competitors; in another, disagreement upon what were considered infallible customs and rules, or a supposition that the United Typothetæ of America was organized and fostered by the large and wealthy offices for the purpose of driving out or crushing the weaker; because we *were not* organized for the purpose of regulating the printing business upon such a basis as would insure ample remuneration, or that we had been unable to furnish the full measure of relief desired where there had been some local disturbances, were a few of the objections urged against the formation of new, or a revival of some dormant, societies in several cities that had hitherto expressed a desire to co-operate with us.

Early in February we mailed the following circular letter to the secretary of each Typothetæ:

Dear Sir—The Executive Committee of the United Typothetæ of America takes great interest in the condition of the various local bodies, and, understanding that there is more or less apathy existing, sends out the following questions, which they will be pleased to have you answer, that they may be able to make an intelligent report at the next annual meeting of the Typothetæ, and if necessary, suggest some plan whereby the interest in our organization may be increased.

Accompanying this was the following list of questions:

1. How many firms are represented in your organization?
2. What proportion do they bear to the number of printing firms in your city?
3. What proportion of your membership is book and job, and what newspaper?
4. How often do you meet?
5. What is the average attendance?
6. What interest is manifested?
7. If lack of interest, what is the cause?

8. At your meetings are topics of interest to the trade suggested and discussed?

9. Can you suggest any line of action on the part of the Executive Committee of the United Typothetæ of America which will, in your opinion, be productive of good results?

Please mail reply to AMOS PETTIBONE, Chairman of Executive Committee, Chicago, Ill.

In reply we received reports from twenty-two societies, which showed that about one-half of the printing establishments in such cities are members of the organization, and that they represent about 80 or 90 per cent. of the invested capital. Fourteen of this number report monthly meetings; three, semi-occasionally; three, when called; one, quarterly; one, five times a year. These meetings are fairly well attended, with a reasonable amount of manifested interest.

In answer to the question, "If lack of interest what is the cause?" there is such a variety of answers that we deem it proper to enumerate a few, in order that, as far as possible, we may correct erroneous impressions as to the real objects of our organization.

"Objects have not been understood. Some of the old established firms look upon it as a scheme to effect a combination." "Insane jealousy and personal pique." "Old fogyism." "What is the use of the Typothetæ when members will work at cost or less." "Is a dormant force awakening to activity only in a crisis." "Lack of unanimity, and competition." "In the absence of trouble nothing to draw us together." "The same cause which leads them to work for years without getting ahead—blind to their own interests." "A few hogs think there is no money in it." "Indifference—a failure to appreciate the objects of organization."

In almost every society we are pleased to report that, occasionally, at the regular meetings, papers pertaining to the practical subjects are read and discussed, as we believe in every instance beneficial to each participant, and your committee most earnestly urge the extension of this mode of diffusing information. A few good papers read and fully discussed upon any of the leading lines of interesting topics will prove very beneficial in an effort to extinguish the fires of jealousy and discontent, so that the real objects and true benefits of organization will soon become apparent.

In answer to the question, "Can you suggest any line of action on the part of the Executive Committee which will, in your opinion, be productive of good results?" we have the following from Philadelphia:

"If you could only regulate prices of composition and presswork, which is very important, you would increase membership everywhere."

Troy Typothetæ desires the formation of a committee from their own and Albany Typothetæ to establish a minimum scale for law work.

Toledo, Ohio.—Printed reports of good accomplished in other cities, schedules of prices adopted by other Typothetæ distributed to various branches, would be a good thing.

Worcester, Mass., desires the establishment of some medium for transmission of news and information to local bodies; also, to keep them posted on type discounts, prices of materials, etc.

Minneapolis.—There should be concerted action in defending ourselves from the encroachments of paper-houses and others upon our legitimate fields of operation.

Detroit, Mich.—In our individual case, I would suggest a hypodermic injection of about four gallons of the "elixir of life."

That this case was intelligently diagnosed, a suitable prescription expertly compounded and most successfully applied, is apparent from the fact that within thirty days our good friends were confronted by a demand from the Typographical Union for not only a *nine-hour day*, but an advance in the scale of wages as well. "No dormant force now slumbers in this locality." "The elixir has produced a phœnix." "The advantages of organization are at once apparent." Correspondence with other Typothetæ was immediately opened, asking what assistance could be rendered. The replies were so encouraging that they decided to make a stand for their rights, the result of which was a slight modification in the hours of labor for summer and winter months, without any increase in the scale of wages, settling the questions satisfactorily to all, with every assurance that there will be no further agitation of the subject at present.

The Master Printers' Club, of Boston, present the following:

Resolved, That, in the opinion of this Club, it would be highly useful for the purposes of the ensuing National Convention to obtain statistics of wages, hours of labor, and trade usages throughout the country, as far as it be practicable to obtain them, and put same in form for the information of the Convention.

The Recording Secretary was instructed to obtain this information and forward to Mr. L. L. Morgan, of New Haven, who, in conjunction with Mr. Kellar, of Philadelphia, and Mr. L. A. Wyman, of Boston, were requested to furnish a report on these subjects.

In regard to the suggestions from Philadelphia and Troy, your committee fail to find any warrant of authority for an attempt on their part to establish a schedule of prices, and very much doubt if our friends in these cities would feel bound to adhere to any formulated scale. Certainly in the future, as in the past, the law of supply and demand, measured by the rules for cost of production, with a small percentage for profit, will continue to be every man's independent basis for calculation; therefore he will be loth to take the estimated cost of any other person as his universal rule. Your committee suggest that the regulation of all such matters should be handled by the local organizations.

It will be remembered that, at the June meeting of the International Typographical Union, October 1, 1891, was named as the date upon which they would demand a nine-hour day. Several of our local societies shortly after this passed resolutions urging a change in date of the annual meeting to September, in order that this organization might have the opportunity for discussion of the question, and decide upon a course of action in advance of the date indicated.

It was therefore deemed advisable to call a meeting of the Executive Committee, which was held in the city of Cincinnati, July 17th and 18th, the full committee being present, except Mr. William H. Bates. Mr. Theo. L. DeVinne being present, was elected to fill the vacancy *pro tem*.

After thorough discussion it was decided to furnish the Associated Press with a telegram for publication in the leading cities, to the effect that we were opposed to any change in date of the annual meeting, and that we recommended most vigorous opposition to any movement looking towards shorter hours at this time. The following circular letter was formulated, printed and distributed in sufficient quantities for information of our entire membership:

After a thorough discussion of the questions submitted, it was then and there resolved that it would be unwise to call the annual meeting of the United Typothetæ for an earlier date than the one named at the last annual meeting held in Boston.

United opposition to the proposed nine-hour rule was earnestly advised—

1. Because it will be unequal and unjust in its operation. Under no circumstances could the new rule be made operative in more than one-tenth of our printing-offices. It is unfair to expect that one-tenth of the offices will submit to a disability from which nine-tenths are free.

2. It puts the burden of loss entirely on the master-printer, for it is not possible for the master-printer to get from his employer, the publisher or the buyer of printing, the increase in price which the shorter day and diminished production really demand. When nine-tenths of the offices are working ten hours, and one-tenth of them nine hours, a general or uniform advanced rate is impossible.

3. This loss threatens us as ruinous. It is not, as is claimed by the advocates of nine hours, a loss of one-tenth of our profit; it is a loss of all the profit. The average profit of printing, at present rates and present cost, is decidedly less than 10 per cent. of the receipts.

The office that works ten hours and produces $1,000 within a given time, under the new rule will produce in that time but $900. If it costs as much to produce $900 worth of work as it has cost heretofore to produce $1,000, then there can be no profit. The work will be done at cost or at loss. Any master-printer can readily ascertain what the loss to him will be by a study of his balance-sheet for the past year. If he deducts one-tenth from the production of his last year's business, and charges that production with the regular expenses of that year, he will, in most cases, find that his expenses would have been greater than his receipts.

A proposed shortening of the hours of labor cannot be fairly done unless it is the joint work of employers and employed. In this, as in other matters, the old rule holds good: "It takes two parties to make a bargain." While we recommend opposition to this rule, which has been made exclusively by the employed, without a proper knowledge of the conditions of the trade, we are ready to unite with the employees of our respective offices in any feasible attempt to secure a common advantage by means of mutual concession.

We also contracted for the insertion of the following advertisement in a number of the trade journals and a large list of carefully selected papers throughout the country—

Good job and book compositors employed in country offices who desire employment in large cities will please address, with reference as to ability and character,

UNITED TYPOTHETÆ OF AMERICA, BOX 695,
CINCINNATI, OHIO—

which has resulted in the accumulation of a considerable list of names, which have been properly classified and registered for use as occasion may require, and which prompts us to suggest for your consideration a plan for the formation and conduct of a Bureau of Information and Supply.

OBJECT.—To collect and disseminate information of practical value to the printer, and eventually to work into a Board of Trade in the interest of the local Typothetæ.

DETAIL.—1. To procure the names and addresses of workmen (compositors and pressmen) in interior towns who desire work in large cities, also in places where there is an overplus of workmen, and to keep a record of the same with the view to supply cities when needed.

2. To collate information as to the number of offices, and the men employed in different cities; to acquaint itself as far as possible with the general conditions of trade, and the supply and demand in the different centres of trade.

METHODS.—1. To advertise from time to time for needed information.

2. To seek correspondents in the printing trade in different cities.

3. To issue blanks of every kind needed, with a view to seek information from local societies; answer applicants for work; explain the objects and aims of this bureau, and question local societies on matters of interest.

4. To keep in correspondence with applicants for work, show an interest in their needs, and to supply freely any pertinent information asked for by them or others.

5. To keep in correspondence with the local Typothetæ for the purpose of gathering and supplying information, and furnishing workmen, in times of pressure, from other places.

6. To obtain, so far as possible, from the local societies monthly reports on—
   The state of trade;
   The prevailing conditions of supply and demand;
   The prevailing wages;
   The business outlook,—
and to publish the same for distribution to the societies.

Control.—To be under the management of the Corresponding Secretary, controlled by the Executive Committee, until such time as the growth of the bureau demands a separate establishment.

The Corresponding Secretary to be empowered to employ such clerical labor as may be required to conduct the work.

Revenue.—To be from either of the following sources:

(It is assumed that if the scheme proves a success it will finally be self-supporting.)

1. The Treasurer to be instructed to pay the expenses from the general fund of the society, and any deficiency to be assessed from local bodies.

2. A fund to be raised by subscription among the local bodies in the same way as was the organization fund of 1889.

3. An assessment on each Typothetæ, in addition to its dues, of a sum, *pro rata* of membership, to cover the estimated cost of one year.

It is estimated that the plan can be formulated and put into operation at a cost the first year of less than $1,000.

It will at first be more a matter of study than of labor, and voluntary aid can be commanded for all except the clerical work, printing bills, and postage.

A small fee, charged by the bureau for services rendered the local Typothetæ, would be proper, and in time, if success attended, furnish the income required.

Cincinnati Typothetæ will offer an amendment to the Constitution, providing for an increase in annual dues; which we approve, and recommend its adoption.

There is in the hands of our Treasurer $436.23 to credit of the organization fund. We recommend that this account be closed, and the balance placed to the credit of the general fund.

Your committee are impressed with the great injustice to every printer by the present system of government printing of envelopes, which we most earnestly deprecate, and recommend adoption of the following:

Resolved, That a committee of five be appointed to appear before the proper committee of Congress, at its ensuing session, and urge a repeal of the law permitting this work to be done by the Postoffice Department.

Being of the opinion that the interest in our meetings and the general good would be largely enhanced by our holding secret sessions, the following resolution was adopted:

Resolved, That admission to this annual meeting shall be by card, and shall be limited to the delegates and alternates of local Typothetæ, but that special tickets of admission may be furnished persons whose discretion is vouched for by any delegation, and upon the recommendation of the chairman of the delegation for the city in which applicant resides. In case there is no Typothetæ in such city or town, the chairman of Executive Committee may make such recommendations. We recommend its adoption for this and future meetings.

We recommend the adoption of the following as a standing resolution:

Resolved, That upon the request of any delegation, the presiding officer may declare the Convention to have entered into executive session—and while in such executive session only the following persons shall be entitled to be present:
1. The officers of the United Typothetæ of America;
2. The ex-Presidents of the United Typothetæ of America;
3. The delegates and alternates entitled to seats in General Convention.
4. The official stenographer.

Your committee further report that, in their opinion, the expense of printing the Proceedings of our annual meeting will be materially reduced by a discontinuance of the practice of printing a large number of copies of each day's proceedings during the Convention. Therefore, we have contracted with our official stenographer to furnish, at the beginning of each day's session, a complete type-written copy and duplicate of the proceedings of the preceding day. At close of the Convention the Recording Secretary will have the entire proceedings printed and distributed as economically as practicable. We recommend the adoption of this plan.

We recommend the discontinuance by local Typothetæ of the practice of furnishing men and rendering assistance to firms and corporations outside the membership of our organization, as has been frequently done, and in several instances, to the manifest injury of our own members. We advise the extension of our assistance only to such cities and establishments as are recognized members of this organization.

Your committee would call attention to the certificates prepared for workmen that have been distributed to nearly all of the local societies, and earnestly urge their issue to worthy, competent employees.

Another subject that should be taken up by this Convention is the consideration of some other plan for holding our Conventions than that of having them meet from year to year at the expense of the local Typothetæ. It entails upon the organization a great amount of expense and labor, which can be avoided by having our Conventions meet at some summer or winter-resort hotel, where the proprietor would be very glad to furnish us all the room we might need for holding our meetings, and we would be enabled to devote much more time to the transaction of our business. We suggest this subject as a proper one to be referred to the committee which you may appoint, and request that it report to this Convention before we adjourn.

All of which is respectfully submitted.

      AMOS PETTIBONE,
          Chairman.
      W. C. ROGERS, by
      THEO. L. DE VINNE, *Proxy.*
      C. S. MOREHOUSE.
      E. R. ANDREWS.
      WILLIAM H. BATES.
      GEORGE M. COURTS.
      A. H. PUGH,
        President.
      EVERETT WADDEY,
        Corresponding Secretary.
      W. L. BECKER,
        Recording Secretary.

The PRESIDENT. Gentlemen, you have heard the report of the Executive Committee. If there are no objections, it will be received and accepted. The topical matter in it of course will be taken up later. It has been the custom heretofore to take up the report of the Executive Committee and the President's address and reports of the officers, and divide the subjects contained in them for discussion. What is your pleasure at this time?

Mr. MORGAN, of Cincinnati. I move that it take the same course.

Seconded.

The PRESIDENT. How many do you desire that this committee shall consist of? A committee of three or five? The Chair will appoint a committee of five.

Mr. SLAWSON, of St. Louis. I have had a little experience on that, and the matters treated of in the reports this year are much more voluminous than heretofore, and I do not think a committee of five will be sufficient. That committee will have to subdivide, and we have at least three reports that ought to take up considerable time. I think it will be better to have a committee of nine, and let them subdivide by threes; and one committee take one subject, and another another, and the third one another. Otherwise, it will take all night.

The PRESIDENT. There was a motion to make it a committee of five. Do you offer that as an amendment?

Mr. REES. Are we to understand that this committee is to make reports back to the Convention, or simply to subdivide?

The PRESIDENT. It is a committee to divide and report subjects of discussion to this Convention at future dates.

Mr. REES. If it is simply to divide the work up for other committees, five would be enough.

Mr. LOCKWOOD. I think you will find trouble if you give the matter to different committees. The President's address and other reports treat of the same subjects, and they should be acted upon by the same committee.

The President. Last year the committee was three, and this year I think a committee of five would be enough to handle the matter. As Mr. Lockwood suggests, the topical matter is very much the same in the address of the President and the report of the Executive Committee, which is the most to be considered. All in favor of a committee of five to take up the President's address and Executive Committee's report, to divide the subject-matter, will signify their willingness by saying "aye."

Carried.

It has been customary in the proceedings of the Convention that a committee be appointed at this time to take into consideration the appointment of a meeting-place for next year, and also to report a list of officers later in the Convention. Is it your will that this matter be taken up at the present time?

Mr. Bates. I think it would be advisable to defer action upon that matter until this committee reports upon the report of the Executive Committee, as there is a recommendation in that report as to the holding of future conventions.

The President. In the order of business, the next thing would be the taking up of the reports of committees appointed at the last meeting of the Typothetæ in Boston. The first subject is the report of the Committee on the Evils of Competition. Mr. Waddey is chairman of that committee.

Report of Committee on Competitive Bidding and Code of Ethics.

The committee appointed at the Fourth Annual Convention of the United Typothetæ of America, and to whom was referred the following subject: "To take up the evils that result from competitive bidding and prepare such a Code of Ethics as will tend to elevate the dignity of the trade," respectfully submit the following report:

In the consideration of this subject your committee has endeavored to keep in mind what they esteem to be the true idea intended by the delegate who introduced the subject on the floor of the Boston Convention, viz.: That it is the *evils* which result from competitive bidding that we are to endeavor to correct, or to suggest what may, in some degree, tend to their correction; for it is not to be supposed that an effort could be made by an intelligent body to suppress competition, that being as old as Time itself, and as honorable when done in a manly way as any influence which sways the mind of man in its upward progress. But this ennobling form of competition which has influenced the present and past generations of mankind, "standing upon the shoulders of their predecessors," to delve deeper into the bowels of the earth, to peer further beyond the stars, to dive to greater depths beneath the sea, or to experiment more and more with the subtle influences of chemistry, that the riddle of the rocks may be read, or another constellation added to the starry hosts of the heavens, or other pathways marked upon the trackless seas, or another yoke fastened to the lightning, which man has bitted and bridled and tamed for his use—all in order that the student who burns the midnight oil and rises up with the dawn to continue his work may, in coupling his name with a new discovery, carve for himself such a niche in the Temple of Fame that succeeding generations may surround it, too, with a garland of laurel; this competition, which has lifted men from the meaner forms of life, and enabled them to achieve and hold that pinnacle of excellence which the great Creator in the beginning designed them to occupy,—this is not to be included in "the evils which result from competitive bidding."

Competitive bidding, as your committee understand it, is that custom which obtains with States, counties, cities, corporations, and individuals, of giving out no work unless it is first either advertised for proposals or hawked about from one establishment to another in an effort to ascertain what is the lowest possible price at which any one can be induced to undertake to do it. We doubt if any plan can be adopted in regard to public work which can be an improvement upon a public letting, and what we say has application rather to corporations and individuals, although we have seen some of the most bitter feuds have their origin in scrambles for this class of work. The evils which result from excessive competition are great, and work many disasters to the trade. Amongst these may be enumerated:

(1) *Moral weakness*, in that the bidder so frequently does not have the courage to ask what he knows the work to be worth, so great is his fear that his neighbor will be just a few cents below him, and thus secure what both seem at the time to regard as the last job ever to be gotten by them.

(2) *Mortification and chagrin*, either that we should have seen him whom we had hoped to make a customer, or who, perhaps, has been a customer for a long time, going to our erstwhile friend over the way; or else, on the other hand, when we have had the cutting-knife too sharp, and our proposition is accepted, and we proceed to look over our figures, ascertain that we have omitted the paper, or failed to double the composition in the tabular work, or made a fool of ourselves in some other equally ridiculous way in our anxiety not to miss the job.

(3) *Jealousy, envy, and hatred of our neighbor* and fellow-craftsman who secures the work, and who may have innocently left out an important item, or, through ignorance, have erred in some other way, but whose name henceforth, whenever we hear it, fills us with an uncontrollable desire to get even, and which desire invariably proves a boomerang with which a more deadly blow is inflicted upon ourselves than upon him.

(4) *Inadequate compensation for all classes of work*. It is a well-settled principle with all live mercantile houses, that if you allow each salesman to make prices according to what he thinks should be the percentage of profit proper to be charged on different articles of merchandise to different individuals, he will, in his anxiety to sell goods, very shortly reach a point in his prices that is equivalent to the lowest profit that he thinks his employer will forgive him for making. This, together with the system of reprisals which is developed in our efforts to get even, will soon make a very large minority of all work done in a community a matter of absolute loss.

(5) *Corruption and demoralization of the customer*, who, seeing the weak points in their armor, determines to play one printer against another for his own advantage, and which he does very

effectually, sometimes truthfully and sometimes by misrepresentation—always, however, to his own gain and to the printer's loss.

(6) *Temptation to dishonesty*, in that, after using every means known to secure the order, some will yield and use cheaper materials or furnish a lower grade of work than that contracted for, in order to save themselves from loss.

(7) *Loss of reputation*, for, when a customer learns that a house has done a questionable thing—and you may rest assured there will always be some one near who will point out the deficiencies—he not only takes away his patronage, but spreads the story of how he has been unfairly dealt with.

(8) *Loss of self-respect*, for, although the ignorance or credulity of the customer may enable the sharp bidder to impose upon him goods or work which are not up to the standard agreed upon, the printer, who does know better, cannot quiet the still, small voice of conscience which is continually reminding him that, although he bears a fair reputation in the community, he knows himself to be like a whited sepulchre.

(9) *Poor credit, bankruptcy and ruin*, as a result of that temptation to bid for work for which the establishment is not equipped. There is a weakness among Americans which manifests itself in our business in an unwillingness on the part of the printer to admit that another establishment is better fitted to do certain work than his own. The unfailing results of yielding to this temptation are disastrous in the extreme. The office is compelled to add to its outfit, the cash requisite to do this is lacking, and a load of debt is assumed. The necessary addition is often more than sufficient to consume one or two years' profit, and the mental worry and anxiety incident to it undermine the health and carry the over-ambitious to financial disaster.

Having given a list of some of the principal evils which result from competitive bidding, we should, of course, follow it up with a *recipe* which would work a cure, and this we feel it very easy to do, for if we were only able to raise ourselves far enough above our human frailty to practice at all times, especially in making estimates, the golden rule of doing unto others as we would have them do unto us, we are sure that in cutting for work our knife would never be so sharp; the price would not be so low; the unsuccessful bidder would not have to lie in wait for the next time in order to get even; the temptation to slight work would not exist;

our facilities would not so suddenly and unnecessarily increase; the burden of debt would not be shouldered; and the reward for days of labor would not be nights of sleepless anxiety as to how the accruing bills can be paid. But your committee feel that, were they to suggest such an utopian remedy, they would possibly be considered as begging the question, and they have, therefore, prepared the following code, which appears to them to be an embodiment of what ought to be the theory and practice of the trade:

CODE OF ETHICS.

Recognizing the fact that in the conduct of our business no individual or concern in any community can act regardless of his neighbors and competitors, and that while the spirit of competition has been so deeply imbedded in the human breast and so keenly sharpened by the methods of every-day life as to cause it to enter into and influence every transaction, but at the same time believing there are methods of competition which are clean, honorable and legitimate, whereby we can compete without wronging others, and without demoralizing the business in which we are engaged, the United Typothetæ of America adopts the following rules, and recommends them to the employing printers of the country:

OF OUR DUTY TO OURSELVES.

(1) The Code of Ethics best calculated to elevate the status of employing printers must be evolved by the development of moral and intellectual manhood. We should, therefore, and firmly, resolve to test every *transaction* by the standard of truth and justice.

(2) Take advantage of no man's ignorance, and see that employees are truthful and straightforward, and do not misrepresent nor overcharge the confiding.

(3) It is an absolute essential in honorable competition that we prove ourselves as honorable in every particular as we would have our competitors.

(4) Mix freely with intelligent and honorable members of the craft, and study their ways and methods, and endeavor to get a reputation in the community as an intelligent, honest, first-class printer, whom people can trust with their work without competitive bidding.

(5) Every printing establishment should have a perfect system of ascertaining the actual cost of every job. It is in this way only that the business can hope to be relieved from the deleterious effects of guess prices. Such a system should not only ascertain the facts, but record them, so that they can be referred to understandingly, and the information immediately ascertained.

(6) No establishment should be satisfied with anything except the most exact and systematic book-keeping, and all work should be checked up and charges proved before delivery, and the following made a standing rule: Never permit a charge to be entered on the books that cannot be proved by competent evidence in a court of justice to be a fair competitive price.

(7) The expense of doing business, such as the wear and tear of material, interest on money invested, bad debts, rent, taxes, insurance, book-keeping, and all other items of expense, should be ever before our eyes, and we should never forget that these must be as surely levied on each particular job as its labor cost. Never, under any circumstances, should the minimum cost plus a fair profit be departed from. We should feel here a double restraint: in the first place, to cut cost is *foolish;* in the second place, it is *wrong.*

(8) On no account consent to pay commissions to book-keepers, secretaries, or others who have work to give out. It is demoralizing to both the giver and the taker. Money is passed without a proper equivalent. The agent is selling something he has no right to sell, and unless the printer has a better conscience than is ordinarily met with, the commission is added to the bill, and the customer pays more than he should.

OF OUR DUTY TO EACH OTHER.

(9) When a young competitor enters the ranks welcome him as a new soldier to the field, and help him to any information and assistance which will enable him to overcome the difficulties we had so much trouble in surmounting. Rest assured you can make no better investment of the time necessary to do so, as his gratitude for the kindly consideration will often cause him to repay you in a fourfold way, and where you would least anticipate it.

(10) It should be a duty and pleasure to impart to our less experienced competitors the knowledge we possess, so long as we are satisfied that the information generously given will be honorably used. In this way the element of ignorance which does so much

to demoralize the craft may be partially eliminated, and one of the most dangerous factors of competition destroyed. Remember that knowledge kindly imparted makes a business friend of one who would probably otherwise become a business foe.

(11) The young employer who starts with a small capital, and does most of his own work, should ever remember the honorable nature of his calling, and never make the mistake of supposing that because he does his own work he can do it for less than his neighbor who employs fifty or more hands with a long list of superintendents and foremen. He should rather insist that the work which he does with his own hands will be better done, and therefore he should receive more for it.

(12) When a printer is offered work which he cannot do, his rule should be to decline it, and refer his customer to the office that can do it, and not accept the work, hoping to get some neighbor to do it for him and allow him a commission.

(13) Make no rebates nor allowances to professional brokers or middlemen. If it is possible to help a neighbor out of an extra rush of composition or press-work, do it cheerfully, and divide with him the profit on the work. In this way the temptation to add to the facilities, oftentimes much too large for the work done in a given community, will very often be overcome, as idle machinery makes it almost impossible to maintain any standard of prices which may be adopted.

(14) When estimates are asked for by any person on work done by another printer, with plain intent to find cause for an alleged unfairness of the price charged, they should be invariably declined. It is not safe to criticise any price until one is in possession of all the facts. The work itself when done does not say whether it was done by night or by day, with few or many alterations; but these and other unknown conditions may have controlled the price.

(15) In making estimates we are shooting arrows in the dark, and may unwittingly wound some of our best friends when we have least intended it. If the aggrieved person thinks he has been injured by an estimate which has taken away a valued customer, his proper course is to seek an explanation, and he should always begin with the supposition that the injurious price has been made in ignorance of all the facts, by thoughtlessness or by mistake. In most cases he can reach such an explanation as will pre-

vent a repetition of the error, if it does not bring the lost work back.

OF PRICES AND ESTIMATES.

(16) Every establishment should have a thorough knowledge of what it costs to produce the work it sends out, and should determine what percentage of profit it will be satisfied with. Based upon those two items, it should establish its prices for all work undertaken, whether secured by competitive bid or without a price being named in advance.

(17) A master-printer should not make estimates for work that he cannot do, and when he is devoid of experience in certain branches of printing, should not attempt to price them. It is always unsafe and often unjust to give prices upon a class of work upon which the cost is not positively known and has to be guessed at.

(18) Always have the courage to ask fair remuneration for any work offered, resting assured that it will be more profitable to be without a job than to secure one in which there is a temptation to resort to questionable methods in order to avoid a financial loss in its execution.

(19) Estimates calling for detailed specifications of separate value of the paper, composition, electrotyping, presswork, ruling, binding, etc., should always be refused. These details the customer has no right to. They are the printer's property, and to be swift in giving them away is one of the surest methods of provoking unfair competition.

(20) When requested to make estimates for work, or submitting proposals in answer to advertisements, the intelligent printer should endeavor to never lose sight of the fact that the only price proper to make is the one that he would make were the work intrusted to him without any estimates having been requested on it. His estimated figures should be made on the basis per thousand ems, per token, and per pound for paper that he has adopted for his minimum for the class of work, while carefully studying the subject with the figures of his previous year's business before his eyes, and while safely shielded from the exciting influences which arise when the estimate fiend is so close upon him—always consoling himself when he loses the job with the thought that if he had incumbered himself with the work at a low figure he would have incapacitated himself from doing what may presently come along at a remunerative rate.

(21) A master-printer should always contend that he is entitled, when asked for an estimate, to know the names of all who are to be requested to bid on the work. A glance at the names is often sufficient to show him whether it is worth the trouble to make the necessary calculations. He should also insist upon his right, if he desires it, to know all the prices offered for the work, and to whom and at what price it was awarded.

(22) The man who asks for a bid upon work, and before receiving it shows the figures made by another bidder, should be marked; it can be depended on, if he will show you another's bid he will show yours to a third party. He wants you to do the job, if you will do it for less than any one else.

OF OUR DUTY TO OUR WORKMEN.

(23) In the conduct of our establishments it should be our constant endeavor to elevate the moral character, and ameliorate the financial condition of our workmen who are engaged with us. This interest in his welfare is one of the best methods of preventing strikes and lockouts, which do such untold damage to both the proprietor and the journeyman.

(24) While it should be the firm and unalterable determination of every printer not to be dictated to by labor organizations when their demands are unfair, or which substitute the will of a prejudiced majority for the conservative teachings of common sense and justice, we should be slow to condemn the action taken by the journeymen, as it is possible that the influences controlling them may be more than they are able to resist.

(25) Any action which tends to decrease the rate of wages should be looked upon with as much distrust as is an effort to increase them. We should always remember that the proper place for us to look for remuneration is from the business we do at a legitimate profit, and not from what we can save on the *per diem* of the wage-worker, or from what we can make out of each other.

(26) In the treatment of apprentices or boys who are in our employ, we should be ever careful as to whose hands they are in, as they are often influenced for good or for bad by the example of the foreman under whom they work.

(27) When an apprentice is taken it should be considered our duty, if he prove unapt or unteachable, to advise him to seek another line of trade. It often occurs that a poor printer would

have made a good blacksmith or shoemaker; therefore either trade, as well as the boy, would be benefited by taking him away from the trade for which he is unfitted.

(28) When we conclude that the apprentice we have taken is competent to learn the business, and that he will master it in such a manner as to reflect credit upon those who taught him as well as himself, no effort should be spared to make him all he should be as a workman and a good citizen. By so doing we add to our own happiness, his prosperity, and help the future generation of employing printers along a very troublesome road.

Realizing the magnitude of the subject imposed upon it, your committee, in March last, sent out a circular to every Typothetæ in our organization, calling attention to the subject referred to it at the Boston Convention, and requesting each local Typothetæ to appoint one of its most competent members to prepare a paper upon the subject, which, after being read, should be forwarded to this committee, in order that it might have the aid of the best intellects in our guild in formulating its report. We have felt ourselves indebted, in no small degree, for the papers which have been sent us, and from which, in making up a " Code of Ethics," we have felt at liberty to quote literally or otherwise.

All of the papers are submitted herewith, and your committee hope they will be ordered printed with the proceedings for the enlightenment of the trade at large.

Respectfully submitted,

EVERETT WADDEY,
EDWIN FREEGARD,
H. D. BROWN,
JULIUS FESTNER.

The PRESIDENT. If there are no objections, the report of the committee will be received and accepted. Is it the will of the Convention that it adopt the Code of Ethics recommended by this committee?

It was moved and seconded that it be adopted.

Mr. REES. I hate to talk on every subject; but wouldn't it be well for that special report to also go to the Committee on Revision, and have it revised? It seems to me rather an immature way to adopt a Code of Ethics that has been read over here. While the committee is entitled to great credit for their preparation, still I think it would be well to have it go through the hands of some one for report. I hardly think all of the members back here heard it, and we are voting on something we did not hear. I think it might go to the Committee on Revision.

Mr. RIDGE, of New York. I will second that motion. I do not think it ought to be adopted at once. I only heard half of it, and there are several others who were out at the time of the reading.

The PRESIDENT. It is moved to amend that resolution, and that this report go to the Committee on Revision to have them report upon the topics mentioned as part of this Code of Ethics.

Mr. SLAWSON, of St. Louis. We appointed a committee to make this report. If we are not satisfied with the report prepared by this committee, the proper way would be to refer it back to the committee for revision, and not to put it into the hands of another committee.

The PRESIDENT. I think you are out of order. We have already received the report, and the question is upon the adoption of the Code of Ethics reported by this committee to the body.

Mr. SLAWSON. In the first place, I want to remind the President that the longest time we have got for business is about twelve hours, with an immense amount of business to be transacted in that time. If we refer this to a committee, the result is that we will not be any better able to vote on it than we are now. If we adopt it now and look at it for a year, it is an easy thing to change it next year, and therefore I am in favor of adopting it as it is.

Mr. REES. As I understand, the committee was appointed to prepare a report on the evils of competition, and not to adopt a Code of Ethics.

Mr. WADDEY. The instructions were to "to take up the evils that result from competitive bidding, and prepare such a Code of Ethics as will tend to elevate the dignity of the trade." That is the instruction to the committee. They have endeavored to do that work. They apologize for the poor way in which it has been done.

Mr. REES. I will admit that I am in error in regard to the Code of Ethics, but still I do not think that there is anything that I can object to in it. But it seems to me that a deliberative body that comes here with an object in view, if they were going to adopt a Code of Ethics to govern their members, would have some discussion of the Code of Ethics—they would not have a committee of two, or one that prepares the report, adopt the same. They make their recommendations to the Convention, and it is the deliberation, the discussion and the final result of the Convention which is supposed to have any influence whatever on its members. When a report is made here, it is in the power of the Convention to do as it sees fit with it. It is a paper before the Convention just exactly the same as when a member offers a resolution, and nothing else.

The PRESIDENT. I think that the report of the committee was received and accepted, and the original motion was to adopt this Code of Ethics. A substitute was then moved that this Code of Ethics be referred to a committee before being adopted.

Mr. DONNELLY, of Chicago. We are badly in want of ethics out our way, and I would like to take some home with me. I beg that the report as read by the chairman of the committee be printed at once and we have copies of it to take with us, and that it be incorporated into the Proceedings of the Convention, and that it be accepted as our action.

Mr. POLHEMUS, of New York. My hearing is not very good, but I heard every word of that document. I must say that I never listened to a better written report than that is. [*Applause.*] I agree with every sentence of it, and I rise to second Mr. Donnelly's amendment, that it be printed and distributed among the members as soon as possible.

Mr. ANDREWS, of Rochester. I move that it be recommended to the members.

Mr. WEBB. I arise to a point of order. The whole discussion is out of order. The report has not been accepted.

The PRESIDENT. It has been. I said, "If there is no objection that it would be accepted." There was no objection, and I said that the question was whether the code be adopted, and the discussion is upon that subject, and not upon accepting the report.

Mr. WEBB. If it is the decision of the Chair that the report has been accepted, I would like to know what is the question before the house.

The PRESIDENT. That this Code of Ethics, suggested by the report of the committee, be adopted by the Convention, and the substitute offered by Mr. Rees was that the report be referred to a committee, and the question is upon the substitute offered by Mr. Rees.

Mr. GIBSON, of Omaha. I will say that I did not hear half of the report.

Mr. WEBB. If the report has been received, I want to move, as an amendment to all the motions, that the report be spread on the minutes, and then we can take it up afterwards.

The PRESIDENT. Will the gentleman put the last motion in writing? The Chair cannot carry all these motions in his mind.

Mr. SLAWSON. I make a motion that this be adopted by the body, for the reason that any code would be subjected to revision after we find how it is going to work. I believe that it is a good code, as good as we can adopt.

Mr. MUDGE, of Boston. I move that the matter be laid on the table for a half hour, until the previous motions are put in writing and laid before the house.

This motion, being seconded, was carried by a rising vote.

The PRESIDENT. The next business will be the revision of the Constitution. As this will require considerable time, it will be taken up the first thing after dinner. I would like to read you a communication that we received from the Chamber of Commerce of this city.

CINCINNATI, October 19, 1891.

A. H. PUGH, ESQ., *United Typothetæ of America, Cincinnati, Ohio:*

MY DEAR SIR—I take pleasure, in behalf of the Board of Directors of the Cincinnati Chamber of Commerce and Merchants' Exchange, in extending to the members of the United Typothetæ of America the courtesies of this Association during their stay in this city. Any member of the same, by intimating to the doorkeeper of the Exchange that he is a member of your organization, will be cordially admitted to any of our sessions and to the building at any time.

Yours very truly,
JOSEPH R. BROWN, *President.*

The President then appointed as the Committee on Distribution of Topics, Messrs. W. H. Woodward, of St. Louis; R. R. Donnelly, of Chicago; E. Parke Coby, of

New York; Samuel Rees, of Omaha, and Charles Buss, of Cincinnati.

The PRESIDENT. We have a great deal of business before this Convention, and, as Mr. Slawson says, we have only twelve hours to do this business, and there ought to be no advantage taken of the points of order. Our business will be greatly facilitated by little courtesies; otherwise, we will waste very much valuable time if any other question comes up like this last.

Mr. DEVINNE. In a very short time the revision of the Constitution will come up. It has been my good or bad fortune, as the case may have been, to belong to a great many societies where it has been necessary to tinker with the Constitution about every two or three years, and I must say that I do not know how the time of a deliberative assembly can be worse taken up than in a heated discussion of the Constitution. At the present time I have nothing to say for the old or new form, but I do rise to make this motion, that all debates upon this new Constitution be limited to five minutes, and that no person be allowed to speak twice upon the same subject without unanimous consent.

This motion being numerously seconded, was carried.

The motion in regard to the Code of Ethics being reduced to writing, was read as follows:

It is moved by Samuel Slawson, and seconded by R. R. Donnelly, that the Code of Ethics reported by the Committee on the "Evils that result from Competitive Bidding" be adopted, and that we recommend the observance of the same by local Typothetæ; and that the entire report be printed and circulated at once, and incorporated in the minutes of this body when published.

Carried.

On motion, adjourned until 2 o'clock.

AFTERNOON SESSION.

The meeting was called to order by President Pugh.

The PRESIDENT. The first business before the Convention will be the report of the Committee upon the Revision of the Constitution. There are a number of copies of this report, and it would be well for each member to have it.

Mr. WADDEY. Mr. President, and gentlemen of the Convention, as chairman of the committee having in hand the subject of the revision of the Constitution, I beg leave to present the report which is in the hands of nearly every delegate in the room. I do not know that there is anything that the committee can add to the report, or as an introduction to the report, except to say that the authority under which they were appointed was an instruction by the Boston Convention to report what, if any, changes are advisable to be made in the Constitution of this organization. After considerable correspondence between members of the committee, this report which you have now in hand was formulated and agreed upon. Nearly all the changes which have been made in the Constitution, or suggested by this committee, are changes which, in its experience—and each member of it has been a member of the United Typothetæ of America almost since its organization—would militate in favor of the more effective working of our association, and would aid us in carrying out the objects for which the United Typothetæ of America was formed. I presume, Mr. President, that it is not necessary to read the report.

The PRESIDENT. No, sir.

Mr. WADDEY. I beg leave to call the attention of the Convention to the fact that the Constitution, as it now stands, is printed in the back of this leaflet, and that the report of the committee is printed in open matter, so that changes and amendments can be made without difficulty. I move that the report be taken up in sections.

Report of Committee on Revision of Constitution, United Typothetæ of America.

To the President and Delegates to the Fifth Annual Convention, United Typothetæ of America:

The undersigned, having been appointed at the Boston Convention a special committee "to report what, if any, changes are advisable to be made in the Constitution of this organization," with instructions to report at this meeting, beg leave to submit the following revision as the result of their deliberations. In order that it may be with more facility amended during its consideration, the report has been printed in bill form. Your committee has also thought best to append a copy of the Constitution adopted at Chicago upon the organization of the United Typothetæ of America.

Your committee has given the matter much thought, and has only suggested such changes as in its opinion will materially aid in the management of the organization.

Respectfully submitted,
EVERETT WADDEY,
SAM. SLAWSON,
H. T. ROCKWELL.

RESOLUTION OF RICHMOND TYPOTHETÆ.

At a meeting of the Typothetæ of Richmond, Va., held June 13th, 1891, the following was adopted:

Resolved, That the Typothetæ of Richmond, Va., endorse the report of the Special Committee on Revision of the Constitution of the United Typothetæ of America, and hereby propose the same for adoption at the Fifth Annual Convention, to be held in Cincinnati, October, 1891.

CONSTITUTION OF THE UNITED TYPOTHETÆ OF AMERICA.

PREAMBLE.

The United Typothetæ of America is organized for the purpose of developing a community of interest and a fraternal spirit among the master-printers of the United States and Canada, and for the purpose of exchanging information and assisting each other when necessary. It is voluntary, and not coercive. It does not propose to make arbitrary prices, rates or rules, or to make combinations against customers or the public, or to fix or regulate the wages of workmen, or to coerce unwilling members to the adoption of any measure they do not approve. It is based on the right of the individual as opposed to the arrogated rights of trade societies; and while it disclaims any intent to assume an arbitrary control of the trade, either against customers, workmen or members, its members assert and will maintain the individual right to regulate their own affairs.

CONSTITUTION.

Article I.—Name.

This Association shall be called THE UNITED TYPOTHETÆ OF AMERICA.

Article II.—Membership.

1. Any society of master-printers, containing not less than five members, of any city or town (or in any case where there are not a sufficient number of master-printers to form a society in one town, then any society formed in any county or contiguous territory) in the United States or in the Dominion of Canada, may become a member of this association upon its application for membership being approved by the Executive Committee, and paying into the treasury the initiation fee prescribed in Article VIII.

2. Applications for membership shall be addressed to the Secretary, and shall be in the following form:

. . . . 189 . .

TO THE UNITED TYPOTHETÆ OF AMERICA:

We hereby make application for membership in your body and enclose ten dollars, the fee prescribed by your Constitution. We have at present . . . . members, and have adopted the name of . . . .

. . . . *President.*
. . . . *Secretary.*

This form of application must be accompanied by a list of officers, and the name of every concern or individual who are members of the society making the same.

3. Any society of journeymen printers, or society composed of both journeymen and employing printers, containing not less than fifty members, and whose organization recognizes the cardinal principle of individual right to work for whom and what and where he pleases, may be admitted to auxiliary membership by making application to any annual meeting of this association, and being elected thereto by a majority vote of such meeting. All applications for auxiliary membership must be accompanied by a copy of the constitution of the society making the same.

Article III.—Representation.

1. Members of this association shall be represented in its meetings by delegates in the following proportion, viz.: One delegate for every five members or fraction of five.

2. Auxiliary members shall be represented in this meeting by one delegate for every fifty members or fraction of fifty. Delegates from auxiliary members shall be entitled to the privileges of the floor and participation in debate upon all subjects, but shall not be entitled to hold office or vote.

Article IV.—Meetings.

1. There shall be a regular meeting every year for the purpose of electing officers, the presentation of reports and the transaction of any appropriate business, at such time and place as shall have been determined upon at the previous annual meeting.

2. Special meetings shall be called by the President, at the request of a majority of the Executive Committee, or upon the request of any five members of the association. Such requests shall be transmitted to the President in the form of duly certified copies of resolutions adopted by the five (local societies) members aforesaid. The place for holding such special meeting shall be selected by the President.

Article V.—Officers.

1. The officers of this association shall be a President, six Vice-Presidents, who shall be selected as follows, viz.: one from the New England States, one from the Middle States, one from the Southern States, one from the Western States, one from the Pacific

States, and one from the Dominion of Canada; a Secretary, and a Treasurer, who shall be elected at the regular annual meeting. The officers of the association shall also constitute its Executive Committee.

2. All elections of officers shall be by ballot, and in open convention.

Article VI.—Duties of Officers.

1. It shall be the duty of the President to preside at all meetings of the association, appoint all committees not otherwise ordered; acting as chairman of the Executive Committee, admit new members, and issue charters upon compliance with the terms set forth in the official form of application; approve all bills against the association, and attend to such other duties as are elsewhere specified.

2. The Vice-Presidents shall be denominated, when elected, as First, Second, Third, Fourth, Fifth and Sixth Vice-Presidents, and shall, in the event of the death, resignation or disability of the President, assume and execute the duties of his office in the order named, until the next meeting of the association.

3. The Secretary shall keep correct minutes of all the transactions of the association, and shall send notices to each member of all annual and special meetings; shall conduct the official correspondence of the association; shall give special attention to the organization of additional local societies by furnishing information to persons and firms interested in the movement; shall receive applications for membership and reports from members; shall certify the correctness of all bills to the President for approval, and at the annual meeting shall present a general report of the leading transactions of the association during the preceding year.

4. The Treasurer shall hold in trust all moneys and other property of the association; shall pay all bills certified by the Secretary and approved by the President; and shall present a detailed statement of the finances at every annual meeting, or whenever required by a majority of the Executive Committee.

5. The Executive Committee shall have general supervision over all matters connected with the interests of the association, and shall have power to pass upon and accept new members.

6. The Executive Committee shall meet at such times and places as the President may select. Five shall constitute a quorum. They shall have power to fill vacancies in their own number.

7. No officer of the association, other than the Secretary, shall receive any compensation for services, and the salary of the Secretary shall be determined by the Executive Committee.

Article VII.—*Committees.*

1. The Finance Committee shall consist of the President, Secretary and Treasurer, and no debts shall be contracted in the name of this association unless previously authorized by this committee.

2. An Auditing Committee of three shall be appointed from the delegates at each annual meeting, whose duty it shall be to examine the books, accounts and vouchers of the Secretary and Treasurer, and report thereon.

3. Special committees upon correspondence, the state of the trade, or any other question interesting to members, may be designated as occasion requires.

Article VIII.—*Revenue.*

Each member shall, upon admission to the association, pay into the treasury ten (10) dollars as an initiation fee, and shall also pay, on or before April 1st of each and every year, as annual dues, a sum equal to one dollar for every one of its members.

Article IX.—*Amendments.*

This Constitution shall be abrogated or amended only at a regular annual meeting of the association, by a vote of two-thirds of all the delegates present, such amendments having been proposed by one or more members by filing said amendment with the Secretary, who shall serve notice upon all the members of the proposed amendment at least thirty days in advance of the annual meeting.

ORDER OF BUSINESS.

1. Calling the roll.
2. Reading minutes of previous meeting.
3. Reports from officers.
4. Reports from standing committees.
5. Reports from special committees.
6. Motions and resolutions.
7. Miscellaneous business.

Mr. W. H. Woodward. The Committee on Division of Subjects have a report which I suggest be taken up now, and while the body is considering the Constitution the Chair can make the appointments.

Mr. Woodward then read his report as follows:

Report of Committee on Distribution of Subjects.

The Committee on Distribution of Subjects contained in the officers' reports beg leave to offer as follows:

That all matters and recommendations in the reports of the President and Executive Committee relating to the subject of labor be referred to a special committee of five.

That that portion of the President's report referring to the death of prominent members of this body be referred to a special committee of three to report suitable resolutions.

That that portion of the Executive Committee's report which relates to an executive session of this body be adopted without further reference.

That that portion of the Executive Committee's report which refers to the subject of a bureau of information be submitted to a committee of five to report at this session.

That a committee of three be appointed to report on some feasible means of influencing the government to discontinue the printing of envelopes.

That the plan as recommended by the Executive Committee for holding future conventions of the United Typothetæ of America be referred to a committee of three.

That so much of the Executive Committee's report as refers to the meagre results in increasing the list of local Typothetæ throughout the country be referred to a special committee of five to report at our next session.

That the communication from the "Baltimore Yearly Meeting of Women Friends" be referred to a committee of five editors.

That the Chair appoint a committee of three to formulate a circular to local Typothetæ on the subject of negligence on the part of local secretaries in not making prompt and full reports in response to the requests of the Corresponding and Recording Secretaries.

That that part of the President's report which refers to the expenses of the officers and Executive Committee be referred to a committee of three.

That so much of the report of the Executive Committee not herein referred to committees be approved.

W. H. WOODWARD, *Chairman.*
R. R. DONNELLY.
E. PARKE COBY.
SAMUEL REES.
CHARLES BUSS.

The President. You have heard the report of the Committee on Distribution of Subjects. If there is no objection, it stands approved as read.

We are about to discuss this matter of the alterations of the Constitution. You remember, Mr. DeVinne made a motion that discussion be limited to five minutes, and no member be allowed to speak twice on the same subject without unanimous consent. Any motion to commit or lie on the table will receive prompt action, and any amendments to be made must be reduced to writing and read by the Secretary. I think that this will facilitate the work and save time. Also, any original changes will be amended in writing.

It was then resolved that the report of the Committee on Amendment of the Constitution be read section by section, and acted upon, and then adopted as a whole.

Mr. Waddey. I would like to ask for information before we begin this. In construing the resolution adopted this morning, upon motion of Mr. DeVinne, is it the sense of this body that no speaker shall be allowed to speak more than once upon each section, and that he can speak once upon each section?

The President. Yes, sir.

The Secretary then read the preamble in the report of the committee.

The PRESIDENT. Gentlemen, what will you do with the preamble?

Mr. FITCH. I move that the Secretary read the preamble as it at present stands in the Constitution, for comparison.

The Secretary then read the existing preamble.

Mr. REES. I move the adoption of the new preamble as read.

Seconded.

The PRESIDENT. It has been moved and seconded that the preamble, as amended by the Committee on Revision of the Constitution, be adopted as read. Any remarks?

Mr. FITCH. I move as a substitute that the preamble as it now stands in the Constitution be continued as the preamble for the Constitution in the future. It seems to me to be less diffuse.

This motion was seconded.

Mr. FITCH. It explains the objects of the society more concisely and briefly and clearly than the proposed amendment.

The PRESIDENT. Gentlemen, are there any remarks on the substitute offered by Mr. Fitch, of New York?

Mr. SLAWSON. I understand that we already have a Constitution, and if we do not adopt this amended preamble the other preamble will stand, necessarily, and just so far as we do not adopt a new provision in the Constitution the old provision will stand. Hence, there is no necessity for that motion. If we adopt this, the other falls. If we do not adopt this, the other stands as it is already.

The PRESIDENT. The point made by Mr. Slawson is well taken. The question will be upon the original motion.

Mr. FITCH. There isn't any doubt that the position taken by Mr. Slawson is correct. I made the motion in order that the members present should have their attention more especially called to the two preambles, and that making the motion would perhaps be a shorter way to call the attention of everybody to the difference. I withdraw the substitute.

The PRESIDENT. Are there any further remarks on the original motion of Mr. Rees?

Mr. BALKAM, of Rochester. It seems to me that the first line of this preamble should be changed. It starts out with saying that the United Typothetæ of America is organized for certain purposes. The next assertion is that the name of the association shall be the United Typothetæ of America. It seems to me that that is not a correct arrangement. I suggest to the committee that a slight change in the preamble might be made to advantage.

Mr. DONNELLY. I am in favor of adopting the new preamble because it specifies more clearly than the old the nature of the organization. It states that it is not coercive. The old preamble is all right, but it does not go far enough. This goes farther, and shows the spirit of the organization, and I am in favor of it on that account.

Mr. LOCKWOOD. I have no particular objection to this new form. I really think that it is unnecessarily extended and verbose. The objection of the gentleman from Rochester, it seems to me, is very well taken, and it should be rewritten, so as to conform to the style of the original preamble. The additional matter explanatory of the objects of this society is unobjectionable, but at the same time I do not see that it is necessary as a whole. I prefer the original preamble as originally written attached to the original Constitution, and I shall vote for the retention of the old form.

Mr. GIBSON, of Omaha. The only objection I see to this is, as my friend says, it names the United Typothetæ of America. I would say that "this association is organized," and leave out " the United Typothetæ of America " in the first.

Mr. WADDEY. The committee accept the amendment offered.

Mr. MORGAN. Was there a motion to adopt the preamble?

The PRESIDENT. It is up for discussion. There is a motion that the preamble as presented by the Committee on Revision be adopted.

Mr. MORGAN. Then I make a motion to leave out all of lines 2, 3, 4, 5, 6, 7, 8, 9, 10, to the word "approved." Commencing with "it is based on the right," etc., I would leave in.

The PRESIDENT. I think that your motion is in the nature of an amendment to this, and if put in writing it will be clearer, as ruled by the Chair.

Mr. MUDGE, of Boston. It strikes me that, after four years of successful existence, as we have already proved, the dignity of this body precludes any long argument in this way, and it strikes me that the original preamble as written first in Chicago is good enough.

Mr. GILBERT, of St. Louis. I am satisfied that four out of five of the gentlemen are satisfied, and I think that a great deal of time would be saved in this Convention if we could get some sort of preliminary vote to show it, because I think it would show at once that the majority are satisfied with the preamble, and that the amendments are to a particular man's fancy as to the wording, and it would save time if we go to the preamble at once.

Mr. MORGAN. I withdraw my amendment.

The PRESIDENT. The question is upon the new preamble.

Upon request of Mr. Morgan, the preamble to the old Constitution was read by the Secretary.

The PRESIDENT. I think that as this is a change of the Constitution and the vote will be almost about equal, I would suggest that the Secretary call the roll, and it will save the calling of the roll afterwards.

Mr. MORGAN. I move to commence with the old preamble, and add to it that portion of the new commencing with "It is based on the right," etc.

The PRESIDENT. The question is now on the motion of Mr. Morgan. Those in favor of the preamble of the Constitution as it stands now, with the addition of the new preamble from lines ten to fifteen, will signify it by saying "aye."

The President declared the motion carried, when a division was called for. The result of the standing vote was fifty-six "ayes" and forty-one "noes."

The President then declared the preamble to stand, with the original intact, and with the addition of "It is based on the right of the individual," etc.

Mr. LOCKWOOD. I am sorry that I have got to call the attention of the Convention to Article IX. of the present Constitution, which calls for a two-thirds vote of all the delegates. You will find that that will stop you from amending this Constitution very materially. I call for a two-thirds vote.

Mr. BATES. I will ask if that does not relate only to the Constitution as a whole and not to the amendments.

Mr. LOCKWOOD [reading]. "This Constitution shall only be abrogated or amended— "

The PRESIDENT. This is only as to the report on the amendments, and it is only necessary for a majority vote to make them, but when it comes to the Constitution it will require a two-thirds vote.

Mr. LOCKWOOD. I shall take exception to that, if it is your ruling. [Reads section complete.] It cannot be amended in any way—no one word in the Constitution can be changed—except by a two-thirds vote.

The PRESIDENT. I conferred on that point with your Secretary, and he said that he took the opposite side. I agree thoroughly with you, and he with this ruling.

Mr. LOCKWOOD. Who made the ruling?

The PRESIDENT. The Secretary. I acknowledge the error in it, because no word of the Constitution can be amended, and I presumed that that would be upon the adoption of the Constitution as amended when we were ready to adopt the whole of it.

Mr. WADDEY. I rise to the point of order that the preamble is not the Constitution.

Mr. WISE, of Dayton. We have to go further. The amendment has been carried.

The PRESIDENT. I rule Mr. Wise out of order, because the vote upon the preamble has been carried. It is not a part of the Constitution, and there is nothing in the Constitution to prevent the amendment of the preamble by a majority vote.

Mr. WISE. While the amendment has been carried, the preamble has not been carried; I raise that point of order.

The President. The vote was put upon the adoption of the report of the committee, and I declared that we had passed it by a majority vote. Am I right?

Mr. Wise. The amendment has been adopted, but the preamble as amended has not been put to vote.

Mr. Morgan. The Convention has voted on the addition to the first preamble to the Constitution. Now then, sir, will you just put the motion and adopt the whole?

The President. I rule Mr. Morgan out of order. The point of order is not well taken.

Mr. Woodward. To avoid any delays about this matter and any questions as to the two-thirds vote, I move that we go into Committee of the Whole, and report back to this Convention.

This motion prevailed.

Mr. Mudge was then called to the chair.

Mr. Rees. I move that we adopt Article I. of the Constitution.

This motion prevailed.

The Chair. We have now got to Article II. of the Constitution.

The Secretary then read sections 1 and 2 of the report of the committee.

Upon motion of Mr. DeVinne, the discussion of these two clauses was taken up first.

Mr. Morgan. I want to change the amount of membership fee for an association from ten dollars to twenty dollars.

The Chair. Do you offer that as an amendment, Mr. Morgan?

Mr. Morgan. No, no. I withdraw that, because we have not come to it.

The CHAIR. Did you hear the motion as made and seconded?

Mr. MORGAN. My motion will come in on Article VIII.

Mr. WADDEY. As I understood Mr. DeVinne's motion, it was that the first and second sections of Article II. be adopted.

Mr. DEVINNE. I want a vote taken on them because there may be difference of opinion on section 3.

Mr. WADDEY. Did your motion include the first and second sections?

Mr. DEVINNE. It did.

Mr. WADDEY. Of course, the motion of Mr. Morgan in regard to changing the amount of initiation fee would come in there.

Mr. MORGAN. I withdrew that.

The CHAIR. There is no motion before the house.

Mr. WEBB. I move that in section 2 the word "ten" be stricken out and leave it blank.

The Secretary then read the proposed section with the word "ten" omitted.

The question of its adoption was put and carried.

A MEMBER. I propose an amendment to section 2, so that it will read: "This form of application must be accompanied by a list of proposed officers." I do not see how they can be officers until the organization is chartered by the United Typothetæ.

The CHAIR. The question now stands on the amended motion. The Secretary will read it as amended.

The SECRETARY [reading]. "This form of application must be accompanied by a list of officers and the name of every concern or individual who are members of the society making the same."

Mr. LOCKWOOD. If these different societies applying for admission to this Typothetæ have only *proposed* officers, they are not eligible; they must have officers; they must be organized. It seems to me that it is uncalled for to put in that word.

The CHAIR. Those in favor of the motion as amended will manifest it by saying "aye."

A VOICE. There is no amendment.

The CHAIR. The amendment has been passed, sir. The Secretary will please read the amendment.

The SECRETARY. "This form of application must be accompanied by a list of proposed officers," etc.

Mr. DEVINNE. I must submit the question before the house is the adoption of the first and second sections of this article. I submit that this is the only question before the house at present.

The CHAIR. That is exactly the way I put it. The amendment, making the alteration that we did, becomes a part, as we understand, of your motion now.

VOICES. It has been withdrawn.

The CHAIR. It has been carried; and the motion that now stands before the house is on the adoption of those two clauses. Am I right, Mr. DeVinne?

Mr. DEVINNE. That is right.

The CHAIR. Those in favor of that will manifest it by saying "aye." As I understand it and declare, the two clauses are passed, with the amount of dollars (in small print) stricken out.

Mr. DEVINNE. That is the only change made.

The Secretary then read section 3 of Article II., and its adoption was moved.

Mr. SHEPARD, of Toronto. I wish to move that clause 3 of Article II. be referred back to the committee, for

the purpose of being expunged. I am opposed to the
adoption of the clause, and I do not believe that it is any
advantage to this association or members of the Printers'
Union to allow auxiliary members upon the floor for any
purpose whatever. I say that it is contrary to the spirit
of the preamble of the Constitution, which says that this
Typothetæ is an organization to promote a spirit of fraternity among the master-printers. I respectfully submit
that you cannot promote a fraternal spirit by the antago-
nistic influence which would be introduced here by giving
your employees the right to talk here, and giving them
the same effect here you do your members, while you deprive them of the right to vote in this organization. I
think that it would tend to create differences that do not
exist, and increase those that do exist, and I do not believe
that there is any association of journeymen printers on
this continent that will recognize your right claimed in
this preamble, " to work for whom and where they please."
We know that they work from an entirely different principle. They work for no one unless he recognizes the
Union, and while they have the power, I know that they
will not allow any man to work for you who does not
belong to the Union. Now, sir, it can hardly be expected
that they will abandon the principle which has become
to them a law, and as dear to them as their daily existence. Certainly you do not hope to win them over to
your way of thinking, because the journeyman printer
would lose his own right hand rather than go against the
law of his club, or violate the commands of his leader.
Another thing, you have here a delegate for every five
members of this Typothetæ, and you require these Unions
to have fifty members for one delegate. You allow them
to take part in the deliberations of the body, and give

them the same privilege that you do your members, but you prevent them from holding office. If I know anything of the stuff the average printer is made of, I venture the assertion you will not find one in a hundred who will avail himself of the privileges you offer. If the object be to promote a better spirit between the master-printers and employees, I think that this could be better done by meeting them on common ground, and discussing all questions of differences and mutual interests at times and places to be appointed by their respective clubs.

Mr. WADDEY. I wish to say, sir, in behalf of the committee reporting this resolution, that not a member of this committee has been urgently in favor of this resolution. I need not explain this to this Convention—certainly not to those who were present at the Boston meeting, where the amendment was first offered to our Constitution. I have stated upon more than one occasion that unless this recommendation receives the hearty endorsation of the Chicago delegation, that I, as the member of a committee that wrote and prepared it, would not vote for it.

Mr. P. F. PETTIBONE. It is perhaps due the Chicago delegation that a word be said about this. Whether any one is urgently in favor of it, I do not know. Certainly I know this to be true, that we have no desire to force any such provision as this upon your body, or to unnecessarily obtrude it upon its consideration. I do wish, however, and think it is due to us and to our sense of justice, to call attention to the fact that this provision says: "Any organization which recognizes the cardinal principle of the individual's right to work for whom, where, and what he pleases, may be admitted to auxiliary membership." If I rightly understand the gentleman from Toronto, he was speaking of these auxiliaries as if they expect the rights claimed by labor organizations. They certainly do not. They are opposed to such organizations as those he so clearly defines. As I said, I think that none of us wish to obtrude this against the better judgment of the members of the Typothetæ. It will certainly have a tendency to do this: it encourages the formation of societies such as we have in Chicago, and which we know have been of great benefit to us as employing printers. We know it is of advantage to the employee, and we know, also, that it is of advantage to us. It is not necessary, as it would hardly be proper, in this presence, to state all the ways in which it would be a benefit. We are not disposed to urge upon the people of this or any other city to adopt anything of the kind; but we say to you frankly that we believe if you should undertake to foster this sort of society that we have in Chicago you would find it greatly to your advantage. Now, there is already suggested in some of the reports that have been made a proposition for executive sessions. We can readily see that there would be topics coming up in our Convention that we would not care to discuss in the presence of these auxiliary members, if any such there should be. Going into executive session would deprive the auxiliary members of the right of the floor. They would have the right and privilege of the floor when the subject of discussion was such as could be easily and properly discussed before them.

Mr. SLAWSON. I was a member of this committee, and I expressed a doubt as to the utility to this body or to the society that is being proposed to be taken in as an auxiliary body. The only reference to this as an auxiliary matter is in the latter part. That seems to define the question of membership. But in the first part it seems that they are to be admitted to membership. If they are admitted to membership, and afterwards they are claimed to have only an auxiliary membership, it is not a fair thing. [The speaker's attention is here called to the provisions of the article.] Well, I did not read this right, but the point is this: there is another organization that is composed exclusively of printers. That is the "Protective Fraternity." They embrace in their doctrine that they will work for whom and what price they please, and they are just as much opposed to strikes and unions as this Beneficial Society of Chicago. I think the Beneficial Society is an excellent institution; I think the Presbyterian Church is an excellent institution; but I do not think that they ought to be admitted to this floor because they are based upon identical principles with ours. Now, we could admit the Editorial Association. Their object is to foster the printing business and so is ours; and although their interest is not exactly in the line of ours, they are working on the same plan we are. Still I do not think that we could benefit their organization or our own. We would be setting a dangerous precedent that, in two or three years, would be hard to get rid of, and I think the better way is to drop it now.

Mr. BATES. I have one remark to make. What has been the experience of those who have adopted this plan? We come here with this provision in our organic law recommended by the Chicago delegation. We know that they are loyal and true to the core to the interests of the Typothetæ. They have tried that, and their experience is that it is a good thing and should be encouraged. I think we ought to encourage it in our organic law, and in deference to Chicago I shall certainly vote for it as it stands.

Mr. POLHEMUS, of New York. I am really astonished that such a thing should be offered. This is an association of employing printers, and I think we should remain so, and no other body of men have any right to be associated with us. I do not want to make any complaints about it, but I shall certainly lose all interest in the association if this is passed and these people are admitted as auxiliary members.

Mr. McNALLY, of Chicago. I wish the Convention to understand that the Chicago delegation does not insist on this. It would be in very bad taste for them to do so. The pressure on the Chicago master-printers by the men who constitute this Beneficial Association has been very strong to get recognition from the Typothetæ. The pressure is more from the workmen than from the employers, and I do not want the Convention to understand that the Chicago delegation will be in any way put out if this is not carried. We have no feeling about it in any way.

Mr. WADDEY. The motion before the house is the amendment of the gentleman from Toronto, that this section be referred to the committee with instructions to expunge it. It seems to me that the easiest way would be to expunge it right here. This committee that undertook to revise the Constitution is not begging you to adopt this provision. They have recommended it, and if the wisdom of the Convention sees fit they can vote it down and pass on to something else.

Mr. MORGAN. There is a motion made to adopt section 3 of Article II. I cannot see anything to hurt in this resolution. I want to say right now, it is not a bad idea; it is a good idea. It is a good thing to have an auxiliary. It is a good thing to have those people leave

Typographical Unions and enter on our side, and that is the first step. It cannot do any harm. I regret to hear my old and distinguished friend exercise any feeling on this kind of thing. It is for the purpose of helping the society of master-printers of the United States. Now, our friends from Chicago have an idea that it would help. Now, wouldn't it help? Now, really, it would help us. Whenever you can get a good journeyman—a sure enough printer—he does not want to be associated with the men in these Typographical Unions. There is just as much pride in a journeyman printer as in the master-printer, and whenever that individual feels that he can step over to the master-printer's station, he will get there; and I take it, after thinking it over and reading it over three or four times—it required a little thought, and we do not want any of us to get angry—it is the first entering wedge to throw disaffection into the Typographical Unions of the United States, and I am in favor of the proposition on that very point. I heard the report this morning of the Executive Committee, and it was a wonderful report. Then I heard the report of the committee we have so much talked about, on ethics, and the committee recommended this proposition as nearly as you could do it. I want to say it is a good thing, and I am going to vote for it.

The SECRETARY. I have an amendment, offered by Mr. DeVinne, changing the words "individual right" to "right of the individual."

The CHAIR. That is a question of grammar.

The amendment is put and carried.

Mr. WEBB. It seems to me the proper way to get at this question is to vote directly on the amendment. We can vote down the amendment, and while I fully sympathize with the remarks made by Mr. Shepard, for the purpose of getting at this question I move to lay his amendment on the table. His amendment is to refer back to the committee in order that they may expunge it.

The CHAIR. That motion is not before the house. The motion has been amended as the Secretary just read it, and the question has been called for. Those in favor of the provision as amended will say "aye."

Lost.

We will now take up Article III. of the revision.

On motion of Mr. Waddey, section 1 of Article III. was adopted. The Secretary then read section 2 of Article III.

Mr. ROCKWELL. I suggest to the chairman of the committee to withdraw that section of Article III.

Mr. WADDEY. The committee withdraw that.

The CHAIR. If there is no objection, it is withdrawn. The question now comes on Article IV.

The Secretary then read section 1 of Article IV., and its adoption was moved.

Mr. PUGH. There is one amendment that should be made to this section, and that is, "unless the majority of the Executive Committee deem it wise to change it." I will explain that, by stating that when the Executive Committee met here in July there were resolutions passed by at least half a dozen of the local members of the United Typothetæ that this annual meeting be held in September in place of October. There was a ruling made that it would have been absolutely impossible to call the annual meeting of the Typothetæ at that time, and had a regular meeting been called, we would have had to call it on the 20th of October. A body whose powers are of the character of the body that this body is, has placed itself in a position not to be able by any force of circumstances or contingencies that may occur, to change the date of the annual meeting after it has been determined; and I think it should be placed in the hands of the Executive Committee, if they think it wise to change it, that they could change it to some other time than that set at the last annual meeting.

Mr. WADDEY. The committee accept the amendment.

The article as amended was then adopted.

The Secretary then read section 2 of Article IV.

Mr. WADDEY. I move the adoption of the section, and beg leave to call the attention of the Convention to the only change, which is the addition to the old Constitution of the part commencing with line 4.

The section was then put and carried.

Section 1 of Article V. was then read by the Secretary.

Mr. WADDEY. I move the adoption of that article, and beg leave to call your attention to the fact that the only change made in the old Constitution is merging the Corresponding and Recording Secretary into one office, and dropping the additional Executive Committee of seven members, and constituting the six Vice-Presidents (who now have absolutely no duties to perform), together with the President and Secretary and Treasurer, the Executive Committee. I beg leave to say, also, that it is the opinion of the committee that by the adoption of this amendment of our Constitution, we will increase the efficiency and working capabilities of the officers of the association.

Mr. PUGH. I would like to interrupt the gentleman, and read a telegram just arrived from Pittsburg:

PITTSBURG, PA., October 20, 1891.

To A. H. PUGH, *President United Typothetæ of America, Scottish Rite Cathedral, Cincinnati, O.:*

Pittsburg Typothetæ, now in session, sends greetings to United Typothetæ of America. Strike here not yet declared off, but employers jubilant. We are still "in it." Have Uncle Joe Eichbaum make further remarks.

H..J. MURDOCK,
President pro tem.

Mr. WADDEY. I started to say, sir, that the working of this organization is certainly abnormal. We have a President who is almost a figure-head in the interim between this Convention and the holding of the next annual meeting. The chairman of the Executive Committee has the absolute control of the affairs of this organization. Now, sir, if you put a man at the head of this organization, you make him responsible. Then it is an abnormal condition of things to put some one else in authority in the interim, while this man will sit at the foot of the table and some one else take the head and call him to order. I feel that the condition of things is disjointed, and that it is not in harmony with natural laws even, and the best way to change it is according to the report of the committee. If the Convention decides otherwise, I hope it will make the President an *ex-officio* chairman of the committee anyway.

The CHAIR. The motion is that this section of Article V. be adopted.

Mr. PUGH. I have heard what Mr. Waddey has to say in referring to the chairman of the Executive Committee, and think the officers as they are, with the exception of one Secretary, cannot be improved upon. The Executive Committee, as you all know, is a very able board of hard-working men, and you need a chairman for them; and as for the President, he is not a figure-head by any means. The correspondence the President has to answer and his calling of the Executive Committee, and the amount of business he has to learn in getting thoroughly acquainted with the association and wants of the Typothetæ throughout the country, keeps the President busy. The organization has grown to such an extent that we should not curtail the officers of the association. The Vice-Presidents have been the figure-heads. We cannot give everybody a place. The Vice-President was a very beautiful place to put these men; they appeared on the letter-heads, and in case of necessity they can appear on the staff. We should have men who, in case of disability of the President, are able, as he is, to fill the place. We should have an Executive Committee, and these men should be from different points throughout the country, to lend it a wide influence. The Executive Committee should be gathered from not to exceed four hundred to five hundred miles from the place where the President lives, so that the committee can be brought together at little expense.

Mr. WADDEY. If you will allow me a minute, the President of the organization has not the power to call the Executive Committee together.

Mr. PUGH. So far as the power of the President goes to call the Executive Committee I am not sure. He has always worked very closely with the chairman of the Executive Committee, and I think there will be no trouble about that. I do not think the time has come to eliminate from our list of officers the Vice-Presidents, nor do I think it is well for Vice-Presidents to be members of the Executive Committee—and I do not think you ought to place the head of the Executive Committee in the President's hands. I think he has power enough. It might be well to have only one Secretary; but if you have the President a member of the Executive Committee and the Secretary also a member, you will have your business well done. I trust that with this one exception Article V. in the old Constitution will stand.

Mr. SLAWSON. The old Constitution I think is all right with the amendment proposed, and with the further amendment that we insert the words "so far as practicable" after the clause "the Vice-Presidents shall be selected." It might happen that we may not have a man available on the Pacific Coast, and it might be that we would not have a man in the Southern States, and it might be that we would not have a man in the Dominion of Canada; and we might have a man in any one of these places who would not be suitable, but if we do find a man that is suitable we can use him, and so I move to put in the words, "so far as practicable."

Mr. DONNELLY. That is to be stricken out where it says all officers of the association shall be members of the Executive Committee, etc.

The CHAIR. The amendment as suggested is being written out now.

Mr. ENNIS. I think the President has enough to do without being on the Executive Committee. I move to amend the amendment so far as making the President a member of the Executive Committee. It should be left the way it is now.

The CHAIR. That should be in writing, according to the vote this morning.

Mr. ENNIS. My motion is that the words "so far as practicable," as offered by Mr. Slawson, that the Executive Committee consist of seven members (Constitution, Article V.), and that all reference to the President, be omitted in connection with the Executive Committee. I now move you, sir, that the motion prevail.

Mr. DeVinne. If Mr. Ennis will allow me, you have made no provision for the Secretary and President as members of the Executive Committee. I move that the resolution already before the house be passed with these words added: "The President and the Secretary shall be members of the Executive Committee, *ex officio.*"

The Chair. I think that is incorporated in the article as read.

Mr. Lockwood. We are going right around to the old article, and I think if we vote this down we will have just what we want.

By request the Secretary read the article in the original Constitution.

Mr. Fitch, of New York. I move that the last section as read, excepting with regard to the Secretary and Corresponding Secretary, be adopted as a substitute for the last amendment.

This motion prevails.

The Chair. The motion before the house is to adopt the old article as an amendment.

Mr. Waddey. There was one point which I failed to call the attention of the Convention to—the fact that the Treasurer ought to be a member of the Executive Committee. There is no question as to that, and I think the omission of the Treasurer was an oversight.

Mr. Pugh. I agree with Mr. Waddey; there is nothing which the Executive Committee wants to do but what it is important for them to know the state of the finances, and there is no doubt but that the Treasurer who is elected will be of as good calibre as anybody else.

Mr. LOCKWOOD. It was not an oversight in the beginning. It is a very simple thing to get a report from the Treasurer whenever the state of the finances is necessary to be known. I think this is right as it is.

The motion as amended was then put and carried.

The Secretary then read section 2 of Article V., which was adopted.

The Secretary then read section 1, Article VI., the adoption of which was moved by Mr. Waddey.

Mr. LOCKWOOD. It has been stated that the President of the association is a figure-head. If you adopt this you make him Czar. It makes him supreme.

Mr. SHEPARD. Mr. Waddey may strike out the sentence "chairman of the Executive Committee."

Mr. WADDEY. There is nothing which has been adopted which says anybody else should be chairman of the Executive Committee. Article V. of the original Constitution, which was adopted as a substitute, says that the officers of this association shall be a President, six Vice-Presidents, a Corresponding Secretary, a Recording Secretary, a Treasurer, and an Executive Committee of seven, who shall be elected at the regular annual meeting. It does not say who shall be chairman of the Executive Committee.

Mr. SHEPARD. The chairman of the Executive Committee can be elected by it, and I move that the words "as chairman of the Executive Committee" be stricken out.

The CHAIR. You have heard the motion of Mr. Shepard, that the action be adopted to strike out the words "as chairman of the Executive Committee." What is your pleasure?—Carried.

The CHAIR. The question before the house is on the motion of Mr. Waddey as amended.

Mr. WADDEY. We are taking action upon a very important subject. In the first place, as at present constituted, the detail by which a new member is admitted to the organization is that the application must be addressed to the Secretary, and it must be passed upon by the Executive Committee. This is a routine matter which never has been complied with, and never will be complied with. It has been done by the chairman of the Executive Committee, and no Typothetæ yet has had an application passed upon by the Executive Committee to my knowledge. I wanted to give the President the chairmanship of the Executive Committee, and put sufficient authority in his hands to give the association an actual ruler during the interim; and as I understand the amendment the article will read, "appoint all committees not otherwise ordered and admit new members," etc.

The CHAIR. In order not to have any misunderstanding, the Secretary will read the article as amended.

The Secretary then read the article as follows: "It shall be the duty of the President to preside at all meetings of the association, appoint all committees not otherwise ordered, admit new members and issue charters upon application, approve all bills against the association, and attend to such other duties as are elsewhere specified."

Mr. TAYLOR. I move to strike out the amendment, and adopt section 1 of Article VI. of the old Constitution, and that will leave the matter of the new members in the hands of the Executive Committee.

The CHAIR. Do you offer this as a substitute motion?

Mr. TAYLOR. I do.

Mr. DONNELLY. In section 5 of the same article you will find that this power is vested in the Executive Committee, and I think it might as well be stricken out of the duties of the President.

Mr. LOCKWOOD. Mr. Waddey probably forgets that at the first meeting there was a motion made authorizing the chairman of the Executive Committee to accept new members and issue charters, and it is for this reason that the question of admission has not been of late placed before the whole committee. The simplest way out of this thing is to leave the whole clause as it stood before.

The CHAIRMAN. The substitute motion of Mr. Taylor is before the house.

This motion was then put and carried. Section 2, Article VI., was then adopted.

Section 3 of Article VI. was then read by the Secretary.

Mr. LOCKWOOD. You overlooked the fact of the reference to the President, "who shall certify the correctness of all bills to the President." I make a motion to amend by striking out in the ninth line the words "to the President for approval." The section before gives him the sole power to approve.

The SECRETARY. Section 1 of Article VI. was lost, and the first section of the old Article VI. does not refer to this at all.

Mr. TAYLOR. I submit that the rejection of that clause will leave Section 3 of Article VI. in force, which covers the matter, and which gives the Secretary the authority to see that the bills are correct.

Mr. LOCKWOOD. I am sorry that I have to speak so often, but you will find that we will have to come back to the old arrangement of the Finance Committee. You have taken away the right of sole approval from the President, and you will have to come back to the Finance Committee. The Finance Committee calls for the President and Secretary to approve all bills. Now, I find by striking out the words, "to the President for approval," will make it chime with the old clause that you have passed.

This motion was seconded.

The CHAIR. The motion is made and seconded that the clause "to the President for approval" be stricken out.

Mr. WADDEY. As I understand this matter, we have adopted Article VI., which declares that it shall be the duty of the President to preside at all the meetings of the association, and to attend to such duties as are elsewhere specified. The object of the committee in adopting this resolution as it appears before you, that the Secretary shall certify the corrections of all bills to the President for approval, is, that they may be properly checked before they go to the Treasurer for payment, and that the money may be properly drawn from the treasury. The certificate of correctness of bills to the Treasurer, as suggested by Mr. Lockwood, would cut that out, and the result would be that this Finance Committee approve all bills. It seems to me that this would be in better shape, and "chime in," as he expressed it, with the object that we have in view.

Mr. LOCKWOOD. I notice, in looking ahead a little, that the clause providing for the Finance Committee defines it as being made up of the President, Secretary and Treasurer.

Mr. WADDEY. This does not provide for the approval of bills.

Mr. LOCKWOOD. I withdraw my amendment.

The CHAIR. There is no question before the house.

Mr. WADDEY. The motion is to adopt section 3 of Article VI.

The Chair then put the motion, which was carried, whereupon the Secretary read section 4 of Article VI.

Mr. WADDEY. I move the adoption of this section, and beg leave to call the attention of the Convention to the fact that the only difference between the old Constitution and the new Constitution is, that the old Constitution does not have in it the words, " by the majority of the Executive Committee," and the old Constitution does not say who has the authority to require the statement from the Treasurer.

Carried.

Section 5 was then read by the Secretary, and, on motion of Mr. Waddey, adopted.

The Secretary then read section 6.

Mr. WADDEY. I move the adoption of this section, and call attention to the fact that the changes consist in making five a quorum, instead of six. The committee consists of nine members, and five should be a quorum, instead of six.

Carried.

Section 7 was then read. Upon the statement of Mr. Waddey that there was no change in the section other than the word "corresponding," the motion by him to pass the same was adopted.

Mr. DONNELLY. You will find the committee that will be appointed by the Chair were to take into consideration the expense of the Executive Committee. I do not know whether you will call it salary or not.

Mr. PUGH. There is a resolution in the report of the Executive Committee, and there will be a committee to report on this, and I do not see any other place to bring this matter up in regard to the expense of the Executive Committee in case we have a meeting.

Mr. DONNELLY. That is what I was speaking about; but I did not think that this was a question of salary.

Mr. PUGH. Where do you propose to add this section? This must come in some place.

The question was then put and the article declared adopted.

Section 1 of Article VII. was then read by the Secretary.

Mr. WADDEY. I move the adoption of the resolution, and call the attention of the Convention to the fact that the only change is this, in inserting "Treasurer," instead of Recording Secretary; and the idea that the committee had in mind in drafting that section was that we would be able thereby to keep our expense always within our income, as no debts would be contracted without the consent of the committee, and, therefore, there would always be a balance in our treasury. This is not provided for now.

The section was then adopted, as were also Sections 2 and 3.

The Secretary then read Article VIII.

Mr. MORGAN, of Cincinnati. I move that line two be changed from $10 to $20 and that $2 be substituted for each member instead of $1. This is done with the idea of meeting the expenses of the Executive Committee traveling here and there.

The motion was seconded.

Mr. WADDEY. I will call the attention of the Convention to the fact that we have some very small associations—one organized in Lafayette, Ind., with five members, which will make the per capita tax $4, while we have one in Pittsburg, and we take the whole thirty-four members for $10 for the lot.

Mr. MORGAN. It is what we have to do and ought to do, as you are making changes and you are adding expenses to the association, and you ought to do it. It is necessary. If any body of printers in the United States cannot pay a fee of $20 to this association and $2 a year, it is not, I think, a body of men that we want. I do not think that they mean it. I ask for the adoption of the amendment.

Mr. SLAWSON. We have to get more revenue, and the question is whether we do get it by saying it should be $10 for ten members and less, and for all above ten members it should be $15, and for all above twenty-five members it should be $50. Where there are fifty members it would come lower for them to pay $50 than for five members to pay $20, and I move that it should be graded in this way, and that it be $10 for any number of members constituting the local society less than ten members, and $1 for each additional member, and if it goes up to fifty it is $50.

Mr. MORGAN. I accept this.

Mr. ENNIS. I suggest that Mr. Slawson make it $1 for each member.

Mr. MORGAN. I say that each member should, upon admission into the association, pay into the treasury $2 for each member of the local association as an initiation fee.

Mr. LOCKWOOD. I suggest to make it read "a sum equal to $2 for each member."

The Secretary read the section as follows: "Each member shall, upon admission to the association, pay into the treasury two ($2) dollars *per capita* as an initiation fee, and shall also pay, on or before April 1st of each and every year, as annual dues, a sum equal to $2 for every one of its members."

A MEMBER. There is no penalty in regard to non-payment of dues, and I want to amend it so it should be that any local Typothetæ being in arrears over two years should be dropped for non-payment of dues.

Mr. WADDEY. The committee accept the amendment.

A MEMBER. I move that the word "membership" be inserted for "initiation." There is no initiation in this association. This is no secret organization.

Mr. REYNOLDS, of Dayton. I think it would be a very easy matter for new members who expect to come in to get the membership fee down to $5. They are just organizing, and they could pay $2 and increase their membership afterwards. As it is the object of this association to increase the revenue, it seems to me it could be better borne by older and larger local organizations that are already members. Those that we may expect to get in now will necessarily come from the smaller places. It seems hardly right for them to pay a higher membership than we do. I think it would be better to increase the dues of the older associations.

Mr. WADDEY. I would like to reply to this, that at present, by the old and the new Constitution, a Typothetæ cannot be organized with less than five members, and accordingly we get a membership fee of $10 anyway. I hardly think that we ought to contemplate that any number of master-printers would be willing to stoop to such a way of escaping the amount that we ask as initiation fee, and I for one would not be willing to go on record as one to suppose that this would be possible.

Mr. REYNOLDS. Why should we ask this little association in Lafayette, Indiana. Of course they pay $10, but if they had eight or nine members they would pay $15 or $16 or $18, while Pittsburg with thirty-four members will come in for the job lot at $10.

Mr. WADDEY. I did not say job lot.

Mr. REYNOLDS. They are job printers. [*Laughter.*]

Mr. MORGAN. We did not know at first what was necessary. We have members who have spent hundreds of dollars to come here, and we have imposed upon gentlemen of this association. This committee was appointed for the purpose of revising the Constitution and seeing how much stronger we can get on. Any person who cannot afford to pay $2 as a member of the Typothetæ in any village or city in the United States ought not to have a wife or a baby or any association whatsoever; because he ought to love the association as he loves his wife. You belong to the Odd Fellows and Masons and all that sort of thing, and pay your dues there, and you ought to pay them also in this association. I hope that the members will vote for this increase of fees.

The CHAIR. All in favor of the adoption as read and as changed by the last amendment will say "aye."

Carried.

The Secretary then read Articles VIII. and IX. and the Order of Business, which were adopted as read.

On motion, the Committee of the Whole then arose, and the Convention resumed its session, with President Pugh in the chair.

Mr. Mudge, as chairman of the Committee of the Whole, submitted the report of this committee in favor of the adoption of the Constitution as amended, whereupon

President Pugh put the motion to adopt the report of the Committee of the Whole, which motion was carried.

[This report, which is the Revised Constitution of the United Typothetæ of America, is printed in the Appendix to these Proceedings.]

The Auditing Committee then reported as follows:

CINCINNATI, October 20, 1891.

To the United Typothetæ of America:

Your committee appointed to audit the accounts of the Treasurer, beg to report that they have performed the duty assigned them, and find the accounts correct.

C. B. WOODWARD.
W. S. BEST.
A. M. GEESAMAN.

On motion, the report was received and filed. The President then announced the different committees to whom subjects were assigned as follows:

On recommendations in the reports of President and Executive Committee relating to the Subject of Labor:

Messrs. C. H. Blakely, of Chicago; J. S. Cushing, of Boston; J. C. Rankin, of New York; Joseph Eichbaum, of Pittsburg, and Julius Festner, of Omaha.

On Mortuary Resolutions:

Messrs. W. J. Gilbert, of St. Louis; W. W. Pasko, of New York, and C. J. Krehbiel, of Cincinnati.

On Bureau of Information:

Messrs. Edwin Freegard, of St. Louis; W. S. Best, of Boston; Wm. Johnston, of Chicago; J. W. Wallace, of Philadelphia, and H. O. Thudeum, of Indianapolis.

On the Printing of Envelopes by the Government:

Messrs. Geo. M. Stanchfield, of St. Paul; W. H. Bates, of Memphis, and L. G. Reynolds, of Dayton.

On Place for Holding Future Conventions:

Messrs. C. M. Skinner, of St. Louis; H. T. Rockwell, of Boston, and C. S. Morehouse, of New Haven.

On Plan for Increasing Number of Local Typothetæ:

Messrs. E. A. Johnson, of Providence; Chas. C. Giles, of Troy; L. D. Myers, of Columbus; Chas. M. Rousseau, of Detroit, and C. H. Brandon, of Nashville.

On the Negligence of Officers in Local Typothetæ in Supplying Information to Officers of the United Typothetæ of America:

Messrs. Thos. Knapp, of Chicago; M. N. Price, of Minneapolis, and E. W. Matson, of Chattanooga.

On Expenses of Officers and Executive Committee:

Messrs. W. F. Balkam, of Rochester; John Polhemus, of New York, and Bruce Brough, of Toronto.

In reference to the Bureau of Information, it was resolved that the committee report at this session of the Convention.

The recommendation of the Committee of Distribution was that the communication of the Society of Women Friends be referred to five editors.

The President requested that if there were five editors present he would be obliged if they would come forward.

On motion, the Secretary was instructed to reply to the communication, and to state that "The American Newspaper Publishers' Association" was the proper place for this communication, although we are in hearty sympathy with the object proposed in the communication.

Mr. SHEPARD. I do not want to say anything to embarrass the committee appointed to choose the place of the next meeting, but I wish to call the attention of the Convention to the fact that at the last Convention at Boston, it will be remembered by most of you that Mr. Barton made a request of those present then to pledge themselves to come to Toronto next year, and I am here on behalf of the Employing Printers' Association of Toronto, to repeat the invitation we then gave you for the Typothetæ of 1892 to have their Convention in our city.

I may say to you that the proposition has been very enthusiastically received by our people, and, although we cannot expect to play the host in the munificent and royal manner that has been done in other cities, I can assure you that you shall receive a hearty and hospitable welcome. Although Canada is believed by a large majority of your people to be an inhospitable region, where savages and bears abound, I would like to tell you that we have had some experience in entertaining outsiders from your side of the border. Last summer some of your school teachers, including the high commissioner at Washington and professors of your colleges, swooped down on us in numbers of nearly twenty thousand; and later we had the florists of the United States, and yet we were not inconvenienced. It is true, the supply of pemican and bear's meat was entirely exhausted, and it was a question whether further supply could be obtained by a dog train in time for next year; but, fortunately for us, the McKinley bill prohibits the exportation of hen-fruit from Canada, and through the kindness of Mr. Blaine, in the delaying of the squadron, our fisheries will be likely to produce enough to supply a reasonable amount of this article, and if, as an additional inducement, the American cruisers will keep away from Behring Sea, we may be able to present a sealskin or two to the ladies who come with you. [*Applause.*]

The International Congresses go a good way to wipe away prejudices on both sides of the line. Why should they not continue? Does not the same blood run in our veins? Are we not of the same Anglo-Saxon stock? Are we not by common education, by common civilization, by the tie of common brotherhood, one people? And should we not try to cultivate a spirit of brotherhood and good feeling, and to obliterate each other's prejudices and antipathies—those prejudices and antipathies that dispel like the dew before the morning sun when we get to know each other more intimately? And, therefore, on behalf of my colleagues and the people of Toronto, I invite you to come to our city next year, and you will have a hearty welcome, and I know you will go away with a better knowledge of our people and our country. [*Loud applause.*]

The President then read a communication from the Cincinnati Type Foundry.

OFFICE OF THE CINCINNATI TYPE FOUNDRY,
CINCINNATI, OHIO, October 20, 1891.

The United Typothetæ of America are, collectively and individually, cordially invited to visit the Cincinnati Type Foundry, 201 Vine street, at any time during their stay in Cincinnati.

The President then read a communication from Mr. Pears, of Pittsburg.

Mr. TAYLOR. I move that the letter be received and filed, and that it be published in connection with the minutes of this meeting, in order that we may show the good results of the Typothetæ in one city.

This motion was seconded.

The PRESIDENT. Motion is seconded that the Pittsburg Typothetæ be wired that we congratulate them on their Typothetæ and on the happy results of being members of the association.

Carried.

Mr. DONNELLY. I know that some will object to publishing this letter, as it might hurt the feelings of the employees of some of our offices. I run a non-union office, but I respect those that run a union office, and I ask that Mr. Taylor withdraw his motion, or that part of it. If we have to fight it is all right and well, and we want to band together to fight, but we do not want to make a fight.

Mr. TAYLOR. I wish to say that I run a union office, but I do not see where the objection would come in. It is only an expression of what can be done.

The PRESIDENT. It is out of order, but can be reconsidered.

Mr. GALLISON. I want to call attention to the fact that the Proceedings of the Fourth Annual Convention must be approved, and that this session is not properly in order till the records of the previous meeting have been approved.

The PRESIDENT. The Fourth Annual Convention is vanished and all its functions. The officers which were elected to come into existence here, and this body of delegates, have no authority to pass upon the minutes of any other body which does not exist.

Mr. GALLISON. I call your attention to the order of business, which provides that the minutes of the previous meeting should be approved.

Mr. SLAWSON. It refers to the minutes of the previous meeting, but not to the previous Convention. I move a reconsideration of this last vote. I do not think it is proper that it should be a part of the minutes.

Seconded.

Mr. PEARS. When I sent that letter I had no idea that it was to appear in the minutes. I thought it was information that the Secretary would like to know.

The motion to reconsider was then approved.

Mr. TAYLOR. I will withdraw it, and wish to express my idea of putting this in the minutes. In the city of Memphis we had our entire force walk out of the office.

I had given instructions to the foreman to discharge an incompetent man. There was a clique in the office, and one that run the local Union, and they carried their proceedings a little too far, and at 1:30 they decided to go out. It is just such actions as this that I think the publication of this letter would have a good moral effect upon.

It was then agreed that the telegram of congratulations should be sent to Pittsburg, but that the letter should not be published.

Mr. Waddey here read a telegram, which was ordered to be sent to Pittsburg.

On motion, adjourned to Wednesday morning, October 21, at 9:30 o'clock.

SECOND DAY'S PROCEEDINGS.

MORNING SESSION.

The Convention was called to order by President Pugh.

On motion, the President's address and report of the Executive Committee were read as a part of the minutes, and the reading of the rest of the minutes was dispensed with.

The President here appointed the Committee on Nominations and on the place of holding the Convention next year, to report at the Thursday morning session. The committee was as follows: John C. Rankin, Jr., of New York; W. P. Dunn, of Chicago; A. C. Bausman, of Minneapolis; Stewart Scott, of St. Louis; Theo. Sproull, of Pittsburg, and F. H. Mudge, of Boston.

The Secretary here read a telegram, dated San Francisco, October 20, as follows:

SAN FRANCISCO, CAL., October 20, 1891.

A. H. PUGH, *President United Typothetæ, Cincinnati, O.:*

California greets Typothetæ. Longitude separates bodily; with you in spirit. AI ROLLINS.

Mr. PETTIBONE. I move that a telegram acknowledging this be sent, expressing our congratulations, and regrets at their not being able to have the delegation present with us this session.

This motion prevailed.

Mr. WADDEY. I have here a telegram from Pittsburg:

PITTSBURG, PA., October 21, 1891.

EVERETT WADDEY, *Secretary National Typothetæ, Scottish Rite Building, Cincinnati, O.:*

Morning *Pittsburg Dispatch* states Pittsburg delegates refused admittance to Cincinnati Convention. Communications to Pittsburg evening papers denying same should be sent immediately. Strikers believe it and are jubilant. It hurts us. Make it strong.

HARRY P. PEARS.

The PRESIDENT. You have heard the dispatch from Pittsburg. What is your pleasure? Shall it be answered?

Mr. WADDEY. I have prepared the following reply:

Pittsburg delegates here, and admitted at first session of Typothetæ of yesterday, and were greeted with applause. Additional delegates arrived this morning, and are now in session with us.

On motion, the transmission of this reply was ordered.

The PRESIDENT. There is another dispatch received.

The Secretary then read the following dispatch from Toronto:

TORONTO, ONT., October 21, 1891.

To W. A. SHEPARD, *Burnet House:*

Important business engagements prevent my being with you. Do your utmost for Toronto for '92. We can guarantee the association great welcome. C. W. TAYLOR.

The PRESIDENT. Is the committee appointed yesterday on the manner of holding Convention ready to report?

Mr. DONNELLY. I would like to suggest that Mr. Waddey hold on to that telegram for an hour or so.

Mr. WADDEY. I would like to state that the telegram sent as congratulations to Pittsburg was sent last evening, and will doubtless appear this morning.

The PRESIDENT. Is the committee on the manner of holding future Conventions ready to report?

Mr. SKINNER, of St. Louis. I ask that the reading of the report of the committee be laid over until the report of the nominating committee has been made.

The PRESIDENT. The next is the committee on reports of death of prominent members of this body. Is that committee ready to report?

Mr. PASKO. The other two gentlemen did not know that they were on the committee.

The PRESIDENT. The next will be the committee on government printing, of which Mr. Stanchfield is chairman.

Mr. STANCHFIELD. I was unable to get the committee together. I would like to have a little more time.

The PRESIDENT. The next will be the committee to which was referred all matters relating to the question of labor, of which Mr. Blakely is chairman. Is that committee ready to report?

A MEMBER. I think they are now engaged in their duties.

The PRESIDENT. The next committee is that to which was referred so much of the report of the Executive Committee as relates to Bureau of Information, of which Mr. Freegard, of St. Louis, is chairman.

The report of the committee was then read as follows:

CINCINNATI, October 21, 1891.

The committee to whom was referred the scheme of the Executive Committee for establishing a Bureau of Information and Supply, report that they have considered the proposal as detailed, and recommend that the same be put into operation during the ensuing year, under the control of the Executive Committee through the office of the Secretary.

. The amount of work required in carrying out this matter will undoubtedly be very large, and the committee therefore suggests that the Secretary be empowered to employ such assistance as he may deem necessary, the means of providing necessary funds for this expense being left to judgment of the Executive Committee.

We would advise the Convention that the work of the first year will be largely experimental, but that the results of the first year's existence of the Bureau would provide information and experience sufficient to warrant the Convention of 1892 in determining whether or not such a Bureau should become a permanent feature of our organization.

       EDWIN FREEGARD,
       WM. JOHNSON,
       H. O. THUDEUM,
       JOHN W. WALLACE,
       W. S. BEST,
            Committee.

On motion, the report of the committee was accepted and adopted.

Mr. ANDREWS. It seems to me that it would be necessary to incur considerable expense in doing that work, and the Executive Committee ought to draw upon the local organizations for some funds to meet it. It does not seem to me that the ordinary revenue of this body will cover the expense of it.

Mr. FREEGARD. In reply to that, the Executive Committee itself suggested several ways of raising funds, and we simply put it back upon them to do so.

The PRESIDENT. The next is the report of the committee on the expenses of the officers and of the Executive Committee.

Mr. Balkam, the chairman of the committee, handed his report to the Secretary, who read it as follows:

Your committee to whom was referred that portion of the President's address relating to the expense of the Executive Committee, would respectfully report that, in their opinion, such legitimate expenses should be paid by the organization, and respectfully offer the following for your consideration:

Resolved, That from and after this date the members of the Executive Committee present vouchers to the Treasurer for their hotel and traveling expenses while engaged in United Typothetæ business, and that the same be paid from the funds of the association.

W. F. BALKAM,
BRUCE BROUGH,
JOHN POLHEMUS,
Committee.

Mr. BALKAM. I move its adoption.

Mr. PASKO. I want to rise here to correct an error which we seem to be likely to fall into, in the use of the abbreviation U. T. A. for United Typothetæ of America. This is an error that is being made by other bodies over the country, and I do not think that we should tolerate it. You know the story of the old lady at the prayer meeting who prayed for the Y. M. C. A. and the A. B. C. D. M. The old lady understood her prayer, but it was not a very intelligible one, and we do not want to fall into that habit. After long experience the religious bodies have stopped it, finding it very offensive, and we should stop it here and have no more U. T. A., but United Typothetæ of America.

The motion to adopt the report was then put and carried.

The PRESIDENT. I have here the report of the committee, of which Mr. Ennis was chairman, which I appointed to meet the National Editorial Association at their meeting in St. Paul in July last.

The Secretary then read the report as follows:

Report of the Delegates to the National Editorial Convention.

To the President and Members of the United Typothetæ of America:

Your delegates appointed to attend the Seventh Annual Convention of the National Editorial Association, held at St. Paul, July 14, 1891, would respectfully submit the following report and suggestions:

As the pioneer delegation, selected by President Pugh, to represent the interests and dignity of our association, we desire to express our appreciation of the high compliment thus reposed.

Our departure, stay and return will, we trust, in no wise mitigate your esteem. The welcome given us, although strangers in strange places, the round of pleasure and delightful entertainment (and no less instruction) are graven on our memory.

The chief interest claiming the attention of the Convention was the country newspaper. With this subject the United Typothetæ of America has no concern save in the matter of apprenticeship. We conceive great good could be expected were a system evolved whereby our cities could draw from contiguous towns, having job departments, with large or small investments, where young men graduate as compositors and pressmen more or less perfect—their efficiency more marked in the art of printing—retiring only from their tutelage, with a good and sufficient certificate given for workmanship and good conduct—be happy in morale and permanent in good results.

Bankruptcy legislation is of no less importance to the United Typothetæ of America than the subject as presented to the National Editorial Convention. Where can you find a case where a printer obtained a *pro rata* distribution of money among the bankrupt's creditors? Waste of time and hopes dashed has been, these many years, the reward of any effort to obtain any part rightfully his.

A uniform commercial probate law ought to be in force, protecting the rights of the debtor as well as the creditor, preventing the waste incident to the delay and uncertainty of litigation.

The printing by the Government of return requests on envelopes is undoubtedly wrong, both in principle and practice, and your representatives would respectfully suggest that support and co-operation, financial and representative, be given in an effort to secure a repeal of this injurious and obnoxious law.

Government of a people should be confined to true democratic limitation—protection of life and property—leaving to individuals the privilege to engage in industrial pursuits for profit. A suitable amount of money should be obtainable to be given a committee to assist Mr. Jewett, Chairman of the Legislative Committee of the National Editorial Association, urging upon Senators and Representatives the legislation the United Typothetæ of America demand.

Your attention is asked to the various libel laws in the several States. It is the experience of many printers that suit for defamation, asking for large damages, is not of infrequent occurrence Where the imprint of the printer is unconsciously given, attack is made against him in the absence of an unknown author—an onerous responsibility, entirely out of character with the profits obtained from its mechanical construction.

Regarding this subject it was the voice of the Convention that an amendment be enacted to the present libel and slander sections, as they now exist in some States: "Provided that proof that the words spoken or published are true shall be a complete defense to all actions of libel or slander, except where physical or mental infirmities are maliciously exposed or ridiculed." Or this: "Unless actual malice be proven, no libel shall be maintained against the publisher of any paper, unless the complainant has first given such publisher notice that the words complained of are false, and the publisher has failed to retract the words complained of, as fully and publicly as first published, in the first issue of the paper after the notice, and opportunity is offered."

As joint members of the United Typothetæ, we cannot pass the opportunity offered, without commending the wisdom of our brother, W. J. Gilbert, of the St. Louis Typothetæ, in advocating a mutual interest and fraternal visitation in Convention time, of the National Editorial and United Typothetæ Associations. Your delegates were among those that enjoyed the prayer given by Bishop Ireland, the thrice hearty welcome of the Governors of Wisconsin and Minnesota, and no less remarkable and beautiful response of President Stephens—a masterpiece of oratory, from beginning to close, foreshadowing the spirit and method that marked this gathering of the brainy editors of America.

Without instruction, your delegates were at no loss to comprehend what their duties were—observers largely; instructing those dominating public sentiment and opinion with the principles and workings of their honored society, and showing a recognition of the claim of our organization as co-workers in the inflexible right to govern affairs of business without interference on the part of employees.

The trip, by far, excelled any previous event of the sort—continuously lavish and generous, without regard to cost or time.

Acquaintance with many of the delegates of this remarkable Convention will ever be a source of pleasure. Your representatives, too, will dwell about Madison, St. Paul and Duluth, in the long time to come—Duluth, city built upon rock, where nature has played strange freaks that rival the cunning of man's touch in the wild play between rock and lake; waters springing from rocky sides, gurgling, splashing, sparkling in the sunshine; fit resting spot for the recipients of your consideration.

These recommendations and suggestions are respectfully submitted for your careful consideration.

     RICHARD ENNIS, *Chairman.*
     FREDERICK BARNARD, *Sec'y.*
     F. L. SMITH, Minneapolis.
     T. L. PRICE, St. Paul.
     WM. C. SWAIN, Milwaukee.

Thanks are due to members of Typothetæ of St. Paul and Minneapolis for special attention.

Mr. DONNELLY. Other members of the committee cannot be present and they wish me to make some remarks. Mr. Barnard, who was a delegate to this meeting, was prevented by circumstances from attending. He wished me to state to the Convention that he would like to impress upon them the desirability of acting in unison with the editors, because in the matter of libel, to some extent it affects those who print briefs and documents; that the editorial body took hold of them warmly in the matter of urging that the Government discontinue the printing of envelopes, and he said that, although it was of little consequence to them, it was of importance to the Typothetæ, and that the hearty manner in which they took hold of this matter ought to induce us to take hold of the libel matter.

The PRESIDENT. While upon this subject I wish to inform you that the Ohio Editorial Association is here by a committee appointed from their association by Mr. Cappellar, those gentlemen are here. They are Mr. Price and Mr. Amos, and in the name of the body I welcome them here to our meeting.

Mr. WADDEY. I will read the telegram suggested by the Convention to send to San Francisco: "The United Typothetæ of America extends fraternal greeting, and regrets absence of the California delegation."

Mr. Knapp, chairman of the Committee on Issuing Circular to the Local Typothetæ, then read his report, as follows:

> During last year the officers of the United Typothetæ complained of considerable neglect at the hands of local secretaries in getting replies to communications, thereby causing great inconvenience in administering the affairs of their office. Therefore, it is particularly desirous that in future you answer all correspondence addressed to you from this body without any unnecessary delay, thereby assisting them in prompt work, that we may not be confronted with the same complaint at our next Convention.
>
> THOMAS KNAPP.
> M. N. PRICE.
> E. W. MATSON.

Mr. ROCKWELL. We have not heard the report of the committee.

The PRESIDENT. There are plenty of seats in the front, and I do not think there should be any lobbying in the rear. [*Laughter.*]

The Secretary then read the report, which, on motion, was received and adopted.

Mr. LOCKWOOD. I move that the Secretary be instructed to forward a copy of that resolution directly to the secretary of each local society. It should be put before the secretaries of the local societies in a direct manner, so that there can be no excuse that they never saw it or heard of it.

Carried.

Mr. GILBERT. I move that the chairman of the committee of the Editorial Association be invited to address us for five minutes from the platform.

Carried.

It was stated that Mr. Ochs went to Chattanooga the evening before.

The PRESIDENT. Will Mr. Gilbert be kind enough to escort Mr. Price to the platform for a five minutes' address.

Mr. Price was introduced by the President and received with great applause.

REMARKS OF MR. PRICE.

Mr. President and Gentlemen—In behalf of the National Press Association I want to thank you for this reception, and for the kindness in inviting us to be present at your deliberations. Self-preservation is the first law of nature, and the object of this association is to look out for self-preservation; but I am glad to find that in the law of live and let live you have learned all the departments of the word, not only to live but to let the other fellow live. Your deliberations seem to have in mind the laboring man who is in your employ, so that you see that he has fair play. Also, I see you have in mind to let the public live if the public will let us live, by not seeking to get exorbitant rates, but fair rates. This is along the proper line, I think. It is with pleasure that I find that you are in touch with the National Press Association, which also has the same important work of elevating the art preservative. I am not the orator of the National Press Association, John Amos, of the delegation that is here, being the principal of the number, and I will not take up your time any further, but thank you for the kindness bestowed upon us. [*Applause.*]

The PRESIDENT. Gentlemen, I have the pleasure of introducing to you Mr. Amos, of Sidney—an Ohioan, by the way.

REMARKS OF MR. AMOS.

Mr. President and Gentlemen—I haven't got my oratorical part here. Mr. President, for the first time in my life I have made the discovery that I am an orator. I do not think that any other person ever discovered that except Brother Price; and I may say that the members that are here this morning will make the discovery that I am not. I want to say, however, that nothing ever afforded me more pleasure than when I received notice from Mr. Page, the Secretary of the National Editorial Association, that I was appointed a fraternal delegate to meet with this association. I hardly knew what the objects of this association were, and I began studying them. I have learned a good deal more about it since I came in here, and I find that you are in touch with the National Association, working not only for the good of the—I was going to say the good of the order, and I think I might say so in here; but working for the good of the press, and that you as publishers and we as editors are engaged in a work in the interest of harmony all over this country. The better we get acquainted with each other, the more we understand the businesses that are in sympathy with each other, the more we can accomplish, not only for ourselves, but also for the public. Now, we are working for the public as well as for ourselves—and ourselves especially—though the more we can accomplish the more good we accomplish. I think the five minutes are up that were assigned me. [*Applause.*]

Mr. Theodore L. DeVinne, as delegate to the American Copyright League, read his report as follows:

Report of Delegate to American Copyright League.

United Typothetæ of America:

Your delegate to the Copyright League would respectfully report that, during the winter of 1890–'91, he attended many meetings and aided in the deliberations of that body. He found it necessary to write frequently to the Typothetæ of different cities, urging them to solicit the Congressmen and Senators of their respective districts to make renewed exertions for the passage of this bill. These efforts were reasonably successful. In the face of determined opposition, the bill passed the House of Representatives by a decided majority.

It was hoped and believed that the passage of the bill through the Senate was assured. Unfortunately, the bill met with amendments made in the interest of lithographers and copper-plate printers, which seriously menaced its passage. It was only after strenuous exertions that these impediments were surmounted. During the last hours of the session the bill, as amended, was adopted by both houses, signed by the President, and by him made operative on the 1st of July.

It is a matter for congratulation that this tardy act of justice has become a law; but it is a pleasure to know that the Typothetæ of the country have been nearly unanimous in their petitions for its enactment.

As the bill went in force on the 1st of July, it is too early to make any report as to its operation; that it will be beneficial to American printers cannot be doubted.

As nothing further remains to be done concerning International Copyright, your delegate respectfully requests to be discharged from any further consideration of the matter.

     Yours fraternally,

          THEO. L. DeVINNE.

Mr. Morgan, of Cincinnati, moved that the report be received and spread upon the minutes, and the committee discharged.

Mr. SLAWSON. I would like Brother Morgan to include the thanks of this body. Although I was not in sympathy with the act particularly, I think the work done by Mr. DeVinne and those with him deserves the thanks of this association.

The amendment was accepted, and the motion carried as amended.

The PRESIDENT. I will call upon Mr. Ennis of the Committee on Copyright, which was appointed July last. The Secretary will read its report.

Report of Committee on National Copyright Law.

Your Committee on Copyright Law have carefully examined the subject, and while of the opinion that there is great necessity for amending the acts of Congress under which copyrights are now obtained, have not at their command sufficient information to justify them in submitting any concerted plan of action.

They ask for further time, and would deem it a favor for any gentleman of the Typothetæ to write out and send to them as early as practicable any opinion he may entertain on the subject.

      RICHARD ENNIS, St. Louis;
      THEO. L. DeVINNE, New York;
      ANDREW McNALLY, Chicago;
      H. T. ROCKWELL, Boston;
      EVERETT WADDEY, Richmond;
       Committee on National Copyright.

Mr. MORGAN. I move that the report of the committee be received, and that the committee have further time. Carried.

Mr. ROCKWELL. Mr. President, I suppose that one of the most important topics which we shall have to consider and, possibly, to discuss, will be the attitude we shall take towards shorter hours, upon which we have a committee now deliberating. I understand that they will have the report ready during the day, and it seems to me that every member should know when it is to be considered, so that everybody can be here. I move that the report of that committee be made the special order of business for this evening at 8 o'clock.

This motion prevailed.

Upon motion, the Pittsburg delegation were invited to take seats on the platform. Messrs. Pettibone and Waddey were appointed to escort the gentlemen to the platform, which was done amid great applause.

The PRESIDENT. Mr. Sproull will only be too happy to address you. He commenced, when he left Pittsburg last night, to write up his remarks, and I see he has got them ready. He knew he would be called upon.

Mr. SPROULL. Instead of this being what our worthy President says, it is a telegram I sent to Pittsburg a few minutes ago. I suppose you wish to know simply with reference to the attitude of affairs in Pittsburg. I know from the assurances of sympathy since I came on this floor you are deeply interested in the progress of affairs there now. The strike there commenced about the 28th of September. There was no organization there, and there was a feeling of distrust and a feeling of antipathy between the different printers—so much so that they were almost afraid to be seen going in and coming out of each other's offices. When persons came into my office I thought that they came to get some points in regard to my business instead of some good for me. However, when we found that there was a common danger, we had to unite and join for action, and immediately all the larger concerns in Pittsburg, with the exception of two, formed an organization, which we called the organization of the Employing Printers of Pittsburg. Mr. Kerr took the position that to make such an organization effective, it would be necessary to form a connection with the United Typothetæ—a local organization was not sufficient. After talking the matter over, we concluded that if we could obtain entrance into the United Typothetæ of America we would apply for such a branch organization there. As a result, you know we made our application. We have been received here to-day as the infant organization of the United Typothetæ of America. In reference to our strike, and in reference to the manner in which we got to our present position, it is simply this: Somewhere about the fifteenth day of September—my office is a Union office—one of my compositors, who had been many years in my employ, came to me with a schedule. I took it up and looked at it and laid it down, as I had done several times before; and he said: "Mr. Sproull, we mean business this time." And I said: "That is all right; that is all I cared about it." He said: "I wish you to understand the situation thoroughly. It is nine hours or a fight. Which are you prepared for?" I took it up and looked over it carefully, and I found a number of demands which made it impossible for any employing printer, from one end of the country to the other, to comply with and exist; and we commenced talking among ourselves, and there were various objections made. Some objected to the nine hours. Some objected to eighteen cents increase per over-hour; but the thing which made us the most sensible of the need of organization was that the last clause of the circular said that every difficulty between employer and employee should be settled by the committee of the local organization in that office, and if they could not settle it, then it should be settled by Typographical Union No. 7. That we would never agree to. This is not a question of forty-five cents, or of nine or ten hours, but it is simply this: Shall we manage our business to suit ourselves? Now you want to know the result. We have received a great deal of encouragement. Chicago sent Brother Knapp to give us advice, and we received a good deal of good advice. The President of the association took his time to come up there. Philadelphia aided us, and New York aided us, and the Secretary of this organization at Richmond sent encouragement, and we received such encouragement that the heart of not one member of our association failed him, and we stood there man to man, and did not budge an inch, and we propose to run our business to suit ourselves, and according to the principles laid down by your President in his address, and not simply to live, but to let live. [*Applause.*] One word more. What success have we had? Within four days after it was known we had secured membership in the United Typothetæ of America, the largest firm in Pittsburg came and said: "Gentlemen, we want to join you." Three days before, when they were asked to become charter-members and to sign the petition that we had for signature, they refused, and said there was no use in it. Within four days they wanted to become a member. The next largest firm had signed the schedule, and instead of having a big job list, they found the hook empty. They took their signatures off the paper that they signed with the Typographical Union, and they came humbly and asked us if we would not take them into the Typothetæ. [*Applause.*] We stand here not simply as we started, representing two-thirds of the Pittsburg employing printers, but to-day nine-tenths of them are in the organization, and they are there to help you with financial assistance if necessary, and to do anything that you ask us to do. [*Applause.*] One word more. I was a little better off than my brother-printers. One of them had two men that stayed with him, and I had two-thirds, and they came around to me and said: "How is it that your men stayed?" I had an open office, and they could not pull them out or drag them out. As a result of that open office, I have only put on seven men of those who came from Philadelphia. The Union has begged them, and tried to intimidate them, but every one of the seven men has stayed with me, and they are going to stay as long as I want to keep them. To-day you cannot drive my employees away. I wish you would drive two or three of them away, they are so poor. We have in Pittsburg all of our offices running two-thirds full. We have all the pressmen we need to be going on, and do all the business possible for us to do. The only thing lacking is the matter of about twenty or twenty-five job compositors. The press-rooms are crowded with men—all the feeders we want—and of the one hundred and seventy men that went out, all the places are full except twenty to twenty-five job compositors. Gentlemen, we won this fight, not simply because we stood together, but also because we joined the United Typothetæ of America. [*Loud and long-continued applause.*]

Mr. Eichbaum was called upon for an address, and responded as follows: Well, Mr. President and gentlemen, I do not think there is very much left for me to say. Brother Sproull has hashed this matter up in a manner that certainly ought to be satisfactory. I agree with him that a better thing never happened to us than to get into this association. I will say this: that while I am probably as well known a man as there is in Pittsburg, and know as many, the large bulk of our printers I did not know by sight, and many of them I had not heard of. I am happy to say that we now meet in the most fraternal relations, and the lion and the lamb lie down together in the most beautiful manner. I am firmly convinced that we are going to stay there. There are other things to be gained than the mere matter of business. Personal friendships are a great thing with me, and I appreciate them highly; and I may state that outside of actual business matters, we have many things that we would not have had without this strike, and I bless God that they made this strike. I am rather a peacefully inclined man, but if any fighting is to be done, I am ready to go in. In 1873 I took the front of the business when there was not a grievance against our office. I am happy to say that in seven weeks Typographical Union No. 7 had no existence. Now they are going out with the Knights of Labor. Pittsburg is a smooth running place. It has got a bad name, but it don't deserve it. We get along smoothly all the time.

I hope you are pleased with the Pittsburg delegation. We flatter ourselves that you will be satisfied, because they are all good looking men. [*Laughter.*] I will tell you something you don't know: this delegation is happily constituted—about half Methodist and half United

Presbyterians. The Methodist part, of which I am one, does the thinking, and the Presbyterians do the talking.

Mr. BALKAM. It is very unpleasant to drop so abruptly from such pleasant matters to the business I desire to bring up. I am informed that some time during the summer it seemed necessary for the President to call a meeting of the Executive Committee; that they met here, and came from all parts of the country, and, as you all know, paid their own expenses. Now, sir, I move that the members of the Executive Committee be requested to present vouchers for their personal expenses at that meeting, and that those vouchers be audited and paid at this meeting.

The TREASURER. If this motion carries I will have to be provided with some funds. I do not propose to pay this out of my own pocket, and I haven't the funds to settle those bills now.

Mr. BALKAM. I will add this—" when we have funds." I know Mr. Russell's straitened condition, and we do not desire him to pay it out of his own pocket.

The PRESIDENT. There were nine members of this committee, and one of them had no expense; that leaves eight. I think the expense will be something less than $400; and as I understand that our worthy Treasurer will not accept the office another year, he will have that much less to turn over.

Adjourned to meet at 8 o'clock P. M.

EVENING SESSION.

The Convention met and was called to order by the President.

The chairman of the Committee on Labor announced that he was ready to report.

The Convention went into executive session, at the unanimous request of the delegation from Richmond. The stenographer was ordered not to take notes of the proceedings.

After the executive session was over, it was resolved that the reports of the Committee on Labor be received and spread on the minutes.

On motion, adjourned to Thursday morning, October 22, at 10 o'clock.

THIRD DAY'S PROCEEDINGS.

MORNING SESSION.

The Convention was called to order by President Pugh. On motion, reading of the minutes was dispensed with.

Mr. AMOS PETTIBONE. As there is nothing else before the Convention, I desire to offer a resolution. The preamble to the Constitution sets forth that, among other things, this organization was formed for the purpose of assisting each other when necessary. I think it is a subject that interests us all, and we are not unmindful of the fact that our friends in Pittsburg are in trouble; that they and their cause have been very seriously misrepresented through the statements that have been published from time to time, not only in the papers of this city, but in Pittsburg and other localities, whereby the status of the Pittsburg delegation as related to this Convention has been, and is now, represented in such a way as to work serious detriment to our interest. I move the adoption of this resolution:

Resolved, That the United Typothetæ of America approve and endorse the action of the Pittsburg Typothetæ in resisting the recent demand made by the Typographical Union of that city, and that we pledge them our hearty support in every practicable form.

The resolution was adopted.

Mr. MCNALLY. Would it not be advisable to have that resolution given to the Associated Press? I make that motion.

Mr. SPROULL. I must say, gentlemen of the Typothetæ, the Pittsburg delegation feel very grateful for the interest you are taking in our affairs there, and we thank every one of you very heartily. Before, however, you pass this resolution I would like to offer one amendment, which I think will be accepted. I find already that the action which you took last night in executive session is being changed, until by the time it reaches Pittsburg to-day, it will be so mutilated and changed that nobody will understand it; and in that connection I would like to add this as an amendment also, that the action that was taken with reference to the executive council and their letter and our answer, be made public and given to the Associated Press.

Mr. McNALLY. I accept the amendment.

Mr. WADDEY. I wish to call the attention of the Convention to the fact that this matter received last evening the attention of the full Executive Committee. If a report has been printed showing a garbled statement of the correspondence between the gentlemen who sent the communication on yesterday and our reply, we have the documentary evidence and can easily correct it. The committee came to the conclusion that it would be improper for us to give the correspondence to the Associated Press or to give it to the local press; and I merely wish to say, before the Convention votes on this question, that this matter was very fully discussed in the Executive Committee, and we thought it was better, inasmuch as this was a communication received by us and answered, that nothing further ought to be done with it until we saw, by some overt action of the body calling themselves a committee of the Typographical Union, that something else is necessary. I still feel, as a member of the Executive Committee, that it was the part of wisdom, and I think that the motion as originally made by Mr. McNally should prevail. I hardly think it is necessary to say anything more than to call attention to the fact that it would be going out of our way were we to adopt the suggestion of the gentleman from Pittsburg. We have passed a resolution and pledged ourselves to stand by the Pittsburg delegation, and I think that that is all that the dignity of this Convention calls upon us to do. I think that your Executive Committee has ample power under the Constitution, and if there is any misrepresentation as to the attitude of this Convention towards the Pittsburg trouble, they can give the entire correspondence, and it seems to me to be a matter to be considered hereafter, and I think it is better not to give that correspondence away until we see what action they take.

Mr. AMOS PETTIBONE. As one of the Executive Committee, I desire to express my sentiments in harmony with those of Mr. Waddey, and to say that that action was one of the reasons which prompted the drafting of this resolution, thinking that that would fully cover the ground. The Union people in Pittsburg are already aware of the fact that this association has not denied admission to that delegation. Now, if they shall send statements up there that misrepresent the condition of affairs, we are in position to take them up and do precisely what we did yesterday, and have them in such form that there can be no possible mistake. It seems to me that the adoption of this resolution is giving it out without getting any good out of it at this time.

Mr. Shepard was here called to the chair.

Mr. PUGH. I desire to express my views in full harmony with Mr. Pettibone and Mr. Waddey. I think that the resolution which was offered by Mr. Pettibone fully covers the ground. It is conservative, and such as should come from a body of this character. I do not think we should take action on this matter and place ourselves on record. I think that the resolution of Mr. Pettibone adopted by this body shows to the country, if necessary, the position that we hold in reference to the gentlemen from Pittsburg. I think they cannot fail to see that this body, through its officers and individual members, have done their utmost to help them out in this matter, and I do not think there ought to be anything more done.

Mr. SPROULL. I assure you that the Pittsburg delegation appreciate everything that is done. You have already done more for us than we had any reason to expect you to do. For that we thank you. But it is not simply as a member of the Typothetæ that I arise and speak on this question. It is for the purpose of putting you in the proper light before the community at large. It is not for the benefit of the Typothetæ at Pittsburg, but for this purpose: that the moment that they give utterance to their unjust lies, that moment you can give it a denial. It is very well to follow a lie twenty-four hours after it is started, but a good deal better to follow it up immediately. It is not for the benefit of the Pittsburg Typothetæ, but for the United Typothetæ, and to put the matter straight before them.

Mr. DONNELLY. We have the ammunition, and there seems to be a feeling that the ground is covered by the resolution which Mr. McNally moved to give to the press. Is it not well to hold the ammunition and use it when necessary? It is a good thing to have your ammunition. When it is fired it is lost. I hope the gentlemen from Pittsburg will be satisfied with the original resolution, which I shall vote for, and at the same time I do it without any discourtesy to them, and because I think it is the wisest course.

Mr. SMITH, of Pittsburg. Mr. Chairman, I very much dislike to hear so much stress cast upon what you so much desire to do for the Pittsburg delegation. As a member of the Pittsburg delegation, and without any consultation with the other delegates in this matter, I say to you: Suppose this Convention should legislate upon some other subject, regardless of the Pittsburg strike, and the motion was made that it be given to the press, can you conceive, or can you give me any practical reason, why it should not go out? Last night I made a motion in this Convention that these members of the Typographical Union be notified that they could not appear here while an outrageous strike was in progress in Pittsburg, and I made a motion that that action be sent out broadcast. In the multiplicity of motions that followed, that motion was not put. I went before the Executive Committee, and they decided that they would reserve action until we saw what the enemy did. Now, it makes a little difference. If I saw fit I would telegraph that action to the Pittsburg papers without asking this Convention. In deference to the Convention I have not done so. This Convention legislates and takes action, and it should have the heart and not be afraid to send it out to the world. It was a dignified and honorable action.

Mr. WADDEY. I wish to say in reply to Mr. Smith, that when a gentleman differs from me it does not necessarily constitute cowardice on his part that he should be unwilling to let his action be known. That is putting a feeling in his mind that has never existed in the mind of any member of the Executive Committee or of the association. The United Typothetæ of America has never, when it has taken a stand upon any subject, been afraid to give the widest publicity to it, and I wish to call the attention of these gentlemen to the fact that their judgment in this case does not meet exactly with ours. We feel that they understand and know all about the affairs of Pittsburg. But we have all been through this same thing. We had it in Chicago, and we had it in New York, and we had it in Boston, and we had it in St. Louis. It was only a question of a difference of judgment in this matter, but when you speak of being afraid to let the action be known, you are putting motives in the mind of the Executive Committee which I assure you has never existed there.

Mr. SPROULL. Before withdrawing my motion I would like to say one word of explanation. It is in justice to the Executive Committee of the United Typothetæ of America. Last evening some of us met the Executive Committee and this question was brought up, and we saw that we did not agree with them, and inasmuch as they think the matter ought not to be published, I withdraw my motion, and second that of Mr. McNally.

The motion of Mr. McNally was then put and carried.

The report of the Committee on Government Printing of Envelopes, of which Mr. Stanchfield, of Indianapolis, was chairman, was read as follows;

Report of Committee on Government Printing of Envelopes.

To the United Typothetæ of America:

Your committee, to whom was referred that part of the Executive Committee's report in reference to the matter of free printing of stamped envelopes by the Government, do hereby report as follows:

That each local Typothetæ be requested to appoint a committee from their organization to bring the matter to the attention of the representatives in Congress from their district, and that the President of the National Typothetæ of America select a committee of one from each State, so far as he can, who shall make an effort to enlist the aid of the Senators from their State.

It is further suggested by this committee that the local Typothetæ act in this matter previous to the meeting of the next session of Congress.

And it is further requested that the Secretary of the National Typothetæ mail a copy of this report to the Secretary of each local organization, prefacing said report with the following matter:

It is probably not generally known, even to the job printers of this country, to what extent free printed stamped envelopes are furnished by the Government, but your committee have ascertained that it is *enormous*, something over 250,000,000.

We believe that the law under which the Postoffice Department acts in this matter can be repealed or so modified as to return the work of printing these envelopes to those to whom it properly belongs—*i. e.*, the general job printers of this country—if the matter is brought to the attention of our representatives in Congress and in the Senate of the United States in a pointed manner. Your attention therefore is called to, and you are earnestly requested to take such action as is set forth in, the following report of the national committee on this subject.

GEO. M. STANCHFIELD.
L. G. REYNOLDS.
W. H. BATES.

Mr. LOCKWOOD. I notice that there is used by the committees in their reports the title National Typothetæ, and we ought to be called by our proper title.

The report of the committee was adopted.

The report of the committee on so much of the Executive Committee's report as related to the manner of holding future conventions of the United Typothetæ of America was then read, and, on motion, adopted as follows:

The committee to whom was referred the suggestion of the Executive Committee as to forming a plan for determining the location of future sessions of the United Typothetæ, beg leave to report—

That in view of the facts that the locality for the next session is determined, and that there is a strong probability of the next succeeding Convention being practically located before we separate, there is no immediate necessity of considering a change of policy; but in view of a possibility that at no remote day there may be a cessation in the stream of invitations for this body to accept the hospitalities of local associations, it is desirable that we should be prepared with a plan which will meet the necessities of the case. We therefore recommend that the Executive Committee take this matter under consideration at their convenience, so that, whenever the occasion arises, a plan may be in readiness for the action of this body.

C. M. SKINNER.
H. T. ROCKWELL.
C. S. MOREHOUSE.

Mr. GALLISON. I offer the following:

Resolved, That a committee be appointed by the President of the United Typothetæ of America to join with the American Trade Press Association in its effort to obtain free admission to Canada of trade journals printed and published in the United States.

I know a great many of the members of this body are publishers of trade journals, and some are printers, and as printers they are naturally interested in the prosperity of the people that own the papers. By a strict construction of Canadian laws the trade journals are subject to duties, and I know of several instances where the people in Canada have notified the publisher that they were compelled to discontinue their subscriptions by reason of the duties imposed upon their admission to the country. The Trade Journal Association meets on the 30th of this month and will endeavor to have something done in Congress. The publisher of the *Dry Goods Economist* called my attention to it. I know the moral support of this great body would be a great advantage to them.

Mr. SHEPARD. I think you are mistaken as to the duty on trade journals coming in the mail.

Mr. FORTIER. The strict construction of the law requires a tariff on the bundle. I think that they never discovered it until the McKinley bill; and when they found that they could not get hen fruit through and some other things, they tried to find somewhere that they could retaliate. It was not the intention of the department to enforce it, but it is enforced in some places.

Mr. SHEPARD. I receive several trade journals, and I know that Mr. Lockwood, as publisher of the *Bookmaker*, can say that his circulation in Canada is free.

Mr. LOCKWOOD. My own experience is to this effect: that the only publication I ever remember being charged duty on was the *Export Journal*. The Canadian authorities do not seem to care to have American export journals go through without duty. We have had no trouble with our other papers whatever; at least, I have never heard of any complaint. However, I should like to vote for Mr. Gallison's resolution.

A MEMBER. Isn't this a question of reciprocity, and would it not be advisable to refer this to Mr. Blaine? [*Laughter.*]

Mr. FORTIER. There are no duties on any paper addressed to the subscriber, if they are wrapped up in one parcel for one postoffice. If there are four or five or a dozen copies of one periodical parceled up, they might be held for duty; but if they are addressed to single subscribers I do not think that it is charged.

Mr. Gallison's motion was then carried, and Mr. Gallison appointed chairman of the committee.

The PRESIDENT. Amongst the duties assigned to me by the Executive Committee in July last, was the appointment of the chairmen of some committees, and among them was that of a committee on typesetting machines, of which Mr. J. S. Cushing is chairman.

Mr. Cushing not being in the hall at that time, the matter was passed over.

Mr. Crutsinger here read a paper on "Electricity in the Press-Room," which he had been requested to prepare.

Paper on Electricity in the Press-Room.

The subject of "Electricity in the Press-Room," or, rather, in the sheets as they pass through the press, is one which has engaged the attention of scientific men, and at times, ever since the advent of the present style of heavily sized and highly calendered papers, has nearly worried the life out of practical printers.

Judging by the heavy sprinkling of gray hair among the members here present, there are many who, like myself, remember well the time when soft rag paper, *properly dampened*, was used on book and catalogue work; there was no such thing as electricity on the press thought of.

That electricity does exist on the press now, is a fixed and often a very disagreeable and unprofitable fact.

How electricity gets into the paper probably does not interest us so much as does how to get rid of it; yet it might be well to say something about how it gets there.

The text-books tell us that electricity is excited or generated by friction, change of temperature or chemical decomposition.

It is generally conceded that the pressure and friction of the calendering rolls through which the paper passes in the machine, during the process of manufacture, are responsible for the generation of the electricity in it. I am informed that the "lay boys," who are usually girls, and the last handlers of the paper before being tied up into bundles, are often overcome by the amount of electricity absorbed into their systems from the paper, and but few of them are able to remain on duty for more than a couple of hours at a time.

But you will say that not all the highly finished papers, as they come from the mill, are so charged; that which we get in summer being rarely so charged, while that which is made in winter is very often so affected. Consequently we are led to believe that the conditions existing in winter are more favorable to the production and bottling, as it were, of electricity in the paper than are the conditions which exist in summer.

In winter, with the temperature around zero, the atmosphere is as nearly dry as it ever gets to be, as the moisture is then congealed and deposited in the shape of frost and snow.

In summer, the air is, during the driest weather we have in this latitude, only comparatively dry.

Air charged with moisture, especially warm air, is an excellent conductor of electricity, while dry air is the reverse.

If you will look into this matter, I think you will find that nearly, if not all, papers in original packages which are electrified will be found to have been made in cold, dry weather. There may be a few days in summer sufficiently dry to produce the same effect, but not many.

When the atmosphere is moist, it carries the electricity off from the paper as generated; and when it is dry, at least a part of the electricity generated is left in the paper.

Again, we find that papers which have exhibited no sign of being electrified, in the original package, and which behave in the most circumspect manner while going through the press on the first side, will, on running it through to print the reverse side, become highly electrified. Some sheets will come back with the fly, while others will shoot under the press and scatter over the floor on all sides of the fly table. That this is caused by electricity is easily proven by bringing the knuckle or a piece of blunt metal in close proximity to any metallic part of the jogger, when a spark will be obtained.

In this case there is little or no electricity apparent in the paper when put up on the feed-board. Going through the press to be printed on the first side seems to slightly charge it, and it is still further charged by passing through the press to print the second side, rubbing on the sheet below, and on the metal-clad edge of the feed-board, and on the fenders.

•

We find in the printing office that this condition occurs chiefly in winter, when the weather outside is clear and cold, and the atmosphere dry, and communication between the atmosphere of the press-room and the outside is shut off by closed doors and windows. It is much more likely to occur in steam-heated press-rooms, where proper attention is not paid to ventilation, causing a hot, dry air, than in rooms heated by stoves, where the ventilation is much better.

There have been a number of mechanical devices invented for the purpose of overcoming or getting rid of this very annoying and expensive trouble. None of them have been, as far as I know, thoroughly satisfactory. That which would produce good results in one office, would be found almost, if not quite, valueless in another, and it looks like no mechanism can be devised for overcoming the difficulty, on account of the very great differences in conditions existing in the different press-rooms.

It may be observed that electricians are not devoting their time and inventive talent to devising methods whereby they may dissipate or get rid of electricity, but rather to holding it for use. They are bending their energies to devise new and better methods of insulation, so that the electricity, which costs them so much to generate, shall not leak out from their wires and dissipate itself in the air and ground. They find, in practice, that close proximity to a metal down-spout or front of building will oftentimes cause a leak which is hard to find and remedy; and a wet or ice-covered insulator may render a circuit wholly unserviceable.

Then, why should not printers take advantage of this propensity which electricity has for getting away? It is in the paper, but will not stay there if a good opportunity is given it to get out.

We find, in practice, that damp paper is never electrified. We find again, in practice, that during the summer, when the atmosphere is comparatively damp and the communication between the air of the press-room and the outside atmosphere is unobstructed by closed doors and windows, we have little annoyance with electricity.

We find the trouble to be serious *only* in the winter, when the atmosphere is more nearly dry than at any other time, and the communication between the atmosphere of the press-room and the outside is cut off by closed doors and windows, and that the worst trouble is found in illy-ventilated steam and furnace-heated press-rooms, where the air is dry and parched.

Now, if we have no trouble in summer, and do have trouble in winter, is it not reasonable to suppose that if we produce the same atmospheric conditions in our press-rooms artificially, during the winter, that exist naturally during the summer, and pay more attention to proper ventilation, we will get rid entirely of this trouble and annoyance?

This, gentlemen, is my suggestion. There are those present who have given it a fair trial, and will, no doubt, be willing to give us the benefit of their experience.

On motion, the paper of Mr. Crutsinger was accepted and ordered to be spread on the minutes and printed in the Proceedings.

Mr. LOCKWOOD. While I think that it is possible to generate electricity on the printing press, I believe that electricity is put into the paper at the mills. It is charged with electricity while in the course of manufacture. For many years we have been in the habit of placing orders with paper-makers, subject to the guarantee, "delivered free from all electricity." That shows that paper-makers will undertake to keep it out if you insist upon it. It is in their power to do it, and they will do it if it is insisted upon in your order.

A MEMBER. I would like to state that a few months ago an article appeared in the *Scientific American*—which does not print anything, as a rule, which is not what it knows to be correct and good information—that this electricity can be avoided by a very simple process. I will state that, in my experience, I have one press which generates electricity while all the others in the same line are entirely free from it, so that I do not think it can be entirely in the paper. I think it is in the press.

Mr. L. G. REYNOLDS, of Dayton. We are not book printers, and therefore do not have trouble with full sheets. We have, however, some Webb presses, and we find that we have more trouble in the summer time than in the winter. We have a copper plate against the wall attached to the press by wires, and we run the sheet in front of that copper plate and up through the press. We have used the plan with the wet cloths too. We have found a difference in rolls of paper that we get from the same mill made about the same time; so the experience of all of us is not alike, nor the experience of the same person at all times with the same paper.

The PRESIDENT. One of the gentlemen here suggests that Mr. Morehouse, at the meeting of the Executive Committee in Cincinnati, in July last, described a very simple means of overcoming electricity in the press-room. I think a description of it will be interesting to the Convention.

Mr. Morehouse described the process, but owing to the fact that many delegates were unable to hear him, by a vote of the Convention he was requested to prepare a description of his plan, and have it printed in the Proceedings. In response to which we have the following:

> The able treatise on electricity, in the paper which has been read in your hearing by Mr. Crutsinger, has told us of all the annoyances with which we are troubled from the highly calendered paper now in constant use on our modern book and job cylinder presses, but no sure remedy has been suggested for the evil.
>
> For the past three years the firm with which I have the pleasure to be connected has applied a series of gas jets behind the fly, as shown in the sketch accompanying, and has found entire relief from the electricity, and very great gain in the drying of fine inks on illustrated work, where formerly "slip-sheets" were required.

This imperfect pen sketch may represent the rear end of a drum cylinder press, or the delivery cylinder of a two-revolution press. The rod A·A is a copper gas-pipe, three-eighths of an inch in diameter, with holes perforated on the top, one and one-half inches apart. The holes should be of such a size as to permit the flame

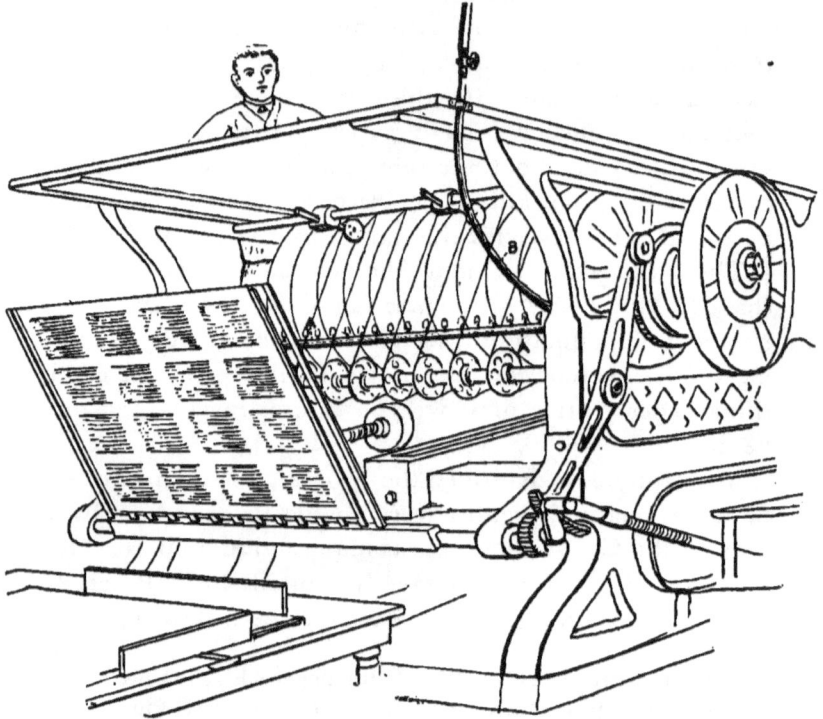

to be about one or one and one-quarter inches in height, with a full pressure of gas on the pipes.

The gas-pipe is suspended at the ends with flat hooks attached to the side frames of the press and connected at one end with a small rubber gas tube (B), and this tube is fastened at the upper end to an iron gas-pipe with a stop-cock attached. In this manner the rubber tube can be detached, and the copper gas-pipe easily removed, if required. Care must be used to place the gas-pipe at such a distance from the delivery cords or tapes, and from the fly while in position to receive the printed sheet, as not to endanger burning them. Rarely will the full pressure of the gas be found necessary to accomplish the warming and drying of the paper enough to overcome all electricity, or to insure the sheets from "setting off" in work where a large quantity of ink seems necessary.

Formerly, and for several years, steam was applied by us in the same manner as now suggested for gas, with excellent results so far as the printing was concerned. The objections were the rusting of the bright parts of the press, and when several presses were in use with the steam at the same time, the air of the room was injurious to the throats of the workmen. By the use of the gas these troubles are avoided.

The expense of fitting a press with this appliance is very trifling, and the experiment well worth a trial.

Mr. RIDGE, of New York. I have tried with success various ways of overcoming the electricity ; but I think the best way is to speak to the paper-dealer.

The chairman of the committee on typesetting machines stated that his report was quite long, and asked permission to simply read the introduction to the report and give a digest of its contents, and that the report be printed in the Proceedings, where those interested could read it at their leisure.

On motion, the permission was granted, the paper read as proposed, and, on motion, ordered to be printed with the Proceedings.

Report of the Committee on Typesetting Machines.

To the United Typothetæ of America :

GENTLEMEN—Your committee to whom was referred the subject of typesetting machines, have spent considerable time and research in endeavoring to get information that would prove of value to those contemplating their use.

We have examined into the working of many of the machines known at the present time; but as there was to be a contest of machines in the city of Chicago, under the auspices of the American Newspaper Publishers' Association, we hoped to obtain from them certain statistics in time for insertion in this report, which we now find are not immediately obtainable. Their figures of the amount of composition performed, and also information as to the general detail of the work, will not be ready for several weeks.

Through the courtesy of James W. Scott, of the Chicago *Herald*, we have copies of that paper for the use of the Convention, showing samples of the work performed by the several machines in the contest.

Extracts from the Chicago *Sunday Herald* of October 18, 1891 :

ROGERS TYPOGRAPH.

The Rogers Typograph was invented by J. R. Rogers, of Cleveland, Ohio, September 4, 1888,—many improvements having been made on the machine since. Of these a number have been suggested by Mr. F E. Bright, the superintendent of the Rogers Typograph Company's factory. In its latest improved form it consists of two parts, an assemblage and distributing mechanism, and the casting mechanism. The assembling and distributing mechanism consists essentially of wires, which spread out in fan shape at their rear portion and converge into a common vertical plane in front. These wires are fastened to a light iron frame, which is pivoted so as to tip forward and back something like a Remington typewriter carriage. This frame and the wires it supports stands at an angle of about thirty-five degrees. On these wires, at their upper or rear extremity, are the matrices suspended by an eye. They are strung on the wire like beads on a string, all those of the same letter being on one wire. By a very simple mechanism the matrices are relieved by touching a key on the keyboard precisely like a typewriter. The matrices then by their own gravity slide down the wires to the forward portion of the machine, where the wires are in the common plane before mentioned. When a line is assembled the casting mechanism comes into play. This consists of two parts. First the mould, which is brought forward against the matrices, or female type. This mould has an aperture just the size of a line of type. The secondary part of the casting mechanism is the melting-pot, which contains about thirty pounds of stereotype metal, kept in a liquid state by a small gas-burner. The melting-pot has a spout adapted to fit into the mould and also a force-pump attachment, which ejects the metal into the mould and the faces of the matrices by the operation of the machine. When the line has been assembled by touching the keys on the frame before described, thereby assembling into a line side by side the matrices, the mould comes forward against these matrices, the spout of the melting-pot closes into the mould, the force-pump in the melting-pot ejects just enough metal to fill the aperture in the mould, making a type-bar, or stereotype line plate, or, in printer's phraseology, a "slug" bearing the characters on its edge to print a single line. The melting-pot is then withdrawn, the mould opens, and the completed line, hard and solid, though still warm to the touch, is shoved by a mechanical finger into a galley. The wire frame containing the matrices is then tilted back and the matrices slide back simultaneously by their own weight, so that the assemblage and distribution are both accomplished by gravitation. This is the simplest possible method of assemblage and distribution, and is the most prominent feature of the machine. The spacing is automatically accomplished by little discs about an inch and a quarter in diameter, which are thrown in by the action of a key between each word. These spacers are composed of two screw-shaped faces, which, when the cam is caused to revolve, spread the line to a predetermined limit. This is done entirely by the machine and the operator pays no attention to it. There are a number of other devices upon the machine, one of which is very simple and yet important. By its action the machine will not work unless the operator has put in the right number of spaces and letters to fill the line. In case too many or not enough are put in, the machine refuses to work, so that accidents upon it are almost impossible.

MACMILLAN TYPESETTING MACHINE.

The MacMillan typesetting machine was invented by J. L. MacMillan, of Ilion, New York. The inventor is a native of New York, having been born at Cambridge thirty-two years ago. The MacMillan system of mechanical composition has been a growth from a small beginning, which dates back to the year 1883, when the first attempt to set type mechanically was made by the present company. The first machine which left the works was sent to the office of the Utica *Morning Herald* in 1885. An important feature of the typesetting machine is, that the key-board is an exact reproduction of the Remington typewriter, an advantage that can be enjoyed by no other company. Owing to the small number of keys used, and the consequent conciseness of the key-board, operators acquire skill in much less time than is required to learn large key-boards. Remington stenographers readily adapt themselves to the machine. The forty keys of the board communicate with the eighty characters in precisely the same manner as a typewriter. The typesetting machine is quite compact, the parts are all accessible, the motions seem positive and safe, the pressure of the keys very easy, approximating a typewriter in this respect. The line of set-up matter is directly in front of the operator, and he may see every letter take its place, add any character not in the machine, or make a correction when wrong keys are struck. For daily newspaper work the machines are made with the justifying attachment fastened to the frame, and the type is justified as fast as set up; but for book, magazine, and periodical work, not requiring special dispatch, a separate justifying machine is provided. On this latter class the operator of the typesetting machine sets the matter into a "storage galley," which is provided with a number of walls about twenty-four inches in length, which serve to separate the lines. As soon as a galley is filled it is removed and a fresh one put on the machine. The filled galley is then proved, corrected, and taken to the justifying machine, which feeds the long lines automatically to the spacer, who justifies it into lines of the required length. The distributing machine occupies, perhaps, a little more room than two ordinary type frames. It distributes from 10,000 to 25,000 ems per hour, owing to the size of the type. The distributor consists of a rotary disc, which has eighty-five inside distributing radial channels. The type are distributed, by means of nicks on their side, directly into removable brass channels, and are all ready for use on the typesetting machines. The wards that make the combinations for the nicks are small rolls at the mouths of the outside or receiving channels. The rolls, like the outside and inside sectors, are of hardened steel. The inside channels are straight grooves, in which the type is placed, with a follower and spring to hold the type against the rolls or wards by which the type passes into the receiving channels. Where the machine is used as an adjunct to hand composition, the type are deposited into tin boxes, which are emptied into the compositors' cases. When so used the size of the distributor is reduced one-half. The type is specially nicked for the distributor, and each type has two little nicks on its body. They vary in depth from two hundredths of an inch on the nonpareil bodies up to three hundredths of an inch on small pica. When new fonts are used they are cast with a nick near the heel of the type, and the machine nicks are made at intervals on the same side; but old fonts have to be nicked on the opposite side. The face of the type does not come in contact with anything in either the typesetter or the distributor, and it is probable that fine text types will wear much longer than when "thrown in" by hand compositors.

MERGENTHALER LINOTYPE.

The "Linotype" (line of type) is the invention of Ottmar Mergenthaler, of Baltimore. The first patent was issued March 17, 1874, and there have been over a dozen issued to it since. A linotype machine is a type-making rather than a type-setting machine. Instead of using movable type it uses movable matrices, which are placed automatically to form a line of matrices, by which a solid line of type is cast. Each letter, space and punctuation mark has its individual matrix, which is made of brass. The die is cut into the edge of the matrix at a certain distance from the bottom, so that when the matrices are in place the alignment of the die is perfect.

The operator places the matrices in position by fingering a keyboard, which resembles that of a typewriter. When a key is depressed it permits the corresponding matrix to drop from the particular tube, which contains a number of similar matrices, and takes its proper position in the line formed in a holder on the left of the machine. A mark cut into the holder designates the full length of the line of type which the machine is gauged to make. When the operator sees that the line is complete he presses a lever, and the assembled line of matrices and spaces is transferred to the face of the mould.

Sometimes the line is not quite long enough, and then the ingenious devices used to separate words come into play. These "justifiers" are slender wedges of steel. As the line of matrices moves toward the face of the mould the steel wedges are pushed up, and thus spread the matrices enough to make a full line.

Connected with the mould is a melting-pot containing molten type-metal, which is kept in a fluid condition by a Bunsen gas-burner. When the matrix for a line of type is in position, the molten metal is fed automatically against its face, filling the mould, where it solidifies and becomes a linotype bar, bearing on its edge in relief the characters corresponding to the line of matrices. An automatic stripping device withdraws the linotype bar, which is then placed automatically and trimmed to the right proportions and ejected on to the pile of linotypes previously made.

While all this is going on another automatic device lifts the line of matrices and justifiers and carries it to the top of the machine, where it is made to travel back over the row of tubes. As the line travels along, the matrices are distributed automatically, each matrix finding its own tube, into which it drops, ready to be used again.

ST. JOHN TYPOBAR.

The St. John typobar is the construction of R. H. St. John, of Cleveland, Ohio. Mr. St. John is a native of the Buckeye State, and is fifty-nine years old. When a boy he learned the trade of watchmaker and jeweler, which he followed for fifteen years, since which time he has been a mechanical engineer. The "typobar" constructed by him was first patented September 2, 1890. Many improvements have since been patented, but the principle and general form of the machine remains as his mind first conceived it. The typobar is the only exponent of the cold metal process or cold type-bar. The producing of the line of matrices which form the type, the justification of the line, and the distribution of the matrices after use, are done automatically, and require only one second in the operation. The action of assembling the matrices is positive and practically instantaneous; they all travel the same distance, guided to their positions by the same kind of mechanism and the same amount of force, and only in the order of their releasing. In case the wrong matrix is released an ingenious device permits of a correction being made before completing the line. The absence of all heat above the machine avoids all danger of molecular adhesion of two metals brought together in a heated condition whereby the line of type would be made defective. Likewise there is an absence of all evils attendant upon continual heating and chilling of the matrices and the parts surrounding the impression chamber. As the line of type is formed from cold metal, by compression, there is no expense for gas or other means for melting metals. The type-bar is made up of two parts: one, a permanent base or blank, to be used over and over, and is in theory part of the machine, the other part being a slight strip of type metal, in the nature of a supply, which is mounted upon the edge of the blank simultaneously with the operation of impressing the characters upon it. This type-metal strip is removed from the bar after use and may be remelted and reformed for further use at a very slight expense and without appreciable loss of metal. Moreover, the compression process insures with absolute certainty that every type-bar shall be perfect, as there can be no air bubbles, blisters, chilled metal or defect of impression. The machines are built of the best materials to be obtained for the several parts, and are especially re-enforced at points bearing the greatest strain. All the operations of the machine being positive, direct and automatic, the speed and correctness of the results depend only upon the skill and intelligence of the operator, as the machine will respond to all the demands of the operator. The machine is operated with a keyboard, on the principle of the Remington typewriter. The adoption of the point system of types allies the type bodies to this generally accepted principle. The spacing is done on an entirely new principle, which opposes to the adjacent matrices two sides, which are held as immovable as the matrices themselves, and between which the movable part of the spacer is pushed, thereby avoiding any displacement of the alignment, or of the impression surface of the bar.

Your committee think it better to submit the following reports of the actual operation of machines, rather than to give personal opinions or the claims of the manufacturers.

THE THORNE MACHINE.

J. S. CUSHING & Co., of Boston, with three Thorne typesetting machines (two long primer and one small pica) give their experience as follows:

We have had three machines in operation about three months, during which time no expense has been spared, and no advantage withheld, to run them successfully.

The Thorne typesetting machine requires the services of three persons—an operator, justifier and a distributor. Our three machines together require also the services of a manager, who "makes up" more or less of the matter, and takes proof, and a proof corrector.

The operator must have education, intelligence, and good judgment. She must be able to read manuscript readily and correctly, and have a good knowledge of punctuation.

The justifier must be able to read type at a glance, see quickly what space is required to complete the line, and to detect and correct obvious errors, etc.

The selection of a distributor seems at first glance a very easy matter. While the operator and justifier are usually women, the distributor, owing to the necessity of being on his feet constantly, must be a boy or man. Here again intelligence and good judgment are requisite. A liking for machinery is indispensable, for if the distributor has this liking, he will more readily understand the machine and will give it better care.

Next to a knowledge of machinery, he should have some acquaintance with type. He must realize that any hard substance brought into contact with the face of the type is apt to ruin it and that type is an expensive commodity.

To find this perfect distributor is no light task, and several applicants must be submitted to trial before the right one is found; for if the machine is intrusted to the care of an incompetent or careless boy, the result is sure to be disastrous.

In the case of our machines the operator and justifier have been, with one exception, selected from among the female compositors of the office, and only one operator and one justifier have proved at all equal to the requirements of the machine out of ten who were given a fair trial.

We are now trying the experiment of training fairly educated young women, who are not compositors, to be operators and justifiers.

From sixty applicants by letter, ten were selected and interviewed; and of this number four have been given a trial—two as operators and two as justifiers. After about two weeks' trial it has been found that while the operators do very well, the two justifiers are signal failures, and we have been obliged to fill their places with compositors.

To learn the key-board is comparatively a simple matter, for more depends upon the intelligence of the operator than upon any instruction which can be given.

Below is given a record (for four weeks) of our best team, and the only one whose production approaches to the figures claimed by the manufacturers as the average capacity of their machines. The operator and justifier were both compositors, with two months' experience on the machines, and the distributor two years' previous experience on the machines:

Aug. 17,	9	hours	. . .	23,556	ems.
" 18,	8½	"	. . .	24,752	"
" 19,	9	"	. . .	28,444	"
" 20,	7	"	. . .	20,618	"
" 21,	8	"	. . .	23,348	"
" 22,	4	"	. . .	11,050	"
	45½	"	. . .	131,768	"

Long Primer, 26 ems wide, leaded with 4-to-pica leads. Reprint copy. The time lost was ½ hour for repairs to machine; 3 hours for repairs to motor.

An average of 2,894 ems per hour.

Aug. 24,	9 hours		. . . .	16,250	ems.
" 25,	9	"	. . . .	23,920	"
" 26,	9	"	. . . .	21,684	"
" 27,	9	"	. . . .	21,918	"
" 28,	9	"	. . . .	22,074	"
" 29,	3	"	. . . .	8,089	"
	48	"	. . . .	113,935	"

This is on the same work as the previous week. The falling off is owing to a new distributor, who was not used to the latest design of machine.

An average of 2,373 ems per hour.

Here occurs a break of three weeks, the operator of the team being away on her vacation.

Sept. 21,	7¾ hours		. . .	15,806	ems.
" 22,	9	"	. . .	20,861	"
" 23,	7¾	"	. . .	16,506	"
" 24,	7	"	. . .	18,699	"
" 25,	9	"	. . .	16,738	"
" 26,	8	"	. . .	17,871	"
	48½	"	. . .	106,481	"

With the exception of 10,000 ems, this work is Small Pica, solid, 23 ems wide. Fair manuscript.

An average of 2,194 ems per hour.

Sept. 28, 9 hours . . . 16,491 ems. Small Pica, solid. Same
" 29, 7½ " . . . 15,652 " as above.
" 30, 8 " . . . 20,493 "
Oct. 1, 9 " . . . 22,747 "
" 2, 7½ " . . . 18,929 "
" 3, 8 " . . . 19,021 "

49 " . . . 113,333 "

An average of 2,292 ems per hour.

For the four weeks a total of 465,517 ems in 191 hours—an average of 2,437 per hour.

Week ending October 17th. Product of three machines:

	L. P. Reprint. (A) No. 1.	L. P. Reprint. (B) No. 2.	S. P. MS. Copy. (C) No. 3.
Monday, 9 hours . .	25,825	11,075	
Tuesday, 9 " . .	26,100	12,050	4,160
Wednesday, 9 " . .	27,425	19,500	8,112
Thursday, 8 " . .	25,375	17,925	11,648 (9 hours.)
Friday, 8 " . .	25,370	18,350	12,123
Saturday, 4 " . .	12,575	11,300	

142,670 + 90,200 + 36,043=268,913 ems in 48 hours. 5,602 per hour. 1,867 per hour, each machine.

(A) Team of 10 weeks' experience—both compositors.
(B) " 2 " " Justifier, compositor—Operator, not compositor.
(C) " 1 week's " Justifier, compositor—Operator, not compositor.

The question is naturally asked: Why this small output, as compared with the claims of the manufacturers?

As before stated, every facility to insure success has been given the various teams we have tried. Most of them have reached an average speed of 1,800 ems per hour on leaded matter, but have been unable to raise this after a reasonable length of time. One reason for this was found to be an indifference to machine work, in which case a change was made at once. By the employment of "non-compositors," if they can be trained to do the work, this difficulty will probably be overcome. The team whose record has been given above like the work, and are undoubtedly doing their best to reach a higher average.

The operator claims that much loss of time is occasioned by the blocking of type in the "type-way," or in the "packer." While this is sometimes the fault of the operator, it may be, and is in a majority of instances, the fault of the machine itself. Blocking may be caused by pieces of type, broken in distribution, being carried into the "packer." It is the duty of the boy in attendance (the distributor) to prevent this, but oftentimes he does not detect them in season to prevent the block.

Another cause, directly attributable to the machine itself, is at the point in the "type-way" where the "separator" operates. This "separator," as its name indicates, is supposed to separate the type as it comes along, so that only one at a time can pass into the "packer." When it fails to work properly, a block ensues. Sometimes the operator notices it at the commencement, but the chances are that the copy and the key-board so occupy her attention that the block becomes serious before it is detected.

This blocking causes a delay of some minutes. Many of these in one day, together with such other delays as may occur, affect to a considerable extent the production.

The justifiers in this office are perhaps handicapped by the high grade of spacing required. The fact that the work is done by a machine is not sufficient cause for lowering the standard maintained in hand composition. Because of this careful spacing the operator sometimes has to wait for the justifier to take the line. This delay must be considered with the others, and helps to swell the sum-total.

Not much can be said in favor of "gravity distribution," with no accompanying mechanism to separate the type. To work successfully, the type must be perfectly dry and entirely free from all adhesive substances. In an office where all type is handled by the electrotyper before it reaches the machine, more or less wax is sure to be encountered in the distribution, and then the trouble begins. The type must be taken out of the channels and the wax removed.

During the three months the machines have been run, thirty pounds of type have been rendered useless. Some of it was broken in distribution, and some in the "packer" or in the "vibrator."

Of the wearing parts of the machine, the "carrying belt" requires to be renewed, on an average, about once a week.

The necessity of sending all type and sorts to Hartford, for nicking, has been and probably will continue to be a serious annoyance. Why do not the company furnish "nickers" to the typefounders, and save us this constant source of delay and consequent expense?

Here is a sample bill:—

                Item—Sorts . . . . 50 cents.
                "   Nicking 04   "
                "   Express, both ways 70   "

Mem.—Machine delayed two days!

JAMES H. BUNKER,
Manager Machine Department.

From L. BARTA & Co.:

BOSTON, MASS., October 17, 1891.

At your request, we hand you herewith a report of our 11-point Thorne typesetting machine. We have not had a very long experience, and have only run one machine, which we put in last April.

We cannot say, so far, that we have got very enthusiastic over it; the best that our team can do with good copy is 2,500 per hour, and on ordinary copy they average 2,000 per hour.

In this we are very much disappointed, as we expected long ere this to have our team turn out 3,000 per hour on ordinary copy, and 3,500 per hour on good copy.

We find that the stoppages are quite numerous each day on account of the small mechanical devices getting out of adjustment or order, the wires getting tangled, the type and small round belts are continually breaking; in fact, there has got to be a good deal of care exercised.

If the type does not come back from the foundry very clean indeed, it will bother the distributor by clogging the slots. In regard to the small production, we have been taught to believe that it is very much due to the stupidity of our team; but we have what we thought two good girls and a boy, all three having worked in the business for quite a while, and we have tried to improve the production by having the justifier and the distributor change places.

Extract from WEST PUBLISHING CO.'s letter of February 9, 1891, in regard to their Thorne machines:

Replying to your enquiry as to how we are getting along, I am glad to say that our machines are running smoothly and satisfactorily. Our output varies considerably, and has not been so large as it might have been if our operators had not changed about a good deal in the past few months, making new combinations amongst themselves and occasionally introducing new hands. There is, however, a general improvement all along the line, and we do not consider that we have reached our maximum in any respect as yet.

Last Friday, the 6th, there were nine machines running, and the total output was 325,400 ems in seventy-six and two-tenth hours. This is as good a day as we have had, and is excellent in view of the fact that two or three of the teams had not had long experience. Our best week's record is 1,486,600 ems in three hundred and sixty-seven hours, an average of over 4,000 ems an hour for each team. The best single record is 49,100 ems in nine hours; but we are confident that the team which did this can and will do better when some of the other teams push it and imperil the office rooster, which is held as a trophy. Our work is all fifteen picas measure and solid. [Size of type not stated.—ED.]

From GEORGE H. ELLIS, printer and publisher:

BOSTON, MASS., October 10, 1891.

In response to your request for a statement of our experience with the Thorne typesetting machine, I would say that in purchasing our first, or 8-point machine, we did so with the expectation of using it on *The Christian Register*, a weekly publication averaging about 150,000 ems of brevier per week. All the brevier matter for that paper has been set upon the machine for a long time, and during the summer months we were able to put upon it other work, which kept it pretty fully employed, though not to its capacity, except possibly for one week. The measure is fourteen ems pica. A part of the matter was solid and part leaded, but whenever leads were used they were eight-to-pica.

A glance at our books shows to the credit of the machine for those weeks the following figures: 173,716 ems, 200,983 ems, 182,-608 ems, 176,808 ems, and 195,069 ems. The time spent on correcting was respectively as follows: Sixteen hours, thirty-three hours, thirty-four and a half hours, thirty-four hours and thirty-four and a half hours.

We have not yet tested this machine in any way. These figures are simply the results of a week's work, in no case exceeding fifty-three hours. The copy was given to the operator just as it comes from the editorial-room, without office-editing, so that it goes without saying that, were we working for a record under favorable conditions, the figures would be considerably larger In but one case have we timed the machine for a single hour, and then simply for our own gratification, and on copy which happened to be running at the time, with the result of almost an even 6,000 ems in the hour, besides making the change of galley.

Our 11-point machine, having been in operation but a short time, has had no sort of a trial, as we were unfortunate in the character of the work put upon it, proofs of which we were obliged to send to England, and therefore tied up type and prevented steady use of the machine. Our impression is, that we shall never be able to make so good a record on the larger type, but we are entirely satisfied of the practicability and economy of both machines.

It is but fair to say that our own experience teaches that the labor or proof-reading is materially reduced where the copy all passes through the hands of one intelligent operator, rather than through the hands of six or eight indifferent, to say the least, compositors at the case. This is indicated by the number of hours required in correcting first proofs, as it is not our purpose to accept poor spacing or anything but the best of work from the machines, as from our other compositors.

Trusting that this will furnish all the data you wish, I am, &c.

MACMILLAN MACHINES.

By R. Harmer Smith, Superintendent New York Typesetting Co.

To ascertain the capacity of the typesetting machines under average conditions, we requested the only operator we had, of any previous experience, to set type steadily for one month. At the time he commenced the operation he had only run the machines for four months, at rare intervals of five and ten minutes at a time to instruct learners. Previous to the month's work, he had had an equivalent to two months' practice on the present style of typesetting machine. He was, however, an operator of average skill on an old pattern of machine, which differed radically in the arrangement of keys, and in other respects.

The type used was long primer, and it so happened that about four-fifths of the copy was reprint.

His average product the first week was 45,000 ems a day of ten hours, and the last week, 51,000 ems—the average for the month 48,300 ems per day. His minimum product at the outset was 43,816 ems, and his maximum 53,700 ems.

He showed a steady increase from the beginning. His proofs improved during the month, and while the average time of correcting his galleys of about 4,000 ems each was seven minutes at the outset, it was less than four minutes at the end of his work.

This operator is foreman of the machine room, and does not do much work on the typesetter, but can easily reach these figures whenever called on.

The manufacturers of the machines have had a nonpareil machine here, on which he has practiced in anticipation of a contest of machines to be held in Chicago. On this machine the operator is limited by the ability of the justifier to space the lines. These men easily average 5,000 ems an hour solid, and the proofs are very satisfactory. A proof of matter before me with eight-to-pica leads contains 7,600 ems. It was done in an hour, and is fairly representative of their work. It has three turned letters, three transpositions, one extra letter and one wrong letter. The measure is thirteen ems pica, but it must be borne in mind that it is newspaper justification.

All our other compositors were learners, with no knowledge of the machines, and generally no practice in hand composition. A number of those who have attempted to learn, early showed so much indifference and want of ambition to excel, that we replaced them by others.

We have two typewriters, a young woman and a boy about eighteen years of age. Under favorable conditions these operators together produce about 300,000 ems a week. Their wages show the type in the storage galleys costs a little less than eight cents per 1,000 ems, but they were not hand compositors, and their proofs are not satisfactory, it costing about two cents per 1,000 ems to correct their storage galleys, and the reading is enhanced in cost perhaps two cents per 1,000 ems by the foul proof. They are deficient in the case of difficult manuscript, and we do not regard typewriters, unless also hand compositors, as a desirable class to depend on to any great extent for future operators.

One feature which has been disappointing in our experience with the machines is the time required by operators to learn. In the course of two months they attain an average of 25,000 ems a day, and under very favorable conditions 30,000 ems, but do not seem to get above that speed readily. We are not discouraged by this, as we find that operators on other machines have had the same experience, viz.: remaining stationary for some months, but afterwards the necessary speed is acquired by those who continue to practice.

The justifiers, who are generally hand compositors and bring their previous experience to bear, average 3,500 to 4,000 ems an hour, after six or eight weeks' practice, fair book justification. We have not had a long enough experience to say what the justifiers can do after a year's training, but on newspaper justification they do between 5,000 and 6,000 ems per hour.

The distributors have been run by printers, and they acquire the ability to feed into the machine from 12,000 to 14,000 ems an hour after a few days' experience. The product of the distributor depends somewhat on the matter, but an average of from 120,000 to 140,000 ems a day can be maintained. It requires a man to feed the lines to the machine, a boy to take away the cases when they are filled and to replace them with empty ones, and a young woman to examine the cases and correct errors and to place the cases on the racks for the setter. The young woman can attend two machines when skilled. The distribution is now costing about four and one-half cents per 1,000 ems, and we are not encouraged to expect that we shall be able to reduce it to much less than four cents. The breakage of type was considerable at the beginning, amounting to three mills per 1,000 ems for the first 1,000,000 ems distributed, half that sum for the next 2,000,000 ems, and at present amounts to one pound for 600,000 ems of distribution.

The inventor accounts for the excessive breakage at the beginning by the fact that the bur thrown by nicking causes the type to work off its feet in the distributor, and also that the nicks often expose blow-holes in the type, so that the slighest pressure causes them to break.

We cannot state precisely the cost of composition per 1,000 ems, as our work has been irregular because of the changes of operators and replacing them with new ones who, for a time, reproduce the uneconomical condition of the first stages of learning, from unsteadiness of work, so that there is much time lost, and what work is done is often divided among operators in short runs; and because, under such conditions, the pay of the learners is disproportionate to their product. For the last few weeks, however, with all these drawbacks, the account of ems set, as against the pay-roll, gives cost of composition on the galley, corrected, at twenty-six cents per 1,000 ems.

Individual cases may be selected showing the cost to be twenty-two and a half cents, and it is thought that when the operators become skilled it can be done for twenty cents per 1,000 ems, and still have all hands earn as good wages as under the present scale of wages for hand composition, which is eighteen dollars a week or forty cents per 1,000 ems for piece-work. We reach this conclusion, not only because the one trained compositor we have now is capable of and surpasses this result, but from the record made on the old and inferior typesetter, which was discarded for our present machine, by several operators who, after a few months' practice, attained on newspapers an average speed of 4,300 ems an hour, kept up for days and months; and also by the experience of other machines like ours, in which the type falls through channels, upon which operators have attained the average product we name above when they have had sufficiently long and continuous practice to develop speed and endurance.

This demonstrates that a safe average for the typesetters in the hands of persons who have become skilled, seems to be 4,000 ems an hour; the justifiers can easily maintain that, and even a higher speed. The justifier is much less uniform than the compositor in his hourly or daily product. The extremes are greater. The matter varies materially in a book office like ours. One work is free from italics, accented letters, etc., and the justifier runs out from 250,000 to 275,000 ems in a week. Another book is full of such objectionable features, and the justifier works more slowly. If the measure is narrow, or the justification unusually particular, the workman may not be able to do over 25,000 ems per day. With wide measure, and under less stringent conditions, he may reach 50,000. Our experience in the want of accord arising at times between the compositor and the justifier, the first puzzling over a difficult word or sentence, or putting in extra italic or sorts by hand, and bringing the justifier to a stand, or the compositor, in just the mood for playing the keys and assembling the type faster than the justifier can take care of it, brought to a stop and broken up, so that it may be some minutes before he can regain his rate of speed—or it may be a narrow measure through a whole book, keeping the compositor to the slow rate of the justifier—led us to suggest the complete separation of the two processes, and the introduction of another piece of machinery to assist the justifier. We regard the independence of each machine an important advance in mechanical composition.

First.—Each operation, setting, justifying and distributing, depends on labor as an auxiliary to the mechanism.

Second.—The ability of operators varies, and each is free to do all he can.

Third.—The conditions of matter are not uniform.

Fourth.—An interruption in one machine or operation does not stop the others. The practical working of this is shown by the fact that our operator set up a novel of 400 pages entirely by himself. He set up on the machine several storage galleys of matter, then justified it on the machine for that purpose, and afterwards distributed it by machine each day. This could be done by no other system of machine typesetting. At that time his best speed on the composing machine was 3,800 per hour. and he averaged 12,500 ems on the galley, set, justified, distributed, corrected, per day of eight and a half hours.

Fifth.—By setting the matter in the storage galleys, corrections of typographical errors, etc., may be made without overrunning, etc.

Sixth.—The practical working of our office for general composition shows that a uniform amount of work cannot be kept in hand. We may require a person to operate, justify, distribute, correct or make up the matter if he is a competent printer. For this reason we would not encourage an office doing general work to use stenographers, unacquainted with hand composition, on the machines.

These machines were run for several months by us before adoption. On the distributor we had no repairs, nor on the justifier. On the first compositor made of the present pattern, there were several screws and springs that had to be replaced from defective workmanship, but they were made stronger for the latter machine. So far as our experience goes, there is nothing liable to get out of order which the compositor cannot fix in a few minutes, and there is no need to have a machinist on hand after the machines are once adjusted. The probable cost of repair is so slight that we may ignore it.

THE PAIGE COMPOSITOR.

Extract from Inventor's Circular.

The Paige Compositor is a machine that does the entire work of composition, setting ordinary movable type with far greater speed, accuracy and artistic effect than has ever before been accomplished by any method. The machine automatically distributes and at the same time sets the type indicated by the operator; automatically spaces and justifies the matter without mental effort on the part of the operator, places it in a galley ready for use on book or newspaper as desired, records the number of lines set, and leads the matter as and when required—all of which is accomplished by the employment of positive mechanism.

The machine is not to be confounded with any other machine, as it is entirely unique in design, principle and method of working.

It is not a mere typesetting machine. It is a compositor in the truest sense of the word, as it performs simultaneously all the work of a human compositor.

Any good printer can reach a speed of operation in two months' time which will enable the machine to put out 50,000 ems of solid corrected matter in eight hours, as Mr. M. J. Slattery, a first-class printer, with an apprenticeship of less than forty days' practice on the machine has already set 68,121 ems of solid, standard nonpareil in eight hours, which is an average of 8,515 ems per hour.

This machine is now in private practical operation at 42 Union Place, Hartford, Conn. It was completed the 24th of December, 1890, and has been in constant operation since that date without interruption of any kind.

Chas. H. Wood, a printer, twenty-three years old, had only four hours' verbal instruction on the machine. This is his actual record:

No. of Days' Practice.	Ems per Day.	Rate per Hour.	Minutes per 1,000 Ems Correcting.
1	16,038	2,005	1.5
2	19,713	2,464	1.0
3	20,277	2,535	0.7
4	21,951	2,744	0.66
5	22,741	2,843	0.55
6	24,003	3,000	0.42
Total for first week	124,723	2,598	0.75

No. of Days' Practice.	Ems per Day.	Rate per Hour.	Minutes per 1,000 Ems Correcting.
7	25,368	3,171	0.29
8	25,231	3,154	0.204
9	26,529	3,315	0.33
10	27,621	3,453	0.33
11	28,409	3,551	0.217
12	29,898	3,737	0.254
Total for second week	162,046	3,397	0.27
13	30,980	3,872	0.226
14	32,499	4,125	0.289
15	33,298	4,162	0.31
16	34,290	4,286	0.236
17	33,772	4,221	0.266
18	34,813	4,352	0.277
Total for third week	199,652	4,159	0.27
19	34,405	4,301	0.215
20	35,628	4,454	0.21
21	37,179	4,647	0.137
22	36,396	4,549	0.172
23	38,205	4,776	0.183
24	39,042	4,880	0.175
Total for fourth week	220,885	4,601	0.181
25	40,338	5,042	0.14
26	40,843	5,105	0.191
27	41,850	5,231	0.161
28	43,011	5,375	0.172
29	44,078	5,509	0.19
30	42,930	5,366	0.233
Total for fifth week	253,050	5,272	0.181
31	44,334	5,542	0.197
32	45,630	5,704	0.21

As this machine has not yet been put in practical operation in any office, we are unable to give other information than the above extract from the company's statement, which is appended to this report simply as an indication of future possibilities in machine composition.

A serious drawback to the use of typesetting machines in book offices is one which is not the fault of the machines themselves. In an office where there are three machines—modern small pica, long primer old style and long primer modern—it is quite possible for business to be "driving," and yet not be able to keep more than one machine at work at a time. Books are apt to be wanted in old-style pica, old-style small pica, bourgeois, brevier, and, in fact, everything but what the machines are ready for.

Respectfully submitted,

J. S. CUSHING,
L. L. MORGAN,
THOMAS KNAPP,
Committee.

The PRESIDENT. The committee appointed by your President to attend the meeting of the American Newspaper Publishers' Association—Messrs. Lockwood and Cushing—are ready to report.

Mr. Lockwood, as chairman, read the report as follows:

Report of Delegates to the American Newspaper Publishers' Association.

To the United Typothetæ of America:

Your delegates appointed by the President, in answer to an invitation of the American Newspaper Publishers' Association, to attend the annual meeting of said Association in the city of New York, on Tuesday, the 12th of February, 1891, beg leave to report that they attended several meetings of the Association, and also were present at the banquet on the evening of the 13th of February, 1891.

Your delegates received from the officers and members of the American Newspaper Publishers' Association every courtesy and attention. Your delegates, having taken note of the methods of transacting business adopted by the Association, and inquired into the object and organization, deem it advisable that they should take this occasion to refer briefly to the operation of a society which is doing a great work and largely on the same lines as the

United Typothetæ of America. The American Newspaper Publishers' Association was organized in 1886. There are now on the roll of membership 126 offices, which represents 70 per cent. of the number of dailies, and almost 56 per cent. of the circulation of the daily newspapers of the United States. Each member or newspaper pays an initiation fee of $50 and annual dues of $50. The headquarters of the Association is in the city of New York, where there is a regular office in charge of a manager and his assistants.

The object of the Association is to collect information of every possible character of value to the business department of its members. It does not in any way deal with editorial affairs.

This New York office, for salaries and other expenses, costs the Association about $3,000 yearly, which amount is about one-half of the total expenses incurred every year by the Association. This New York office is a general clearing-house for all information obtained, the same being regularly distributed to the members upon application, in special cases, without cost. The information furnished covers all recent details of improvements in mechanical devices, the movement of the labor market, changes in prices, etc. The office has also constantly revised reports from a great many offices as to the number of men who could be called on in cases of emergencies, and is always in a position, in case of strikes, to order by wire all the men needed to any point in twenty-four hours.

The entire management of the American Newspaper Publishers' Association is in the hands of a Board of Directors, composed of the President, Vice-President, Secretary, Treasurer and Executive Committee of five, who have the full power to act for the best interests of the organization. The Board also has power to make assessments not exceeding $50. The members of this Board are paid a mileage of two cents per mile each way. It may be well to note that on the occasion of the annual meeting the members of the Association devote two full days to business, holding frequent meetings, and not allowing the same to be interrupted by any social demands of any character. After the two days' work is done a banquet is held, the expense of which is borne by each individual member.

Your delegates also beg to call attention to the action of the American Newspaper Publishers' Association in inaugurating a typesetting machine contest. This enterprise has been carried to a very successful issue. The contest has only recently closed at Chicago, and in the face of great difficulties and expense—the total cost having been upwards of $2,500. This contest has placed in the possession of the American Newspaper Publishers' Association a vast amount of valuable information bearing upon this important subject, which it is proposed to hold for the sole benefit of its members, no publication of the result being contemplated.

Your delegates have gone into these details thinking they might interest the members of the United Typothetæ of America, and in conclusion would respectfully recommend that the Secretary of the United Typothetæ of America be instructed to open correspondence with the manager of the New York office of the American Newspaper Publishers' Association, with a view to obtain full detail of the working of the Bureau of Information now in full operation, and to assist and throw light upon efforts of a similar character now contemplated by this association.

All of which is respectfully submitted,

HOWARD LOCKWOOD,
J. STEARNS CUSHING,
Committee.

CINCINNATI, O., October 21, 1891.

Mr. ROCKWELL. Mr. President, I desire to offer a resolution, and with the consent of the Convention to state my reasons in advance. It may be deemed unusual or irregular to propose legislation at this moment which retraces the ground covered by former action, and opens up matters which a majority of the Convention assumed to be settled. Of the reports of the Committee on the Hours of Labor presented yesterday, one went perhaps too far in one direction, at least in its phraseology "urging" certain action, while the other, in my judgment, went so far the other way that in its adoption this Convention has not expressed its real feeling and judgment.

Mr. SMITH. I rise to a point of order. How can this argument be made with no resolution before the Convention?

Mr. ROCKWELL. I am perfectly aware that I am proceeding only by the consent of the Convention; but in order to have a motion to discuss, I move the reconsideration of our action upon the report of the Committee on the Labor Question.

The PRESIDENT. The gentleman cannot so move unless he voted in the affirmative.

Mr. ROCKWELL. I recognize that rule, and as I cannot reach the matter otherwise, I will now move my resolution, without reference to former action:

Resolved, That the Executive Committee correspond with the local Typothetæ, and with the employing printers not members of the Typothetæ in places having a population of five thousand or more, requesting an expression of opinion upon the practicability of reducing the hours of labor to nine per day, and report to our next annual Convention.

Mr. President, I am satisfied that this resolution comes very much nearer to the real feeling of this Convention than our former action; and this Convention ought to be able to rise superior to quibbles of parliamentary law in order to express its desires. I hope it may be put to a vote on its merits.

Mr. DONNELLY. To a certain extent that commits us to making a request. If Mr. Rockwell will put into that resolution the word "advisability," it is another thing. The "advisability" is one thing, and "practicability" is another. I ask that Mr. Rockwell will substitute that.

Mr. ROCKWELL. Either word will hold it down; I don't care which.

Mr. SLAWSON. I suggest both "advisability" and "practicability"—both mean something.

The PRESIDENT. Does the gentleman making the motion accept both words—"advisability" and "practicability"?

Mr. ROCKWELL. Yes, sir.

The Secretary then read the motion as amended:

Resolved, That the Executive Committee correspond with the local Typothetæ, and employing printers not members of the Typothetæ in places having a population of five thousand or more, requesting an expression of opinion upon the advisability and practicability of reducing the hours of labor to nine per day, and report to our next annual Convention.

Mr. ENNIS. I move that the word "advisability" be omitted, as tautological.

Mr. DONNELLY. A thing may be practicable that is not advisable. I take issue with the gentleman.

Mr. MCNALLY. If this is adopted, what becomes of the minority report of the committee? It seems to me that this ought to be a substitute for that.

Mr. SMITH, of Pittsburg. The way it strikes me, the resolution nullifies the action on the minority report.

The PRESIDENT. I think it would be well to read that, and unless we go into executive session I do not think we can consider it.

Mr. MORGAN. This does not interfere with the action of the executive session last night. This is a resolution to ask for information and get statistics, and this is the only way we can get it.

The resolution was then adopted.

The report of the Nominating Committee was then read as follows by Mr. Rankin, chairman of the committee:

Report of Committee on Place of Next Meeting and on Nominations.

Your committee respectfully report in favor of accepting the very kind invitation of the Toronto Typothetæ to hold the Sixth Annual Convention of the United Typothetæ of America at Toronto, Canada; and, after consultation with the delegation from that city, suggest Tuesday, August 16th, as the date for opening the Convention.

We further suggest the names of the following gentlemen as the officers of this association for the ensuing year:

President—W. A. Shepard, Toronto, Canada.

Vice-Presidents—1st, E. R. Andrews, Rochester, N. Y.; 2d, J. S. Cushing, Boston, Mass.; 3d, L. D. Myers, Columbus, O.; 4th, J. R. McFetridge, Philadelphia, Pa.; 5th, Julius T. Festner, Omaha; 6th, H. P. Pears, Pittsburg, Pa.

Secretary—Everett Waddey, Richmond, Va.

Treasurer—A. O. Russell, Cincinnati, O.

Executive Committee—Amos Pettibone, Chicago (*Chairman*); Theo. L. DeVinne, New York; C. S. Morehouse, New Haven; W. H. Woodward, St. Louis; Wm. H. Bates, Memphis; A. M. Geesaman, Minneapolis.

JOHN C. RANKIN, Jr.
W. P. DUNN.
A. C. BAUSMAN.
STEWART SCOTT.
THEO. SPROULL.
F. H. MUDGE.

Mr. RUSSELL. Mr. Chairman and Gentlemen—I must decline to serve any longer in the capacity of Treasurer of this organization. I have been here now four years, and it is high time that I was relieved. I do not feel that I ought to labor any longer. I have recommended to the Nominating Committee a very competent and proper person to act in the capacity of Treasurer of this organization, and I was in hopes that they would adopt it, as they knew that I could not serve any longer in the capacity of Treasurer.

Mr. MORGAN. In place of Mr. Russell I nominate Mr. Charles Buss, of Cincinnati, one of the employers of the *Commercial-Gazette* office. If I wanted a treasurer of Cincinnati I would vote for Mr. Buss. I think Mr. Russell's declination ought to be accepted. I ask the substitution of Mr. Buss in the place of Mr. Russell.

Mr. BATES. I believe in adhering to the report of the committee, if we can in any way induce Mr. Russell to keep that position.

Mr. RANKIN. In the meeting of that committee we had no information from Mr. Russell further than the report of the President yesterday, and we knew it to be the unanimous feeling of the Convention to have Mr. Russell in that place. The committee did not want to consider any other name, and decided unanimously to recommend Mr. Russell.

Mr. Mudge was here called to the chair, and it was moved that the Secretary be authorized to cast one ballot in favor of the committee's report.

Mr. RANKIN. The first recommendation is in regard to the place and time of meeting. I move that recommendation be adopted.

Seconded.

In regard to the date, we consulted the delegation from Canada after we decided upon holding the Convention at that place, and they stated that for various reasons the hotels would not be so full at that time and they preferred to have the Convention in August, and that the season of the year would be better for entertaining the Convention.

The motion was then put and carried.

The President declared the sense of the meeting to be that the next Convention would be held at Toronto, August 16, 1892.

Mr. RANKIN. If there is no objection, I move that the Secretary be instructed to cast the ballot of the Convention for the officers nominated.

Mr. MORGAN. I made a motion that Mr. Charles Buss, of Cincinnati, be Treasurer instead of Mr. Russell.

The CHAIR. It was not seconded.

Mr. MORGAN. Mr. Russell seconded it. [*Laughter.*]

11

Mr. RUSSELL. I make a motion that the ballots shall be cast by individual members of this organization for those officers and not by the Secretary. Then we will get at the expression of who is who. .

Mr. T. L. DeVINNE. For the benefit of those members who were not here when the report of the Committee on Nominations was read, I will ask to have it read again.

The Secretary then read the report.

President PUGH (in the chair.) Do you desire that a vote be taken, or the ballot be cast?

Mr. DeVINNE. The Constitution we are working under says expressly that it shall be cast by ballot.

The PRESIDENT. Will the Secretary announce for President Mr. W. F. Shepard, and call a vote on it?

Mr. RUSSELL.. If there is no other candidate for that office, I will suggest that the Secretary cast that vote. There appears to be no opposition When it comes to Treasurer, we will talk about it.

Mr. LOCKWOOD. I believe there were only five names read as Executive Committee.

The SECRETARY. There are six.

Mr. LOCKWOOD. Should there not be seven?

Mr. WADDEY. The old Constitution calls for six, and three *ex-officio* members make nine. The new Constitution puts President and Secretary on, and that makes nine.

Mr. LOCKWOOD. I think we had ten all together.

The SECRETARY. The Constitution calls for seven members of the Executive Committee.

Mr. RANKIN. The committee would recommend as the seventh man on the Executive Committee, Mr. Ai Rollins, of San Francisco.

Mr. PUGH. I rather object to that place. We never would have time to hear from San Francisco.

Mr. LOCKWOOD. How many Vice-Presidents have you there?

The SECRETARY. Six.

Mr. LANDIS, of Memphis. I would like to ask who represents the South in the list of Vice-Presidents? I don't remember hearing one named in the list of Vice-Presidents.

The Secretary read the list.

Mr. LANDIS. I would ask that the committee nominate one from the South.

Mr. ENNIS. I move to substitute the name of Mr. Bruce, of Nashville, in place of Mr. Rollins.

The PRESIDENT. You desire to have a change made in regard to Mr. Rollins? Mr. Rollins was nominated as member of the Executive Committee. Upon that Executive Committee is Mr. Bates, of Memphis, and you cannot put on Mr. Bruce, of Nashville.

Mr. RANKIN. The committee recognize the dilemma in which they are placed, and desire to withdraw to the ante-room.

Mr. SLAWSON. I desire to make a motion that hereafter the Executive Committee be instructed to devise some way by which we will elect our officers through open nomination and election by ballot on the floor. This present method is unusual. It is un-American and liable to lead to bossism. You allow the President to appoint a Nominating Committee, so that practically he can nominate the officers for the ensuing year. I don't say that this has been done, or that it will ever be done, but it can be done, and the power to do that is un-American, and, therefore, I desire to see a change made. There is no law by which this practice exists. It is by virtue of a precedent established in Chicago, and followed at each succeeding session of the Typothetæ from that time to this.

It will be well to look out for this matter, as the time may come when the present system will cast us against the wishes of the majority.

The PRESIDENT. I think your remarks are out of order. All election of officers shall be by ballot and in open Convention is the rule we are under now.

Mr. SLAWSON. Exactly; but we do it by virtue of precedent established at Chicago. There may be choice of ways of doing it, and I prefer that it be referred to the Executive Committee to designate the method of putting nominations before this body by nominating two tickets.

The PRESIDENT. Will you be kind enough, if you are going to make a motion, to put it in the shape of a motion so as to get it properly before the house.

Mr. SLAWSON. I move that the matter be referred to the Executive Committee to nominate officers otherwise than as at present.

The PRESIDENT. It is moved and seconded that the Executive Committee formulate some plan of changing the present method of nominating officers and report at the next Convention of this body.

Mr. McNALLY. I do not understand the motion to be an instruction.

The PRESIDENT. I put it "request." I will repeat it, that the motion of Mr. Slawson is, that the Executive Committee be requested to formulate some other plan than the present one of placing in nomination its officers, and report at the next meeting of the Convention.

Mr. CUSHING. I move as an amendment to that the wording: "The Executive Committee take into consideration the advisability of changing the present method of nominations."

Mr. SLAWSON. I accept the amendment.

The motion, as amended, was carried.

The PRESIDENT. Mr. Theodore L. DeVinne, of New York, has been asked to prepare a paper on book-keeping. This paper has been published in pamphlet form and distributed in the hall. What is your pleasure as to it?

On motion, the paper was made a part of the proceedings, and is as follows:

How to Keep Account of Time.

BEGIN by writing in the order-book as soon as accepted an exact description of the order, and of all the directions concerning it. Trust nothing to memory that can be written, or to the presumed intelligence of the workmen. A record of all the details will be needed if the person who received the order should be absent when special directions are asked for.

Some customers do not know how to give an order, and the instructions needed have to be drawn out by questioning. Some clerks who take orders forget to ask the needed questions. To prevent these omissions, printed order-pads should be provided which contain on them suggestions as to the many different styles of doing every department of work. These order-pads must necessarily be of different wording for every distinct class of work, for it is not practicable to devise a form which will serve equally well for cards, posters, check-books, and pamphlets. For most printing-offices six forms are enough, but no form can be made so complete that it will embrace everything. The form on page 3 is a fair example of an order-pad for a pamphlet.

A fair share of blank must be left at the foot of every printed order-pad for special instructions. The details of the order should be neatly copied in the order-book, in which a liberal space should also be allowed for changes in the order, as for more or less copies, thicker or thinner paper, etc. Every order for a change should be written down and dated, so that the record shall show all the information required. A duplicate of this order-pad should be given to the foreman, who will at once paste it down in a book provided for the purpose. Every subsequent change in the order that may be noted in the order-book as the work progresses should at once be sent to the foreman in writing, who will paste it down with the original order.

Affix a printed number on every separate piece of work. Consecutive printed numbers on gummed paper are usually kept by the stationers of large cities. Let work always be known in every department of the house by its number.

If the order is for a book or pamphlet containing maps, engravings, lithography, etc., each of which has to be done by different workmen and perhaps in another office and on different paper, a separate account should be kept for each of these distinct parts of the work. For example: The text of a book may be numbered as 260; its paper cover should be 261; its maps, if separately printed and inserted, 262; its portraits or its lithography, 263. The use of separate numbers will prevent confusion.

Provide every compositor and pressman with a paper ticket substantially after the patterns shown on annexed pages, which has a blank for the name of the workman, the date, and other blanks in which he can put down the number of the job and the time that he spends on each job. The object of the ticket is to enable the office to get from every workman, in his own writing, a report of how much time he has spent on every piece of work. Under the head of Time of Composition will be put all the time spent by the compositor upon each job, including making-up and stone-work. Under the head of Other Time Work on this job not to be charged to author will be put time lost by accidents, like the piing of any part of the work, or the correction of gross faults of workmanship. If the work has met with accident or has been badly set up, the expense of redressing it in workmanlike form should be assumed by the office and should not be charged against the customer. Under the head of General Office Work, not to be charged to any job, will be entered all the time spent in general distribution or putting the office in order.

Alterations by author are chargeable extras. When the office makes its composition correct to copy, and does its work in a decent, workmanlike style, it has done its whole duty. All changes that are made thereafter by the author as improvements are a proper extra charge. This last item is the one which is most difficult to keep, and the one too often overlooked. Under the prevailing system, or want of system, it is customary for the foreman or bookkeeper to ask compositors, when a piece of work has been done, how much time they have spent in alterations. If the inquiry is postponed for more than one day the compositor will probably largely underrate it. If he is a regular time-hand it does not affect his wages whether he makes the report more or less. Without intending to be unfair or even to be careless, he will unconsciously lean to reporting less time rather than more, for he does not want to be rated as a slow workman. If this reporting of time on alterations be postponed for a week or more, the office will surely lose a large portion of the labor that has been given to the work.

These tickets should be filled out every night before the workman leaves, and returned to the foreman, who will revise them carefully, and see that no error is made by inadvertence. If an error is suspected for time that seems too short or too long, an immediate explanation and rectification can be made at once.

Blanks are left for eight distinct numbers; for while it is not probable

PAMPHLET COMPOSITION. *Duplicate*

Date — October 13, 1891.
Job No. 3345. Name of Job — History of 159th Regiment, N. Y. S. V.
Name and address — William F. Tiemann, 16 Murray St., New-York.

Number Copies — 1000.
Est. number of pages.— 64, and cover of paper.
Number Galley proofs — six sets.
Size and quality of paper, Text — 24 x 38, 70 lb. cream super.
    " " " " " Cover — 20 x 25, 48 lb. Quaker drab.
Size of leaf untrimmed — 6 x 9½; when trimmed — ⅛ in. at head only, side and foot uncut.
Size of type page, including head and foot lines, see marginal sheet.
Type of text — Small Pica No. 20, leaded.
       Extracts or letters — Long Primer No. 20, leaded.
       Notes — Minion No. 20, solid, half measure.
Type of Headings } Elzevir.   Running titles — yes: on left the title, on right
       Subheads }   Folios, side. |the substance of page
       Preface — Small Pica No. 20, double leaded.
       Introduction — none.
       Contents — Bourgeois No. 20, caps and small caps, leaded.
       Index — Nonpareil No. 20, solid, half measure.
       Appendix — Long Primer No. 20, leaded.
       Maps and illustrations. 16 full-page maps, to print separately and tip in.
Head-bands } Make selection from War Series on page 29 of Specimen Book.
Tail-pieces }
Electrotype — two sets of plates, not blocked.
First specimen pages to be ready Thursday,   sent to office.

Press-work. Print in 4 forms of 16 pages each. Paper dampened. Dry Press — yes.
          Illustrations. 16 maps, to print separately in one form.
          Cover in black and red.

Bindery.   Sewed — no.
          Stitched through cover, wire or thread — no.
          Side stitched, wire — cover pasted on.
          Rough edges, trimmed at head only.
Sections of 16 pages, with sigs. in 8s. Inset — yes.

Send proofs regularly to W. F. T. at 739 Dean St., Brooklyn.

Work complete is wanted December 1, 1891.
First form should be ready November 3.
Following forms at regular intervals of four days.
Time on this work, including all time except author's alterations, should not exceed 128 hrs.
                 This is equal to 2 hours per page — 32 hours per sheet.

JAMES W. BOSWELL. August 12, 1891.

Time of	No.	No.	No.	No.	No.	No.	No.	No.	No.
Hours at Work, 10½	1705	1706	1710						
Time of Composition, Make-up and Stone Work	2.	.30	1.30						
Other Time Work on this job not to be charged to author	1.15	.45	—						
Alterations made by Author	.30	2.30	.15						
Extra Reading and Revising	—	—	—						
Overtime, Extra	.30								
General Office Work not to be charged to any job (enter in the last column)									.45

COMPOSITION.

No. of Order.	Description.	Date of First Space.	Time Composition, Type Work, &c. to be done as Type Work.	Other Time Work not to be charged.	Alterations by author, Extra.	Extra Reading, Revising.	Overtime, Extra.
126	3000 Pamphlets, medium 8vo.	Oct. 20	7.	—	—	—	—
		" 21	20.	—	—	—	—
		" 22	—	2.	—	—	—
		" 23	—	—	3.	—	—
		" 24	—	1.30	10.	—	—
		" 25	5.	—	.20	3.	—
		" 26	—	—	—	—	—
127	500 Envelopes	Oct. 21	.30	—	.15	—	—
128	500 Letter Headings	Oct. 21	1.15	.15	.45	—	—
129	Composition and press proofs of title page	Oct. 29	4.30	—	.15	—	.30

PRESS WORK.

Preparing the Paper.	Cutting Envelopes, Extra.	Time of Making Ready.	Running Time on Press.	No. of Impressions	No. of Tokens	Two Pressmen, etc.	Dampening, Extra.	Overtime, Extra.	Remarks.
2.	—	2.15	3.30	3000	12	4	.50*	—	*Corrections on press.
2.	—	2.	2.45	3000	12	4	—	—	
—	—	.30	.50	500	2	—	—	—	
.15	—	.45	.50	500	2	—	—	—	
—	.45	.45	.15	10	—	—	—	—	

J. HUBERT.   August 12, 1891.

Time of	No.	No.	No.	No.	No.	No.	No.
Hours at Work, 10	420	428	430				
No. of Press	3	3	29				
Preparing Paper	.30	.15					
Overlay Cutting	—	—	—				
Hours Making Ready	1.30	2.00	.30				
Hours Running	2.00	1.30	1.00				
Impressions	2000	1000	200				
Tokens	8	4	1				
Chargeable Detentions	—	.30	—				
Dry Pressing	—	—	.15				
Overtime, Extra	—	—	—				

that any compositor will ever be engaged in one day on the composition of eight jobs, it is possible that he may have to give a few minutes every day to the correcting of that number. If he works ten hours, the sum total of entries must amount to ten hours. It is hardly possible for any man who writes down this time to make any serious undercharge or overcharge, either against the office or against the customer. He has no interest in doing so. Practice in keeping these tickets will soon make him exact.

The ticket for press-work contains more headings, as will be seen by the illustration, but it needs no explanation.

These reports of time spent in composition and press-work should be put down in a book especially made for the purpose, which has separate columns on left-hand page for the details of Composition and on right-hand page for those of Press-work. This book, which need not be any larger than the ordinary flat cap folio, should contain under the headings of Number of Order and Description a copy of the more important facts entered in the order-book, for it is not necessary in this book to rewrite all the details. As every blank-line is supposed to contain the record of one day's work in every department, a generous provision of blank must be made for each order at the time of its entry. If a job is estimated to be done in four days, six blank-lines should be allowed for it; if it should be estimated at forty days, then sixty lines should be allowed. It is better to allow too many than too few.

When the foreman sends to the bookkeeper the tickets that have been approved by him, the clerk enters each day, on its dated line and under its proper heading, the sum total of the time spent for the previous day by different workmen, as they have it stated on their tickets.

If unforeseen expenses have been made, like specially purchased sorts, brass rule, or leads; if an excess of ink has been used in press-work; if a form has been stopped for any reason — these irregularities should be noted on the back of the ticket. Acting under instructions, the bookkeeper will decide whether these unforeseen expenses are to be charged against the house or against the customer, and will so enter them on the order-book.

When the time on the tickets has been entered, the tickets can be checked and filed. They should not be destroyed. In case of any disagreement with the customer concerning alterations, these tickets are the best of evidence; for they contain the original entry in the workman's own handwriting of the time he spent on the work, and its correctness as vouched for by the superintending foreman.

By this system an employer or manager can readily compute the expenses of time from day to day. While the work is in progress, he can always give this information to a customer at five minutes' notice. When the work has been done, he can promptly make out a bill without asking one question from any of the foremen, for all the facts that are needed are on the record.

In this book no allowance is made for piece-work. The schedule, billbook, and filed proofs, in general use, are satisfactory enough, and do not require any change. The time-book is intended only to keep an account of the added time-work, keeping separate that which should be assumed by the office and that which is chargeable to the author.

No account need be kept of ordinary reading. Where matter is read but once and revised, a close account of time spent would be of slight advantage; but in offices that have work which calls for two or three readings by different workmen, and these extra readings are caused by alterations, then the cost of the extra reading is of serious importance. The same rule should prevail here that already prevails in composition: the re-reading of matter by copy from a badly marked proof, after the composed matter has been made correct to the original manuscript, is an unforeseen expense which has not been provided for in the original estimate. It should therefore go on the record as a chargeable extra, and the reader should enter the time for this extra work on his separate blank.

No provision has been made for the time spent in ruling, binding, or electrotyping. The ordinary printing-office gets this work done outside, and, as a rule, it gets estimates of this work before it is done. An analysis of cost of labor in such cases is not practicable, nor is it needed. The method of keeping time here presented is confined to the two departments which necessarily exist in all printing-offices. Printers who have electrotype foundries or binderies can, if they so choose, make up time-tickets for time spent in these departments.

Two objections have been made to this system, and indeed to any system which requires a daily record of time spent. It is said to take too much time. I do not think so. Time spent by each workman daily in filling out his ticket need not take three minutes. The time spent each day by a clerk in copying the time-records for fifty compositors and twenty presses need not exceed two hours a day. Indeed, this systematic way of keeping time is really quicker and less expensive than the unsystematic way of waiting until the work has been done, and then gathering up by repeated questionings the hazy recollections of workmen and foremen, or the desultory memoranda of time spent on papers and proofs that have often been mislaid.

Workmen sometimes say that the time-ticket is a practical evidence of the employer's lack of confidence in his workmen. This is an absurd view of the system. Every one will admit that it is necessary that the employer should know exactly how much time has been spent on any piece of work.

It is no more improper to ask a workman to tell his time than it is to ask him to write it. "Time is money" to the workman as well as to the employer. As business is now done, money is rarely given or received without a written memorandum. A clerk in a store who would postpone the entry of a credit sale would soon be deservedly discharged. The compositor who obstructs the making of a proper entry of time spent, which is equivalent to money, is just as great an offender. Any obstruction which prevents the employer from recording and getting pay for the time is as damaging to the workmen as to the employer.

When the work has been done the adding of the different columns will show how much time has been spent upon the work. Now comes the question: How much must be added to pay for the expenses of reading and distribution of the particular job, for which reading and distribution special time has not been kept? In piece composition it is usually estimated that distribution is worth one-fourth that of composition. If a workman is paid thirty cents an hour for composition, one quarter of this should be added for the distribution of the type. The expense of reading and superintendence, also a necessary portion of the expense, will necessarily vary, but it should not, under any circumstances, be put at less than one third of the compositor's time. This would raise the cost of time labor to forty-eight cents. To this account must be added the general expense account of the office, which includes rent, insurance, interest, the wear of material, and other expenses, which will certainly increase the cost to much more than fifty cents. Ordinary time-work which does not require reading may be done for fifty cents; but where that time-work requires the additional services of reader and foreman, the rate must run from sixty to seventy-five cents. As these higher rates are often excepted to, it is better practice to add the reader's time to that of the compositor, and charge the lower rate.

The keeping of a time-book like this takes very little time every day. The information it will give is of the greatest value. The employer who puts in contrast the estimated time and the actual time will find, as a rule, that he has underrated it in the estimate. The author's alterations, which, as he often claims, have not amounted to ten minutes a page, will often be proved by the book to exceed an hour a page. After a year's experience in the keeping of the book, the employer will admit that he has largely overrated the performance of workmen. He may now and then find reason for censuring some workmen for their inefficiency, but if he is just he will find more reason for censuring himself for putting up a standard of performance that cannot be attained. The cost of keeping this book need not be more than one hundred dollars a year. To most employers the record will be worth more than one thousand dollars a year.

The President. The Executive Committee desire me to call the attention of the Convention to one other matter in their report, and that is the matter of workmen's certificates. We have thought there is a great deal of merit in this, and that the local Typothetæ ought to obtain them from the United Typothetæ, and that they should issue them to the class of workmen in whose hands they desire to have them.

Mr. Amos Pettibone. In addition to what has been suggested by the President, I desire to say that the recommendation of the Executive Committee is that they urge the issue of these certificates, which have been prepared and issued, in many instances, to the local Typothetæ throughout the country. They can have them upon application to the Secretary. There is nothing in the certificate that can be objectionable to any workman, and it does seem to me that any wage-worker who shows himself to be a first-class man would be pleased to receive a certificate—whether he be union or non-union—from his employer. It simply sets forth the fact that his employer recommends him as a competent workman who can be depended upon. The certificates are in book form, so that a register can be kept of those sent out if the Typothetæ desire. They are the certificates that the Convention heretofore adopted and that the Executive Committee issued, and anybody can get them by application to the Secretary.

The President. Mr. L. L. Morgan, of New Haven, was requested by our Executive Committee, in July last, to prepare a report upon the subject of hours of labor, wages and trade usages. I understand the report of Mr. Morgan is very exhaustive and complete, and one which will be of great interest to you.

Mr. MORGAN. The committee appointed was Mr. Morgan, Mr. Wright and Mr. W. B. MacKellar, of Philadelphia; a very large part of the work in getting up circulars was done by Mr. Becker, the Recording Secretary, under instructions from the Executive Committee, because they did not think that there would be time for the committee to do their work. Mr. MacKellar has also done considerable work in the matter, so that credit to one individual is hardly a fair thing.

Mr. Morgan then read the report as follows:

Report of Committee upon the Subject of Hours of Labor, Wages and Trade Usages.

United Typothetæ of America:

At a meeting of the Executive Committee, held in Cincinnati, a resolution was adopted that the Recording Secretary obtain such information as he can as to the hours of labor, wages and trade usages; that the same be forwarded to a committee consisting of the undersigned, with the request that they furnish a report to the next Convention.

The appointment came to us at a time when many from whom we should have obtained information were away on their summer vacations, so that the subject has not been given that care and attention which otherwise would have been given it.

In order to make the information of the greatest value, it would require several months' work under proper supervision, and would necessitate the spending of a considerable amount of money for necessary expenses. Your committee, however, present this report, embracing as it does leading cities in all sections of the country, with a belief that the information contained therein will be of sufficient interest and value to compensate for the time and labor expended. The statistical table, while it may take a few moments of your time, will probably prove of interest.

In this table are represented twenty-eight cities. It shows that the hours of labor are nearly uniform, fifty-nine hours per week being the established custom. The weekly wages paid compositors vary from $10 to $21; the average price being from $16 to $18.

The highest rate ($21) comes from Louisville and Chicago; the lowest from Toronto. The rate per 1,000 ems varies from 30 to 45 cents, the average price being 35 to 40 cents. The price per 1,000 ems usually charged customers is from 60 to 65 cents. The wages paid pressmen and feeders differ widely, based upon the amount of skill possessed, and the kind of presses operated.

We find that many women are employed as press feeders. The number of apprentices employed proves generally to be in accordance with the rules of the Typographical Union, though many of the offices entirely ignore the union. In some offices the wages are based upon the general conduct of the employees. Some share profits with their men, and the amount is according to merit and time employed. As a rule no charge is made for standing matter. In some cases a charge is made, depending upon the length of time it is kept standing, and in others the matter is subject to a special agreement with customers.

Credit is generally given the United Typothetæ for much that has been done to benefit the printing trade, and much is looked to from it to still further accomplish results beneficial to the craft generally. It may be of interest here to introduce a few comments made upon the blanks sent out:

"The following holidays we close and pay the men for the day: Fourth of July and Christmas. The following holidays we close one-half day and pay the men for the full day: Washington's Birthday, Good Friday, Decoration Day, Labor Day, and Thanksgiving Day. In the latter, if the men are not here in the morning they get no pay for that day whatever; or if the men do not turn up the next morning we only pay them for the half day they worked the day before."

"Job work is taken at pretty much what the printer thinks the customer will stand, or as low as he thinks will be necessary to get a few cents below the next lowest bidder. This city (Richmond) is in no wise exempt from the folly which characterizes the printing business from Maine to Texas and from Pennsylvania to California."

"General trade usages here is to *see how little can be charged* for composition, and I believe nothing for standing matter. I don't suppose a meaner place for the printing business can be found than Baltimore. Nobody cares here how work is done, so it is done 'cheap,' and can be read."

TABLE OF WAGES

CITIES.	Scale.	Wages per w'k.	Piece-work. per 1,000 Ems.	Overtime.	Pressmen per Week.	Feeders per Week.
1 Louisville	Slid.	$12 to $21.	40c.	None.	$9 to $15.	$6 to $10.
2 Boston	Stand.	$15.	40c.	40c.	$15 to $20.	$6 to $10.
3 Minneapolis	Stand.	$16.	35c.	1½ hours.	$20.	$9.
4 Chicago	Slid.	$15 to $21.	35c. to 37c.	50c.	$21.	$6 to $9.
5 Richmond	Stand.	$16.	40c.	40c.	$12 to $20.	$3 to $6.
6 Memphis	Stand.	$18.	None done	42c.	$15 to $21.	$6 to $10.
7 New Orleans	Stand.	$18.	40c.	15c.	$18.	$9.
8 Little Rock	Both.	$16.	Contract.	1½ hours.	$15 to $20.	$4 to $6.
9 St. Paul	Stand.	$16.	35c.	1½ hours.	$16 to $18.	$4 to $10.
10 St. Louis	Stand.	$18.	40c. to 45c.	1½ hours.	$20.	$8 to $9.
11 Dayton	Stand.	$15.	32c. to 35c.	1½ hours.	$15 to $18.	$5 to $6.
12 Albany	Both.	$15.	35c. to 37.2.	1½ hours.	$12 to $18.	$5.
13 Nashville	Stand.	$18.	40c.	40c.	$18 to $20.	$4 to $10.
14 Milwaukee	Slid.	$14 to $20.	40c.	60c.	$18 to $25.	$3 to $6.
15 Detroit	Stand.	$14.	35c.	35c.	$15.	$4 to $7.
16 Kansas City	Stand.	$17.	. . . . . .	1½ hours.	$17.	$8.
17 San Francisco	Stand.	$18.	40c.	60c.	$15 to $18.	$5 to $8.
18 Portland, Ore.	Stand.	$21.	45c.	50c.	$18 to $24.	$12 to $15.
19 Cincinnati	Slid.	$12 to $18.	30c. to 40c.	1½ hours.	$15 to $18.	$5 to $7.
20 Chattanooga	?	$15.	33.3c.	1½ hours.	$10 to $20.	$5 to $8.
21 Philadelphia	Both.	$16 to $20.	40c.	1½ hours.	$16 to $18.	$6 to $9.
22 New Haven	Stand.	$15 to $18.	35c. to 40c.	. . . . . .	$15 to $20.	$6.
23 Charleston, S. C.	. . . .	$17.	35c.	. . . . . .	$14 to $20.	$3 to $5.
24 Washington	Stand.	$18.	42c.	10c. per M.	$20 to $25.	$6 to $9.
25 Trenton	Stand.	$14 to $16.	35c.	. . . . . .	$14 to $15.	. . . . . .
26 Baltimore	Stand.	$16.20.	.	. . . . . .	$12 to $25.	$3 to $4.25.
27 Omaha	Slid.	$12 to $25.	37c.	. . . . . .	$14 to $25.	$2 to $6.
28 Toronto	Stand.	$11 to $13.	33.3c.	25c. per M.	$10 to $15.	. . . . . .

AND OFFICE USAGES.

OFFICE USAGES.

Time Work.	Extra Proofs.	Standing Matter.	Storage Plates.	Holding Presses.	Week's Work.		
					Days per Week.	Hours per Day.	Hours per Week.
60c.	?	20c.	No.	?	6	10	59
50c.	Yes.	10c.	No.	$1 to $1.50.	6	10	59
50c.	. . . . .	10c.	. . . .	70c.	6	10	59
50c. to 60c.	Yes.	10c. to 20c.	Yes.	$1.	6	10	59
50c.	50c. per hr.	10c.	No.	No.	6	10	58
42c.	No.	?	No.	No.	6	10	59
50c.	No.	10c.	No.	74c. to $1.	6	10	59
60c.	25c. per hr.	5c. per wk.	No.	$1.	6	10	. . . .
60c.	No.	One-third.	No.	60c.	6	10	59
50c. to 60c.	Yes.	8c. to 10c.	Yes.	$1.	6	10	59
?	?	?	?	?	6	10	59
50c.	Yes.	One-third to one-half.	No.	50c.	6	10	59
50c.	No.	No rule.	No.	No.	6	10	. . . .
1½.	?	10c. to 20c.	No.	$1.	6	10	59
50c.	No.	No.	Yes.	$1.	6	10	56
60c.	No.	No.	No.	$1.	6	10	. . . .
60c.	No.	8c. to 20c.	No.	No.	6	10	. . . .
75c.	No.	Yes.	No.	?	6	10	59
50c. to 60c.	No.	?	No.	?	6	10	59
60c.	Yes.	?	. . .	?	6	10	59
50c. to 60c.	Yes.	10c. per M. per week.	No.	$1.	6	10	59
60c. to 70c.	45c. per hr.	?	. . . .	. . . .	6	10	59
75c.	No.	?	. . . .	?	6	10	. . . .
50c.	Yes.	One-fourth	No.	No.	6	9	54
40c.	. . . . .	. . . . .	No.	. . .	6	9	. . . .
50c.	No.	No.	No.	No.	6	10	59
60c.	No.	5c. per M.	. . . .	$1 per hr.	6	10	. . . .
40c. to 45c.	Yes.	Yes.	No.	$1 per hr.	5½	10	54

12

"The Typothetæ has accomplished something towards ameliorating the evils in the business, but much more remains to be done."

"The writer thinks that the apprentice system ought to be greatly improved, and the only way to bring such a thing about is by the united effort of the employers."

"The ability of the average compositor is not what it used to be, and we find it quite difficult to obtain first-class help at any price."

"We work ten hours. Profits are not large enough to allow us to work fewer hours at the same pay, or even at a proportionate reduction in wages, as general expenses would be the same for a shorter day."

"About the only way of obtaining a correct average for this city would be to get a report from each concern."

"Our trade is greatly demoralized in this city. All manner of prices prevailing. A better feeling is prevailing among the trade than before the organization of the Typothetæ. We hope for better terms."

"Acknowledging receipt of your circular of the 11th instant, I should be glad to give you information regarding the methods in vogue in this establishment, were I aware of your object in seeking the same, or the purpose to which it is to be put when obtained. I may safely say that we stand alone, of the large printing houses, in the conduct of affairs under the three heads named by you, for the reason that we entirely ignore the several Printers' Unions and their dictates and regulations; yet, by a simple system of profit-sharing with our employees, we are able to defy the Unions and keep about two hundred employees (union and non-union) attached to our and their own success, resulting in the company having for eight years paid regular quarterly dividends to its stockholders.

"The methods by which this result is attained we claim no patent upon, but on the contrary are always ready to give it to others who desire to investigate it, but we do not care to use type and ink to satisfy curiosity, or to pose as the promoters of a labor system directly opposite to universal custom."

L. L. MORGAN,
WM. B. MACKELLAR,
L. A. WYMAN,
Committee.

Mr. ANDREWS. I move that the report be received and published in the Proceedings, and that the committee be continued.

Seconded.

Mr. PASKO. I would like to ask the gentleman who read this report, where does he get his information? For instance, he says that the wages in Chicago and Louisville are $21. I received a circular from Chicago not so long ago in which they told me the wages were $15, and the report of the International Typographical Union does not show that $21 is paid anywhere east of the Mississippi, except in Washington, and there only to Government employees.

Mr. L. L. MORGAN. I said the highest rate of wages. Now, this report reads in this way: "Wages paid by the week, $10 to $21." That shows the highest to be $21. We sent out inquiries, and that is one of the answers we received. I did not say the average was $21.

Mr. PASKO. Twenty-one dollars is not the highest rate to a considerable number in the United States, but it creates an erroneous opinion; people reading the report ought not to think there is any great number receiving $21 or $22. I don't suppose there is a considerable number of compositors receiving $20; $18 is about all that the ordinary compositor can get. A man, if he is unusually skillful, can get more than $18.

Mr. MORGAN. I don't think the gentleman understands that the tabulated report has the figures, and that these are quoted as the exceptionally high figures. It is simply an exceptional case.

Mr. ENNIS. Where did you get the information that the job printer gets as much as he can for his work? [*Laughter.*] I want to say that that ought not to go to the world from the Typothetæ, for the same reason that we have had several papers which are intended to raise the moral standard of the craft. I move you, sir, to suggest to the gentleman that he withdraw the remark, because there is such a thing as manhood and conscience, and I say we don't want to suggest such a thing as that we take advantage of anybody's ignorance, and if he is not competent to get information as to prices, you charge him three or four or eight times as much as necessary.

Mr. MORGAN. The statement was not made by the committee. It was a quotation from a gentleman who made the remark in a sarcastic way. The gentleman does not appreciate it.

Mr. ENNIS. I say that the remark, sarcastic or otherwise, coming from the most insignificant of the printing fraternity, that printers get as much for their work as they can, would be very injurious.

The paper was accepted and ordered to be printed in the Proceedings.

The PRESIDENT. Mr. Robert Morgan, of Cincinnati, was requested by our committee to prepare a paper upon rollers and their proper treatment. I understand that that is prepared. What is your pleasure in regard to it?

Mr. MORGAN. I ask to do away with the reading of the paper, and that it be printed. It is too long to read here.

The request was granted.

Mr. R. J. Morgan's Essay on Roller Composition: Its Manufacture and Uses.

Mr. President and Gentlemen of the Typothetæ:

I have been detailed to make some remarks upon rollers. To save our time I shall be as brief as possible.

The invention of roller composition is not as well known as it should be. French printers claim to have used it as early as 1818, but the evidence is not satisfactory. This, at least, is certain: roller composition was first used in the potteries of Staffordshire. The putting of a uniform design on a set of dishes with irregular surface could be done only by an elastic material which easily received and readily shed ink. It had been used there a long time before it attracted any attention from printers. Konig & Bauer, the inventors of the cylinder press, were defeated, or at least sadly hindered, in their attempt to print with buck-skin rollers, the only material then in use for inking. Somebody suggested the use of this composition to Bensely, of London, who was interested with Konig & Bauer, and they made the first printing ink rollers, probably somewhere about 1814. It was the only thing needed to make cylindrical printing a success.

There was a strong prejudice against the use of rollers for hand presses. Says Brother DeVinne: In 1846 I worked in the office of William Burroughs, of New York, with a very good hand-pressman of the old school, who always used buck-skin balls for his fine work. He claimed that they were better than any roller ever made.

In 1829 Jonas Booth and Jonathan Seymour, of New York, I believe, were the first to use roller composition in this country.

The earliest rollers of the modern type were glue and molasses rollers, made simply of glue and molasses and nothing else. To say the least for the glue and molasses roller, there is no better roller made at the present day. It possessed a peculiar tackiness that under favorable conditions was exactly right. It took up the ink exactly right, and parted with it to the form exactly right. The favorite combination was strong cabinet glue and New Orleans molasses. This combination cannot be made now as it was in the old days, for the simple reason that for many years it has been impossible to procure honest pure New Orleans molasses. For many years past, no New Orleans molasses has been allowed to reach the consumer until it had been heavily adulterated with cheap glucose. Glucose will dry into a hard mass like gum, and is therefore injurious to rollers. Pure molasses will not do this. But the glue and molasses roller, though apparently very cheap was really a very expensive roller; it only lasted, at its best, for a few days, depending on the weather. In some weathers its period of perfection lasted less than a week; in other weathers it might extend to two weeks. This made it far more expensive than the modern rollers, whose period of usefulness extends for months, and in some few cases to years, to say nothing of the cost of the extra labor involved in the frequent renewals.

Rollers, as made to-day, are made by formulas varying so widely from each other that it would be useless to detail them. Every maker has his own way of attaining the desired effects and results, and improvements and variations are constantly going on. Every now and then new substances and materials are produced by chemistry or appear in commerce, and these are experimented with and results observed, until the manufacture has become a mass of trade-secrets. No firm of roller-makers cares for the trade-secret of ten years ago, for they have become obsolete and worthless. It is only those of to-day that they are interested in.

But the basis of the main difference between the old glue and molasses roller and the rollers of to-day, consisted in the discovery of the utility of the new substance, glycerine. De la Rue, of London, was the first to employ this substance, which was then new in commerce, in printers' rollers. The one great point that was gained by the use of glycerine was simply in the durability of the roller, and nothing else. Glue and molasses rollers dried and shrunk rapidly, a dry, glassy skin formed upon the face of the roller in a few days; this tendency was overcome by glycerine. Glycerine forms about six per cent. of all fats. The fats are broken up by super-heated steam into oleine, stearine and glycerine, and these substances remain separate from each other. The peculiar properties of glycerine are: first, that it never freezes at any temperature, and consequently heat or cold have but little effect upon its consistency, and therefore the rollers in which it is used are less affected by variations of temperature than the glue and molasses roller. Secondly, it will mix perfectly with water in any proportion, but will not mix perfectly with oil. This is singular, as it is extracted from fats and oils. Third, and this is a very important property, it never evaporates. Fourth, it is strongly hygroscopic—that is, it has a powerful attraction for moisture, and will gain notably in weight if exposed to the air. This last property is rather a disadvantage, and is the cause of all the troubles attendant upon the use of glycerine in rollers. It is this property that makes rollers to some extent dependent in quality upon the variations of the weather. Roller-makers say "Give us a substance having all the qualities of glycerine except its attraction for moisture, and we will give you an almost perfect roller."

No substance having the precise qualities we desire exists on the earth—at least it has not as yet been discovered; so we have to do the best we can with the materials which modern commerce affords. An absolutely perfect roller has never been made, and probably never will be in this world. All we can do is to come as near to it as possible with the means at our command; we are always moving nearer to perfection, always getting closer to it, never halting in our march; but we will never get there. As we never had a perfect man on the earth, so we will never have a perfect roller.

And the field of lithographic rollers is still an unexplored one—like darkest Africa. Lithography still is confined to the old leather rollers, hard and absolutely devoid of suction. Give us the substance that will have all the qualities of glycerine without its attraction for moisture, and we will try to explore this field and give a modern roller to lithography. What are the qualities of a perfect roller? Of course its form should be mechanically true and exact. First, it should neither shrink nor swell. Not only does shrinking or swelling cause loss of valuable time in setting the roller properly, but they are always accompanied by a variation in the quality of the roller. Second, the elasticity of the roller, if not absolutely perfect, must at least be good, so that it can adapt itself perfectly to the pressure upon the form. Third, it must have a sufficiently strong affinity for ink to take instantly a sufficient supply of ink from the ink-table. Fourth, it must part with its ink properly to the form. We expect a roller to do all this perfectly, under all our varying conditions of heat and cold, dryness and superabundant moisture. It is a most difficult problem, yet it is wonderful how nearly we can satisfy the conditions. We can overcome the difficulties presented by variations from dryness to excessive moisture almost perfectly; we have made considerable progress in overcoming the difficulty presented by great variations of temperature, but that is still the chief difficulty. It has not yet been entirely overcome, and summer rollers and winter rollers are still a necessity. It used to be, not so long ago, that no summer roller could be got to work at all in winter and *vice-versa*. Now we can produce rollers that will print tolerably well in the opposite season; we have not got there perfectly yet, we can only attain the result much more closely than we used to.

In the making of rollers there are a few simple points to be observed. The composition must never be heated more or longer than absolutely necessary. Everything that contains gelatine and everything that contains saccharine matter is injured by heat. Any good glue-maker will tell you to heat glue as little as you possibly can, for heating rapidly reduces a high grade glue to a lower grade. The highest grades of glue are simply the first slight boilings of the hide and sinew scraps. The glue which is drawn off afterward, after longer boiling, is of a lower grade and cheaper quality.

In similar manner all saccharine substances are changed by prolonged heat.

You want the face of the roller perfect, and therefore you must endeavor to avoid three defects: pin-holes, oil-streaks and chill-streaks. To avoid pin-holes you must allow the composition, after melting, to stand quiet in a proper kettle till all steam bubbles and air bubbles have time to ascend to the surface, forming a scum, leaving solid melted composition beneath. This should be poured from the bottom of the melted composition if possible, or if that can't be done, it should be well skimmed and then slowly poured. This is to avoid pin-holes, which not only interfere with the proper inking of the form, but also render the roller difficult or impossible to clean in changing inks. All difficulty of cleaning takes the time of high-priced hands, and therefore costs dollars every week.

Oil-streaks on a roller are caused by too much oil in the mould. They are a serious defect. Every part of the mould must be oiled, but the oil must be driven as thinly as possible. If any small part of the mould is missed in oiling, the face of the roller at that part will be ruined, and the roller must be re-cast.

Chill-streaks are as bad as oil-streaks, and are caused by cold moulds. The stream of melted composition poured into the mould chills against the cold iron, and the successive waves of composition do not unite. All moulds should be warm enough to prevent any chilling of the composition. Any temperature will do between one hundred degrees and two hundred degrees.

Not only do these defects in the faces of rollers interfere with the best printing and prompt cleaning, but they render the roller liable to tear on the press. The adhesion to the ink-table is very considerable, and much power is exerted in the pull of the roller as it drags across the table. Defects on the face of the roller give the ink-table a chance to start a tear there and pull out a piece of the face.

After a roller is made, it is not done and ready for use until it is seasoned. Seasoning is just as much a part of its manufacture as the casting of it is. No piece of furniture is ready for use or shipment the moment it is varnished, and it is seldom that a roller is fit for use the day it comes out of the roller mould.

Now seasoning is not a matter of hours or days at all, and it must not be estimated that way. Seasoning is solely a matter of toughness, of resistance to the powerful pull of the adhesive ink-table. It is not a matter of time at all, and there is no rule of time by which rollers should be seasoned, three days or a week or two weeks. It depends on the drying qualities of the existing weather. Sometimes a roller will season amply in two days, sometimes in one day—there is such weather—and sometimes they will not season at all, as long as certain weather lasts. When the air is already saturated with all the moisture it can possibly contain and carry, it is useless to expect it to dry a roller rapidly. The seasoning is judged solely by the toughness of the roller, when the end is pinched between the thumb and finger. If it is tough, it will do; if not, it is risky. Soft inks require less seasoning than for stiff inks; winter requires less seasoning than in summer. Do you know that the cold dry days of winter are much drier than the driest summer days? The cold condenses the moisture of the air and removes it.

But after a roller is once properly seasoned, the seasoning should not continue. The less further seasoning the better; therefore, after they are once seasoned well it is best to leave the ink on them as much as possible. This increases the durability of a seasoned roller, or rather it retards its aging. Rollers may often be seasoned while in use. For the first month or so, clean them as soon as the run is done, and set them up in a dry, airy place, so as to season during the intervals of work. A great deal of seasoning can be got this way. But stop the seasoning as soon as possible after the right degree of toughness is once reached. Keep the roller that way.

Now, what rollers are the cheapest? Generally speaking, the best rollers you can obtain are the cheapest.

If the quality of your press-work is twenty per cent. better than that of your competitor, the public is sure to find it out. The public will pay you a better price than it will him, and it certainly will prefer your work at the same price. This is an important business advantage. Even a mere preference at the same price is very important. The public is far better educated in the matter of typography and press-work than it was twenty years ago. No firm wants their catalogues or price-lists to look one whit inferior to that of competitors. Every excellent piece of work is an advertisement, and provokes the question, "Who printed this for you?" You can't have any advertisement whatever equal to excellent work.

Now the roller is the most important thing in press-work; you can have the best presses, new type and a skillful pressman, yet, with inferior rollers, you cannot produce the best work. Now what is the use of expending thousands of dollars on fine presses for the purpose of improving press-work, and then of wasting part of that investment by using inferior rollers? Why reduce the grade of press-work that your press is capable of, to the grade that a much cheaper press, with the best rollers, will produce? There is no economy in that. When a first-class press-builder sells you a good press to perform a certain high grade of press-work, he understands and expects you to understand, that to meet his claims, the rollers must be of the best. He does not expect you to drag down the grade of press-work produced by his press by small economy in rollers. Some rollers may cost a few cents a pound more than others, but it only takes a very slight increase in the excellence of the rollers to far more than pay for the slight difference in cost. What we have to consider is the excellence of the press-work, and the saving of time and wages. It is true that good rollers cost money, as well as poor ones, but they are the very least expense in any job. Mr. Wade used to remark, that as ink was the very least item of expense in any job, it paid well to have the best. This was true, but rollers are a smaller item of expense in any job than even the ink, and it is false economy to have any but the very best. It is also false economy to delay renewing them when any gain in the grade of press-work can be achieved by so renewing them. It is not right to regard rollers as an expense, like rent or light, to be cut down to the last degree at the expense of the reputation of the office for grade of press-work.

Rollers should be regarded as part of the material of each job just as ink is, and should be charged for in the estimate. The increased grade of press-work produced by good rollers certainly justifies this charge for the rollers used. The loss of customers and the slight loss of reputation to the office for slightly inferior press-work—these losses certainly far more than counterbalance any false economy in rollers. Flatly, from an economic point of view, it pays to have the very best, and it is a loss to the office to have anything else. There is another point to be considered. Hands are the most important expense in an office. Help is high, and it takes business and profit to pay the pay-roll. Skilled pressmen are expensive. Most printers, if they kept a fine carriage and a span of horses, would think themselves extravagant; but one skilled pressmen costs more to keep than the carriage and horses. Every hour of his time costs money; a little time wasted or demanded on each job each day amounts to more than the rollers for that press amount to in a year.

He understands his business; he knows the effect he wants to produce and ought to produce: he wants to waste as little time as possible in arriving at that effect; nothing can hinder him more in producing what he wants than inferior rollers. Nothing can hasten his effect more and save his valuable time better than the best rollers. Now, where is the economy in hindering a high-priced man in any way? And if the rollers are not of the best he can't produce the effect he otherwise could, no matter how much time he wastes.

Now, in many good-sized offices the whole cost of rollers is less than the cost of one assistant pressman. In many fair-sized offices it is far less than the wages of one cheap press-feeder; yet employers do not know how much valuable time of high-priced hands they waste by not using the best rollers obtainable.

It used to be that the almanac style of press-work was considered good enough for any ordinary business job, and rollers were used that were long past their best days. It is not so any more. Times have changed, and we must change with them or go to the rear.

In these days of sharp competition, and of a public educated in press-work, we must use the best rollers, and those only in the best period of their existence. As soon as they pass their best, they must be replaced. Rollers are replaced by new ones now-a-days in first-class offices that twenty or even ten years ago would have been considered good enough for several months longer. The demand of the public for the best work only compels this.

Even in country newspaper offices, greater efforts toward the best press-work is more necessary than was formerly the case. The well-printed paper has a clear and distinct advantage, both among subscribers and among advertisers, over its more poorly printed neighbor. This advantage means dollars and cents. It may mean failure or success. Competition and the times drive and compel us toward better press-work. We must keep abreast of the times or be content to fall behind and see our competitors absorb our best trade. The best rollers are a slight expense, compared with other materials we use. They aid in holding customers, and they save the valuable time of high-priced employees.

Many printers are annoyed by jobs done in copying inks; when we can make rollers that will work copying inks well, we can produce rollers that will work in lithographic presses under a spray of water. Copying ink is aniline color ground in a mixture of glycerine and water. Letter-press rollers will not stand water. They are designed to withstand oily inks.

The rule in regard to copying ink jobs is to use the oldest set of rollers in the office, and to add the price of a new set of rollers to the bill.

Mr. W. T. Gilbert, chairman of the committee appointed to prepare suitable resolutions on deceased members, presented the following report:

Report of Committee to Prepare Resolutions on Deceased Members.

Your committee to whom was referred that part of our President's address in reference to the death of some of our members during the past year, beg leave to make the following report:

During the past year our society has lost the companionship of three of our members—two of whom were among our oldest, most experienced and best known members.

Mr. W. C. MARTIN, of New York city, was one of the delegates to the first meeting of the United Typothetæ, and has been with us every session till the present. The oldest of those who met with us, he was also probably the oldest employing printer in the

United States. He began business in 1835, having previously made an unsuccessful attempt in the same way. He was then twenty-four years old; at his death he was eighty. When he began, New York city employed only about two hundred journeymen in our art; the list has now increased beyond eight thousand. He was three years an apprentice before he saw an iron hand-press; the few which were here at that time in use were only in newspaper offices. Power presses had not been introduced into America when his period of service began, and he was in its fifth year before an adventurous printer on this side of the water began making rollers. Rumors of the advantages to be derived from this new process had been floating for several years, but no one in America saw them before 1826. From that time on he witnessed all the changes which have been introduced into the art. Each step he welcomed and adopted, so far as his business would permit. He joined the original Typothetæ of New York, begun in 1863; he presided at meetings of the Master Printers of New York, after the previous organization had gone down. When the society was reorganized in 1883, he was unanimously chosen its President. This was not owing to the extent of his business, which was small, but to his high character, his love of justice, his clear-headedness, and the consideration in which he was held by other classes of citizens.

He was re-elected to the position for eight years in succession, although for the last two or three years he was reluctant to allow his name to be used. He gave strict attention to the duties of this position, and spared himself no labor because he had attained so great an age.

Mr. Martin's work as a printer was excellent. He had been bred a pressman, as well as a compositor, and the work he did in his fifty years of business will compare favorably for workmanship with that of any other house in the country. His work was both faithfully and artistically done. No short count was permitted to go out, even if the whole job had to be set up again. Defective sheets, wrong margins, inferior paper, or other mistakes were not allowed to pass. As a consequence, he not only turned out good work himself, but helped to elevate and strengthen the habit of doing such work among the other printers of the country. Among those who have given testimony to his value in this respect are Mr. Houghton, of Cambridge, and Mr. DeVinne, of New York.

His services to the United Typothetæ were not so great as to his local society; but the sobriety of his judgment, his past experience, and his freedom from personal bias, rendered his counsels of very great value.

His personal character was of the highest; uniting the most rigid integrity with the most lovable of dispositions, his services being always at the disposal of the weak or the needy or of those who had been made the jest of fortune. Whatever he had learned about printing was public property. Young men had only to ask him concerning any doubtful question in the art to have his vast stores of information placed at their disposal. He was pleased with everything that was honest and of good report, and his influence was always on the side of morality, of virtue and of public faith. As a friend, a neighbor, a member of the same society, he was staunch and true. Probably the United Typothetæ could not have lost a man whose death would have sent pangs into more hearts. Delicate and pure in his thoughts, he abhorred vice and clung to those whose lives were good and true, akin to his own strong and kindly nature.

His career is now closed, and we can only express our sorrow that so noble a life should have come to an end. Happy we if we can emulate him.

ROBERT P. STUDLEY, after an illness of more than a year, died peacefully at his home on the 10th of November last. He was an honored member of St. Louis Typothetæ, and was a representative from his city in the Convention in Chicago when the National Typothetæ of America was organized; also at the following session in New York. He went East for medical treatment in the summer of 1890, and at the Convention in Boston of that year participated with great delight in the harbor excursion where he met, for the last time, many of his fellow-craftsmen, for whom he had a sincere regard. We shall miss his good judgment and kindly advice in our deliberations, his zeal for the elevation of our craft and his business courtesy.

During his active business life he passed through much of discouragement and heavy financial losses; yet in all this did he hold fast his integrity. Long ago he had settled for himself the question, "If a man die shall he live again?" And with an experimental knowledge, he could say, with the ancient patriarch, "I know that my Redeemer liveth."

It is meet and right that we, his fellow craftsmen, should thus publicly express our sense of loss in parting from our friend, of our appreciation of his many noble qualities, and his upright life. Although of a retiring disposition, he made hosts of friends, and as a business man probably had a larger number of customers running through a longer period of years than any other firm in St. Louis. His customers became his personal friends.

Mr. HENRY G. SCHEPKER, of the firm of Keating & Co., died February 7, 1891, after a short but severe illness, at the age of thirty-two years. Starting at the lowest round, he was steadily and surely advancing to that high point in the business, to which he devoted his whole mind and energy. He took a deep interest in everything pertaining to the elevation of his chosen profession, and hailed with delight the organization of our society, the principles of which he was always a staunch upholder. He was a delegate from the Cincinnati Typothetæ to the Fourth Annual Convention.

W. J. GILBERT, *Chairman*.
C. J. KREHBIEL.
W. W. PASKO.

Mr. WADDEY. My esteemed friend, Mr. Lockwood, says that I was mistaken, and has called my attention to the fact that the Executive Committee under the old Constitution consisted of seven members—

Mr. LOCKWOOD. Louder. If you are making an apology, I want everybody to hear it. [*Laughter.*]

Mr. WADDEY. I want to call the attention of the Convention to the fact that last year we had only six members on the Executive Committee, and that it is responsible for the error I made.

Mr. LOCKWOOD. I had something to do with the Executive Committee for three years, and I was under the impression that we had ten members—seven regular members and three *ex-officio*. The apology is accepted and placed on file.

The President. Are the Nominating Committee ready to report?

Mr. Rankin. We had no revised copy of the Constitution with us last night, and we were of the opinion that the only change was in the matter of the Secretary. I regret that we made any error in the report.

He then read the amended report as follows:

President.—W. A. Shepard, Toronto, Canada.

Vice-Presidents.—1st, E. R. Andrews, Rochester, Middle States; 2d, J. S. Cushing, Boston, Northeastern States; 3d, L. D. Myers, Columbus, Western States; 4th, George M. Courts, Galveston, Southern States; 5th, Ai Rollins, San Francisco, Pacific States; 6th, E. G. O'Connor, Montreal, Canada.

Secretary.—Everett Waddey, Richmond.

Treasurer.—Chas. Buss, Cincinnati.

Executive Committee.—Amos Pettibone (Chairman); Theo. L. DeVinne, New York; C. S. Morehouse, New Haven; W. H. Woodward, St. Louis; Wm. H. Bates, Memphis; A. M. Geesaman, Minneapolis; W. S. Fish, Indianapolis.

Mr. Rankin. For the position of Treasurer, the committee received information during the recess that Mr. Russell positively refuses to accept the nomination, and we nominated Mr. Charles Buss, of Cincinnati, for Treasurer.

Mr. Morgan, of Cincinnati, moved that the Secretary cast the ballot of the Convention for the officers nominated in the report of the Nominating Committee on a suspension of the rules.

Carried.

The Secretary. I cast the unanimous vote of the Convention for W. A. Shepard, of Toronto, Canada, for President, etc. [reading list of officers nominated by the committee.]

The PRESIDENT. Gentlemen, I wish to congratulate you on the very successful termination of your labors, and also upon the very able ticket which you have presented. During my absence, in consultation with the general ticket agent, there was a report accepted which required the appointment of a committee. I shall leave that to your new President. I desire that Mr. Ennis, of St. Louis, and Mr. Eichbaum, of Pittsburg, escort our new worthy President, Mr. Shepard, of Toronto, to the chair.

President PUGH. Gentlemen, allow me to present to you Mr. W. A. Shepard, of Toronto, the President of the United Typothetæ of America.

President SHEPARD. Gentlemen, I thank you for electing me President of the United Typothetæ of America. It is an honor of which the most distinguished member of this association might well be proud, and I feel very keenly my unfitness to occupy the position so ably filled by the gentlemen who have preceded me in this chair. I accept this position, however, as a tribute to the city and the association I am here to represent, and I will endeavor to preside over the deliberations of this body as best I can. I know and expect I will receive from you a hearty assistance and co-operation in the discharge of my duties. Let us hope that the cloud that is passing over Pittsburg may speedily pass away, and that peace and goodwill may prevail throughout the entire continent. If we practice toleration of each other's views, and employers and employees are willing to act upon the Golden Rule—"As we would that men should do unto us "—there need be no fear of strained relations between labor and capital, and no question of strikes and consequent disturbances of trade and those evils that follow. I thank you, gentlemen, for electing me to this position.

Mr. PASKO. There has been a good deal of complaint at the late time at which we get a copy of our Proceedings. I hope the Proceedings will be pushed through as much as possible. As a means of placing them before a great many who do not see our Proceedings in the usual way, but would see them in the trade journals, I move that proofs of the Proceedings be furnished to as many trade journals as apply for them.

Carried.

Mr. MORGAN. I move that a vote of thanks of this Convention be extended to the retiring President and officers of the Executive Committee, who so faithfully served this association for the last year.

Seconded, and carried by a rising vote.

The PRESIDENT [to Mr. Pugh]. On behalf of the Convention, I desire to present the thanks of the Convention to you, as well as the other officers of the association, for the able manner in which you have discharged the duties of your office.

Mr. PUGH [received with applause]. Gentlemen, I thank you very deeply indeed for this manifestation of your kind regard. One year ago in Boston it fell to my lot, as a representative of the Cincinnati Typothetæ, to receive your unanimous vote for the Presidency of your organization for the following year. I have tried to do my duty, giving all the time and attention I possibly could to its duties; and if there is anything that I have omitted in trying to make the United Typothetæ of America a success, it was not from any lack of heart, but from lack of ability. If you remember my words in accepting the office a year ago: "that we would work hard in Cincinnati to show you our high appreciation of this honor," I didn't consider that the honor came to me individually, for there are so many stronger, better men in our association, but as an honor to the Cincinnati Typothetæ. I have tried as best I could to uphold her in maintaining that place we knew she was entitled to when it came to dispensing her hospitality. [*Applause.*] As presiding officer, I felt that there were two sides to every question, and that both sides should be heard. There is a strong feeling in favor of the nine hour move, not nine hours with ten hours' pay, but nine hours as being a sufficient day to labor, and if it can be reached by the joint concession of the employees and employing printers of this country, it will be a grand result of our organization. I hold that we, as a body, should say that at some future time—say one, two or three years hence—that we will concede it; that we will do it; we will not be driven into it; if you attempt to drive us, we will never concede it, but we will give it to you; this large organization, representing the capital that it does, cannot be driven. Gentlemen, I thank you for your kindness and encouragement to me while I was in the chair. I thought a year ago that I was scarcely worthy of this position of honor. I looked about and saw these men whose influence and name and reputation had been in the mouth of all the world of printers, but I resolved that I would do my duty as I saw it, and if you are satisfied with that, that is all the encomium I desire. [*Applause.*]

Mr. ROCKWELL. I would like to inquire whether Mr. Morgan has still got the floor? [*Laughter.*] If not, I would like to make a motion.

Mr. MORGAN. The permission is granted.

Mr. ROCKWELL. I move that the thanks of this Convention be extended to the Cincinnati Typothetæ for the magnificent hospitality with which they have received us.

The PRESIDENT. It is moved that the thanks of the United Typothetæ be given to the local Typothetæ for the royal manner in which they have entertained us. I am sure that this motion will receive the same unanimous assent that the vote of thanks was given to Mr. Pugh. Will you signify it by a rising vote? [*All rise.*] I do not know whether the chairman of the local Typothetæ (Mr. Krehbiel) is here. If he is here, I desire, on behalf of this Convention, to present the thanks of this Convention for the manner in which you have entertained us during our stay here.

Mr. ANDREWS. Inasmuch as our worthy past Treasurer declines to serve us any longer and retires, I think it is a duty that we owe him—and one which every member of the Typothetæ who has met with the various meetings in the last four years will feel that we owe him—to give a vote of thanks for the very faithful services he has rendered during the entire history of the organization. I move that the thanks of this United Typothetæ be tendered Mr. Russell for his able services as Treasurer during the entire history of the organization.

The PRESIDENT. I will ask you to give the same weight to your vote that you did to the others.

[*All rise.*]

The PRESIDENT [to Mr. Russell]. I have great pleasure in tendering to you, sir, the thanks of this Convention for the faithful manner in which you have performed the important duties assigned to you.

Mr. Russell was loudly called upon for a speech and greeted with great applause as he rose to reply.

Mr. RUSSELL. I am no talker. I had determined that I should not be Treasurer of this Typothetæ any longer, and won in the fight. I am *ex-officio* "out," and I am glad of it. I have done all that has been required of me, I believe, to the best of my ability, and filled the office of Treasurer since the organization. I have got to that age that I am old and I am lazy, and you want in that office some younger fellow to do the work for you. You have taken in as your Treasurer a man who is in every way competent and worthy, and a Cincinnati man who will not have to move with the Typothetæ. Gentlemen, I am heartily obliged that you have relieved me of this office. [*Laughter and applause.*]

Mr. SMITH, of Pittsburg. Indulge me a moment! In your inaugural address, you said that you hoped that the cloud hanging over Pittsburg will be dispelled. I will say that had we not dispelled that cloud, the cloud would have overshadowed the whole Typothetæ. This was not an ordinary fight. You have had no such fight. This was a fight for the eight hours. If it won, you would have to fight it all over the country. We have won. We have telegrams to-day that all our offices are running; otherwise we would have left this place as quickly as possible. We are going to see this thing through. The cloud is dispelled. I am happy to see that there is to be a paper prepared to find out how the cities stand upon this question, and I trust that with the facts we will then have, that a year hence a happy solution of this question may be found. If there is anything that I have said to hurt the feelings of the President, I recall everything of the kind. We want to legislate for these bodies. We meet as friends and we want to part as friends, and it is my belief that there will be no rancor on this point.

Mr. PUGH. I rise again to make just a few remarks before we leave. I am very glad the gentleman just preceding me said what he did. It gives me an opportunity that I have desired. There are some of us who have attended the Conventions from year to year—who were at Chicago when the circumstances surrounding the outlook were also very threatening for some of the gentlemen present. The circular sent out by the Chicago organization was a call to the *employing printers* of the United States. Mr. Russell, of Cincinnati, and myself went as delegates to that meeting. We found the men there in a very serious frame of mind. Since I have been engaged in printing I have run a fair office, not a Union office, employing such help as I saw fit, and paying them a scale of wages they were satisfied with. Mr. Parsons, of Louisville, Mr. Freegard, of St. Louis, and myself seemed to have struck the wrong place. The gentlemen that represented the Union establishments saw that we were correct, and they came around to our way of thinking before the strike was over, and when the Constitution of this society, which was formed at that time, went into effect, it stated that the United Typothetæ of America was formed of local Typothetæ, and these local Typothetæ, in nearly all their constitutions, provided for employing printers without regard to whether they worked "rats" in their offices or whether they worked Union men, or whether they worked for the scale or below the scale or above the scale, or, as Mr. Morgan's correspondent says, "they took all they could get." They were banded together and were all in on the same footing. They were united in the assertion of their rights, and insisted that these rights should be respected. Now a word to the gentlemen from Pittsburg—

than whom, I must say, I have never seen brighter or more honorable, or pleasant gentlemen. They entertained me most royally at Pittsburg when I went there to help them out, and their acquaintance I shall cherish most heartily. They have evinced a determination in the trouble that they are in that was worthy of the cause they were fighting for. I think when they came into this body yesterday, they should not have come in with the idea that the particular phase of the fight that they were engaged in should be made the feature of this Convention. I think that there are some members of this Convention that do not like to have this Union matter thrown in their faces, who consider the proper place for it would be at home. We have tried as far as possible, in this body, not to bring this bitterness into our national meetings, and we want to discuss this matter with freedom among ourselves. We do not want to make war on the Unions. We want to discuss such matters as the best way to conduct our business, the health of employees and their physical conditions, machinery, and such subjects. When any of the Typothetæ get into trouble we want to help it out and encourage it, but we do not want to make its fight the central figure of our Convention.

Mr. WADDEY. I hope the gentlemen will not get alarmed. I am not going to make a speech. I am requested to state, on behalf of the United States Printing Company, who have cordially invited the Convention to visit their establishment, that they should by all means be there by three o'clock. I want to say another thing, that it is not everybody gets a chance to go through that establishment, and he can see things there that he cannot see anywhere else in the world.

On motion, the Convention adjourned to meet in Toronto, August 16th, 1892.

Cincinnati and Suburbs.

On Wednesday, after the morning session, which adjourned at 12 M., all of the delegates and their ladies and guests assembled at the Burnet House, where a committee of the Cincinnati Typothetæ had tally-ho coaches and carriages in waiting. They were promptly filled, and the United Typothetæ of America was driven through the city, up Mount Auburn, across through Walnut Hills and Avondale to the beautiful Zoological Gardens, where a German lunch was served. The ride, which was a most enjoyable one, was enlivened by the cornet of Mr. Adolph Bierstadt, the celebrated soloist, and his assistants. After the lunch at the gardens the party again took their carriages, and the drive was continued through Clifton, the most beautiful suburb on the American continent, returning to the city about six o'clock, in time for dinner. None who participated in it are likely to soon forget its enjoyable features—the mellow radiance of the October sun, the beautiful park with its grass still as green as emerald, and the trees gorgeous in the yellow and red of their autumn foliage.

The Blue Grass Excursion.

Friday morning, after the final adjournment, notwithstanding the fact that Cincinnati hospitality had left nothing undone to fill to the brim its unstinted measure, an excursion had been arranged for the delegates and guests to the beautiful Blue Grass region of Kentucky; and although some of those who had tarried late at the gorgeous banquet of the evening before awoke feeling there would nothing suit them so well as "a little more sleep and a little more slumber," nearly all were on hand at the Union depot to take a special train of the Queen & Crescent route at 8:30, which pulled out promptly on time. Crossing the Ohio, it started on its way through "the dark and bloody ground" of Daniel Boone—to-day the land of fair women and brave men. The railway destination of the excursion was the famous High Bridge over the Kentucky river.

The trip from Cincinnati to this point is one of deep interest. The Blue Grass region is enchanting to look upon at any season of the year. The gold of the grain-fields, and the leaf-coloring which the autumn adds, make the scene one of bewildering beauty. The tourist at this season finds himself surrounded with all the splendors of the New England mountains. The Blue Grass, the Kentucky River cañon, finer than anything east of the Rocky Mountains, form a changing, striking and most varied panorama, which cannot be excelled in any daylight ride in the country; and there is no season in which it gives greater delight than when the autumnal coloring is over plain and mountain ranges. High Bridge spans the Kentucky river two hundred and eighty-five feet above the channel. The abutments are chiseled out of the natural cliffs. The stream emptying into the Kentucky river on the south bank above the bridge is Dix river. Crossing the bridge all visible land on the south bank and west of the railroad for two miles belongs to the Shaker community. Their village of Pleasant Hill can be seen from the track a mile south of the bridge by looking to the northwest.

A short stop was made at High Bridge station, and a few seconds later the train was again under way, finally stopping midway upon the famous High Bridge, from whose dizzy height the interested spectators gazed at the Kentucky river, winding between the high hills on either side, and the houses and people on the river's bank reduced in miniature to mere specks.

In a few minutes the train backed to the northern side of the cliff, and stopped a short while to allow the passengers to enjoy the fresh air and take a nearer view of the beautiful scenery which surrounded them. Many of the passengers got off the train here and gathered wild flowers and red berries.

Engine No. 591, which was waiting at the station, now backed down and coupled to the train, and, after giving the preliminary whistle, which warned the guests to return to the coaches, the conductor called "All aboard," and in a few minutes we were whirling back to Lexington.

At the depot in Lexington a committee were waiting to receive the guests, and, inviting them to the line of special electric cars, they were soon on the way to Ashland. Carriages were waiting for the ladies, and a five-minutes' walk from the end of the street-car line landed the visitors on the green lawn of the former home of Henry Clay. Major McDowell welcomed the guests as they arrived, and when all were gathered on the lawn, Mr. A. H. Pugh, of Cincinnati, the retiring President, introduced Col. W. C. P. Breckinridge, who delivered the following brief welcome on behalf of the city of Lexington and the host of Ashland:

Mr. BRECKINRIDGE. I was so unfortunate as not to be able to be with you last night to respond to the toast—"The Blue Grass and what it Produces." You owe me thanks, however, for disappointing you, because my place was filled by a younger and more eloquent Kentuckian, Mr. John M. Yerkes, of Danville. I shall not undertake to say anything now, except that there is one thing that the Blue Grass produces to the sojourner, and that is a hearty and cordial welcome, no matter how chill the atmosphere may be, for we have no control over the atmosphere, no matter how favorable the day may be; but we have control over our welcome, and by the city and by the host who will entertain you, I am authorized to extend to you a hearty Kentucky welcome, which comes from our hearts as well as our lips. It can be given at no place more appropriate to those who are engaged in perpetuating through living type the fame of men who do great deeds, than at this point, sanctified by one who through seventy-five years of long and laborious life, achieved deeds that give perpetual fame; that will live as long as your type lives to preserve the memory of noble and illustrious deeds. [*Applause.*] And now all that I have to do is to repeat our welcome: from wherever you may come, whatever skies bend over you at home, they bend over you here to-day, for we make you here a home at Ashland. [*Cries of "Bravo" and applause.*]

President Shepard responded as follows:

On behalf of the United Typothetæ of America, I desire to express to you our gratitude for this Kentucky reception. It is a pleasure to us all to visit the homestead of one who was not only one of your first citizens, but one of your most illustrious statesmen. We shall carry back with us most pleasant recollections of our visit to Kentucky, of this homestead, and of your unstinted hospitality.

Mr. Pugh then introduced Mr. Pettibone, of Chicago.

Mr. PETTIBONE. It is perhaps not improper that the acknowledgment and response to the cordial welcome which we have received, and which has been given by him who so worthily represents us as our President—representing us in our entirety as an international organization—I say it will not be improper that that be supplemented by a word on behalf of that large majority of our association who, from their heritage as American citizens, may be supposed, at this hour and in this place, to cherish some sentiments and emotions in these matters, from which our honored President, by the misfortune of alien birth, may be debarred. I shall not attempt to insult the well-known patriotism of our President by suggesting that even these associations and these environments can for a moment stir him from that staunch fidelity to his own country which he has so often evinced. I may say, however, that if ever there was a time when perhaps he might have the glimmer of a hope, or a desire that some time he might move into the United States, it should be here and now. [*Applause.*] It may not be improper, in that connection, to divulge a little matter which he confided to me—when he expressed his firm belief that Canada has a bridge which is at least two feet higher than the one which we saw to-day a few miles from here. [*Laughter.*]

I am reminded just now, Mr. Breckinridge, of a little episode that occurred not many years ago in Chicago, not especially important in itself, but it revealed to me the wonderful depth and breadth of the love which every Kentuckian bears to his State and every inhabitant of this famed section bears to his home. It was on the occasion of a National Convention in Chicago; a famous club from Kentucky had come up with bands and banners and barrels [*laughter*], and had taken spacious headquarters, and were keeping open house in true Kentucky style. One evening, after a delightful reception, as we lingered for a moment before going to our rooms, a gentleman stepped into a chair and gave us a specimen of Kentucky oratory which I am glad to be able to reproduce, for it was engraved upon my memory as indicating that love—and as the first revelation to me of the strength and depth of that love—of which I have spoken. He said: "In the absence of the silver-tongued orator for whom our club is named, and whose eloquent voice we have so often heard in the great councils of our party, I am requested on behalf of the Breckinridge Club of Lexington, Kentucky, to return to the ladies and gentlemen who have favored us with their presence on this and on previous occasions, our sincere thanks. We come from a State and from a section of that State which seems to us a little brighter, a little fairer than any other spot on God's green earth. We think that our skies are brighter, our grass bluer, our horses speedier, our whiskey smoother, and our ladies more beautiful than in any other spot of earth on which the sun shines."

I went away from that speech with two desires: the first that I might meet that silvery-tongued orator; and, secondly, that some time I might feast my eyes on the beauties of that Blue Grass region. The one desire was fulfilled at Chicago on the last anniversary of Washington's birthday, when I heard an oration the like of which I never expect to hear again, and certainly never had heard before. And now, under these delightful auspices, we are permitted to gather on this historic ground; for we do not forget that this is historic ground; we do not forget that the beautiful city which we see from here was so named by the pioneers of Kentucky, because the first American blood in defence of liberty was shed at Lexington, Massachusetts. Nor do we forget, as you have so feelingly reminded us, that here was commenced, nearly a century ago, that wonderful career of him who devoted a half century to the highest service of his country; and my heart thrills with patriotism and pride and gratitude as our train passes yonder cemetery, where the white shaft lifts itself into the still air, and I see floating there the grand flag of our country within a stone's throw of the sacred place where rest the ashes of Henry Clay. [*Applause.*] And here, under the shade of the trees he so loved, and which gave the name to this beautiful domain, which, with that other domain by the sea, are dear to every American heart, to every one who admires eloquence and who admires patriotism, Ashland and Marshfield and the names they suggest will be forever dear. And so, standing under the shade of these trees and of this home, which now shelters those in whose veins runs the blood of that grand patriot, let us with uncovered head remind ourselves of the virtues of that grand man, and renew our allegiance to that grand country and that grand flag for which he lived, and to which he devoted his life.

I am sure, sir, that I express the sentiments of every individual member of our association when I say that Cincinnati hospitality, not content with filling its own beautiful basin to the very brim of its encircling hills, overflowed her river banks and brought us within the hand-grasp of Kentucky hospitality, and with that hospitality has reached its climax. We thank you for your cordial greeting, and shall long remember this as one of the memorable occasions of our lives. [*Applause.*]

The party then passed into the spacious mansion, where an elegant luncheon was served for the next two hours, presided over by the accomplished hostess and her charming daughter, assisted by one of Lexington's most noted belles; details of the visitors surrounding the tables, while others strolled about the grounds.

While the luncheon was in progress a magnificent horse show was given on the lawn, at which Dictator, King René, Bermuda, Fayette Wilkes and several scores of other splendid animals belonging to Ashland and Ashland Park farms were exhibited, to the manifest delight of the assembled visitors.

Ashland never entertained more appreciative guests, and all were loud in praise of the kind reception they received.

Lexington is one of the handsomest cities in the country, being well laid out, the streets shaded with thousands of trees, and many spacious mansions adorn her suburbs. The people are intelligent, educated and refined, and at all times hospitable to the strangers within their gates. It is situated in the geographical centre of the Blue Grass region of Kentucky, and is the capital of Fayette, which, with the adjoining counties, constitutes the larger part of that famous section, and embraces about one thousand two hundred square miles of territory. No area of equal extent anywhere on the American continent, or in the world, has been endowed with greater natural fertility of soil, healthfulness of climate and beauty of rural landscape. More than fifteen hundred miles of macadam turnpike roads, converging upon Lexington, interlace this country and furnish an unrivaled system of intercommunication and facilities for local traffic, and give every farmer easy and rapid access to market.

The Blue Grass region has long been known as the great race and trotting-horse producing region of America. When you come to examine the fastest time on record at various distances, from half a mile to four miles, every animal contained in the list, was either bred in Kentucky, or, if foaled elsewhere, their sire and dam were bred in Kentucky.

After enjoying the bounteous hospitality of Ashland for several hours, we bade adieu to Major McDowell and his family, and re-embarked for Cincinnati at 4 : 30 P. M., feeling well repaid for our visit to the Blue Grass region of Kentucky, and delighted with our ride over the beautiful Queen & Crescent route.

The Queen City was reached in due time, and we were again forced to feel that the saddest of the meeting is the parting.

APPENDIX.

Constitution and Code of Ethics

OF

The United Typothetæ of America.

PREAMBLE.

With a view to developing a community of interests and a fraternal spirit among the master-printers of the United States and the Dominion of Canada, and for the purpose of exchanging information and assisting each other when necessary, the Typothetæ and other societies of employing printers of various cities, through their authorized delegates, do hereby organize themselves into a national association.

It is based on the right of the individual as opposed to the arrogated rights of trade societies; and while it disclaims any intent to assume an arbitrary control of the trade, either against customers, workmen or members, its members assert and will maintain the individual right to regulate their own affairs.

CONSTITUTION.

ARTICLE I.

NAME.

This association shall be called THE UNITED TYPOTHETÆ OF AMERICA.

ARTICLE II.

MEMBERSHIP.

SECTION 1. Any society of master-printers, containing not less than five members, of any city or town (or in any case where there are not a sufficient number of master-printers to form a society in one town, then any society formed in any county or contiguous territory) in the United States or in the Dominion of Canada, may become a member of this association upon its application for membership being approved by the Executive Committee, and paying into the treasury the initiation fee prescribed in Article VIII.

Sec. 2. Applications for membership shall be addressed to the Secretary, and shall be in the following form:

................., 189—.

To the United Typothetæ of America:

We hereby make application for membership in your body, and enclose . . . dollars, the fee prescribed by your Constitution. We have at present . . . . members, and have adopted the name of . . . .

. . . ., *President.*
. . . ., *Secretary.*

This form of application must be accompanied by a list of officers, and the name of every concern or individual who are members of the society making the same.

ARTICLE III.

REPRESENTATION.

Members of this association shall be represented in its meetings by delegates in the following proportion, viz.: One delegate for every five members or fraction of five.

ARTICLE IV.

MEETINGS.

Section 1. There shall be a regular meeting every year for the purpose of electing officers, the presentation of reports, and the transaction of any appropriate business, at such time and place as shall have been determined upon at the previous annual meeting, unless a majority of the Executive Committee deem it wise to change the time.

Sec. 2. Special meetings shall be called by the President, at the request of a majority of the Executive Committee, or upon the request of any five members of the association. Such request shall be transmitted to the President in the form of duly certified copies of resolutions adopted by the five (local societies) members aforesaid. The place of holding such special meetings shall be selected by the President.

ARTICLE V.

OFFICERS.

SECTION 1. The officers of this association shall be a President, six Vice-Presidents, who shall be selected, as far as practicable, as follows, viz.: one from the New England States, one from the Middle States, one from the Southern States, one from the Western States, one from the Pacific States, and one from the Dominion of Canada; a Secretary, a Treasurer, and an Executive Committee of seven, who shall be elected at the regular annual meeting. The President and Secretary shall be members of the Executive Committee, *ex officio*.

SEC. 2. All elections of officers shall be by ballot, and in open Convention.

ARTICLE VI.

DUTIES OF OFFICERS.

SECTION 1. It shall be the duty of the President to preside at all meetings of the association, appoint all committees not otherwise ordered, and to attend to such other duties as are elsewhere specified.

SEC. 2. The Vice-Presidents shall be denominated, when elected, as First, Second, Third, Fourth, Fifth and Sixth Vice-Presidents, and shall, in the event of the death, resignation or disability of the President, assume and execute the duties of his office in the order named until the next meeting of the association.

SEC. 3. The Secretary shall keep correct minutes of all the transactions of the association, and shall send notices to each member of all annual and special meetings; shall conduct the official correspondence of the association; shall give special attention to the organization of additional local societies by furnishing information to persons and firms interested in the movement; shall receive applications for membership and reports from members; shall certify the correctness of all bills to the President for approval, and at the annual meeting shall present a general report of the leading transactions of the association during the preceding year.

SEC. 4. The Treasurer shall hold in trust all moneys and other property of the association; shall pay all bills certified by the Secretary and approved by the President; and shall present a detailed statement of the finances at every annual meeting, or whenever required by a majority of the Executive Committee.

Sec. 5. The Executive Committee shall have general supervision over all matters connected with the interests of the association, and shall have power to pass upon and accept new members.

Sec. 6. The Executive Committee shall meet at such times and places as the President may select. Five shall constitute a quorum. They shall have power to fill vacancies in their own number.

Sec. 7. No officer of the association, other than the Secretary, shall receive any compensation for services, and the salary of the Secretary shall be determined by the Executive Committee.

ARTICLE VII.

COMMITTEES.

Section 1. The Finance Committee shall consist of the President, Secretary, and Treasurer; and no debts shall be contracted in the name of this association unless previously authorized by this committee.

Sec. 2. An Auditing Committee of three shall be appointed from the delegates at each annual meeting, whose duty it shall be to examine the books, accounts and vouchers of the Secretary and Treasurer, and report thereon.

Sec. 3. Special committees upon correspondence, the state of the trade, or any other question interesting to the members, may be designated as occasion requires.

ARTICLE VIII.

REVENUES.

Each member shall, upon admission to the association, pay into the treasury a sum equal to two dollars per capita as an initiation fee, and shall also pay, on or before April first of each and every year, as annual dues, a sum equal to two dollars for every one of its members; and any member being in arrears for two years shall be dropped from the roll.

ARTICLE IX.

AMENDMENTS.

The Constitution shall be abrogated or amended only at a regular annual meeting of the association, by a vote of two-thirds of all the delegates present, such amendments having been proposed by one or more members by filing said amendment with the Secretary, who shall serve notice upon all the members of the proposed amendment at least thirty days in advance of the annual meeting.

ORDER OF BUSINESS.

1. Calling the Roll.
2. Reading the Minutes of the previous meeting.
3. Reports from Officers.
4. Reports from Standing Committees.
5. Reports from Special Committees.
6. Motions and Resolutions.
7. Miscellaneous Business.

CODE OF ETHICS.

Recognizing the fact that in the conduct of our business no individual or concern in any community can act regardless of his neighbors and competitors, and that while the spirit of competition has been so deeply imbedded in the human breast and so keenly sharpened by the methods of every-day life as to cause it to enter into and influence every transaction; but at the same time believing there are methods of competition which are clean, honorable and legitimate, whereby we can compete without wronging others, and without demoralizing the business in which we are engaged, the United Typothetæ of America adopts the following rules, and recommends them to the employing printers of the country:

OF OUR DUTY TO OURSELVES.

(1) The Code of Ethics best calculated to elevate the status of employing printers must be evolved by the development of moral and intellectual manhood. We should, therefore, and firmly, resolve to test every *transaction* by the standard of truth and justice.

(2) Take advantage of no man's ignorance, and see that employees are truthful and straightforward, and do not misrepresent nor overcharge the confiding.

(3) It is an absolute essential in honorable competition that we prove ourselves as honorable in every particular as we would have our competitors.

(4) Mix freely with intelligent and honorable members of the craft, and study their ways and methods, and endeavor to get a reputation in the community as an intelligent, honest, first-class printer, whom people can trust with their work without competitive bidding.

(5) Every printing establishment should have a perfect system of ascertaining the actual cost of every job. It is in this way only that the business can hope to be relieved from the deleterious effects of guess prices. Such a system should not only ascertain the facts, but record them, so that they can be referred to understandingly, and the information immediately ascertained.

(6) No establishment should be satisfied with anything except the most exact and systematic book-keeping, and all work should be checked up and charges proved before delivery, and the following made a standing rule: Never permit a charge to be entered on the books that cannot be proved by competent evidence in a court of justice to be a fair competitive price.

(7) The expense of doing business, such as the wear and tear of material, interest on money invested, bad debts, rent, taxes, insurance, book-keeping, and all other items of expense, should be ever before our eyes, and we should never forget that these must be as surely levied on each particular job as its labor cost. Never, under any circumstances, should the minimum cost plus a fair profit be departed from. We should feel here a double restraint: in the first place, to cut cost is *foolish;* in the second place, it is *wrong.*

(8) On no account consent to pay commissions to book-keepers, secretaries, or others who have work to give out. It is demoralizing to both the giver and the taker. Money is passed without a proper equivalent. The agent is selling something he has no right to sell, and unless the printer has a better conscience than is ordinarily met with, the commission is added to the bill, and the customer pays more than he should.

OF OUR DUTY TO EACH OTHER.

(9) When a young competitor enters the ranks welcome him as a new soldier to the field, and help him to any information and assistance which will enable him to overcome the difficulties we had so much trouble in surmounting. Rest assured you can make no better investment of the time necessary to do so, as his gratitude for the kindly consideration will often cause him to repay you in a fourfold way, and where you would least anticipate it.

(10) It should be a duty and pleasure to impart to our less experienced competitors the knowledge we possess, so long as we are satisfied that the information generously given will be honorably used. In this way the element of ignorance which does so much to demoralize the craft may be partially eliminated, and one of the most dangerous factors of competition destroyed. Remember that knowledge kindly imparted makes a business friend of one who would probably otherwise become a business foe.

(11) The young employer who starts with a small capital, and does most of his own work, should ever remember the honorable nature of his calling, and never make the mistake of supposing that because he does his own work he can do it for less than his neighbor who employs fifty or more hands, with a long list of superintendents and foremen. He should rather insist that the work which he does with his own hands will be better done, and therefore he should receive more for it.

(12) When a printer is offered work which he cannot do, his rule should be to decline it, and refer his customer to the office that can do it, and not accept the work, hoping to get some neighbor to do it for him and allow him a commission.

(13) Make no rebates or allowances to professional brokers or middlemen. If it is possible to help a neighbor out of an extra rush of composition or press-work, do it cheerfully, and divide with him the profit on the work. In this way the temptation to add to the facilities, oftentimes much too large for the work done in a given community, will very often be overcome, as idle machinery makes it almost impossible to maintain any standard of prices which may be adopted.

(14) When estimates are asked for by any person on work done by another printer, with plain intent to find cause for an alleged unfairness of the price charged, they should be invariably de-

clined. It is not safe to criticise any price until one is in possession of all the facts. The work itself when done does not say whether it was done by night or by day, with few or many alterations; but these and other unknown conditions may have controlled the price.

(15) In making estimates we are shooting arrows in the dark, and may unwittingly wound some of our best friends when we have least intended it. If the aggrieved person thinks he has been injured by an estimate which has taken away a valued customer, his proper course is to seek an explanation, and he should always begin with the supposition that the injurious price has been made in ignorance of all the facts, by thoughtlessness or by mistake. In most cases he can reach such an explanation as will prevent a repetition of the error, if it does not bring the lost work back.

OF PRICES AND ESTIMATES.

(16) Every establishment should have a thorough knowledge of what it costs to produce the work it sends out, and should determine what percentage of profit it will be satisfied with. Based upon those two items, it should establish its prices for all work undertaken, whether secured by competitive bid or without a price being named in advance.

(17) A master-printer should not make estimates for work that he cannot do, and when he is devoid of experience in certain branches of printing, should not attempt to price them. It is always unsafe and often unjust to give prices upon a class of work upon which the cost is not positively known and has to be guessed at.

(18) Always have the courage to ask fair remuneration for any work offered, resting assured that it will be more profitable to be without a job than to secure one in which there is a temptation to resort to questionable methods in order to avoid a financial loss in its execution.

(19) Estimates calling for detailed specifications of separate value of the paper, composition, electrotyping, presswork, ruling, binding, etc., should always be refused. These details the customer has no right to. They are the printer's property, and to be swift in giving them away is one of the surest methods of provoking unfair competition.

(20) When requested to make estimates for work, or submitting proposals in answer to advertisements, the intelligent printer

should endeavor to never lose sight of the fact that the only price proper to make is the one that he would make were the work intrusted to him without any estimates having been requested on it. His estimated figures should be made on the basis per thousand ems, per token, and per pound for paper that he has adopted for his minimum for the class of work, while carefully studying the subject with the figures of his previous year's business before his eyes, and while safely shielded from the exciting influences which arise when the estimate fiend is so close upon him—always consoling himself when he loses the job with the thought that if he had incumbered himself with the work at a low figure he would have incapacitated himself from doing what may presently come along at a remunerative rate.

(21) A master-printer should always contend that he is entitled, when asked for an estimate, to know the names of all who are to be requested to bid on the work. A glance at the names is often sufficient to show him whether it is worth the trouble to make the necessary calculations. He should also insist upon his right, if he desires it, to know all the prices offered for the work, and to whom and at what price it was awarded.

(22) The man who asks for a bid upon work, and before receiving it shows the figures made by another bidder, should be marked; it can be depended on, if he will show you another's bid he will show yours to a third party. He wants you to do the job, if you will do it for less than any one else.

OF OUR DUTY TO OUR WORKMEN.

(23) In the conduct of our establishments it should be our constant endeavor to elevate the moral character and ameliorate the financial condition of our workmen who are engaged with us. This interest in his welfare is one of the best methods of preventing strikes and lockouts, which do such untold damage to both the proprietor and the journeyman.

(24) While it should be the firm and unalterable determination of every printer not to be dictated to by labor organizations when their demands are unfair, or which substitute the will of a prejudiced majority for the conservative teachings of common sense and justice, we should be slow to condemn the action taken by the journeymen, as it is possible that the influences controlling them may be more than they are able to resist.

(25) Any action which tends to decrease the rate of wages should be looked upon with as much distrust as is an effort to increase them. We should always remember that the proper place for us to look for remuneration is from the business we do at a legitimate profit, and not from what we can save on the *per diem* of the wage-worker, or from what we can make out of each other.

(26) In the treatment of apprentices or boys who are in our employ, we should be ever careful as to whose hands they are in, as they are often influenced for good or for bad by the example of the foreman under whom they work.

(27) When an apprentice is taken it should be considered our duty, if he prove unapt or unteachable, to advise him to seek another line of trade. It often occurs that a poor printer would have made a good blacksmith or shoemaker; therefore either trade, as well as the boy, would be benefited by taking him away from the trade for which he is unfitted.

(28) When we conclude that the apprentice we have taken is competent to learn the business, and that he will master it in such a manner as to reflect credit upon those who taught him as well as himself, no effort should be spared to make him all he should be as a workman and a good citizen. By so doing we add to our own happiness, his prosperity, and help the future generation of employing printers along a very troublesome road.

PAPERS

RECEIVED BY THE

COMMITTEE ON THE EVILS THAT RESULT FROM COMPETITIVE BIDDING.

CONCERNING ESTIMATES.

THEO. L. DEVINNE, OF NEW YORK TYPOTHETÆ.

Every buyer of printing has a right to know the value of the work he proposes to have done. As a rule he will not give an order until he gets an exact or conditional estimate. He expects the master-printer to name a definite price for a petty card or a large book, for a ream of paper, for a thousand ems of composition or a thousand impressions of press-work. It is the interest and the duty of the printer to give this or similar information and to answer reasonable queries. He would soon have to stop business if he were to stop giving estimates.

The justice or injustice of estimates is largely a personal affair. If the master-printer makes the estimate too low, he must suffer the loss; if he makes it too high, he repels and loses the expected order. Our society does not meddle with individual right. It does not say that the master-printer shall maintain any fixed prices. It assumes that he knows what is the value of the work he is asked to do, and that he will not knowingly do it at loss. It assumes that he is fairly well informed of the usages of the trade and of the rates charged by his brothers in business, and that he will not knowingly try to undercut or overreach. It does not pretend to discipline any of its members for any errors they may have committed in making estimates.

This tolerant attitude of our society towards individual right, and even individual wrong, is always a surprise to the members of other societies, but it is really one of our strongest safeguards. It keeps in our fold members of the most diverse views, and enables them to have an influence on each other which they never could have if they were not fellow-members. It enables us to discuss debatable questions and to harmonize differences of opinion. It certainly does draw us nearer together in individual lines of action. With a view to closing the distance that now exists between many members in the matter of making estimates, these observations are respectfully submitted.

Although the making of estimates is a matter of individual right, it can be made the pretext for great general wrong. The printer who estimates $100 for work usually or generally done at $150, does not only injure his brother printer who has done the work at the last-named price, but he strikes a blow at all the master-printers of his city. He encourages his customer to distrust the fair dealing of other printers. This suspicion is often highly unjust. The undercutter encourages a system of reprisals as well as of competition, from which he is sure to suffer eventually.

A young master-printer, or one not well versed in making estimates, cannot safely deviate from the established rates of the trade. He may think, as most journeymen compositors do think, that an advance of 80 or 90 per cent. on the compositor's charge for 1,000 ems is altogether too high. He thinks so only because he does not know the magnitude of other items of expense necessary for the perfection of the work in this 1,000 ems. He underrates these expenses. Is it wise or safe for any young man to think he can prosper by rates that are refused by the great majority of the trade?

The commonest error is that of overrating the performance of men and machines. There are many compositors who can set more than 1,000 ems an hour, but we know also that the average performance of an office of fifty men on book or job work is less than 500 ems an hour. There are cylinder presses that have done, and can do, on long runs, 10,000 impressions in a day, but we know also that the average performance of cylinder presses in job offices, on long and short runs, rarely exceeds 3,500 impressions a day, and oftener falls below 3,500. Estimates for time work should be based not on the performance of the expert, but on that of the average workman—not on the number of tokens done in the pressroom in one exceptional day, but on the average number of tokens done in the past year. What has been is that which will be. There have been many essays written on the cost of doing printed work, which will deserve study; but every master-printer of one year's experience can learn a wiser lesson from the study of his own account books. If he will take the trouble to find out how many tokens of press-work he did the previous year, and what he got for it, and what was the expense account of his press-room; how many thousand ems he set, how many hours of time-work he charged, and what he got for it, and what the expense of his composing-room was—if he will do this carefully, honestly reckoning interest and depreciation, he will learn more of the cost of printing than he can get from any treatise on the subject. After this has been done, he may possibly think that he can do better next year. Perhaps he can, but not much better. The conditions of work are inflexible. He certainly will not learn that he can do for $100 what others charge $150 for.

A master-printer should not make estimates for work that he cannot do. The master-printer who is not provided with the proper material, and has not had experience in certain branches of printing, should not attempt to price them. It is always unsafe and often unjust to give prices for Greek, music, high-grade color work, etc., on the supposition that these kinds of work are done or can be done at an imaginary rate. One should know and not guess what the rates are.

In my boyhood master-printers used to advertise that they could do "every kind of printing" that might be offered. I know of no one who makes that boast now. Our art is now so complex and has so many branches that no one office dare undertake all of them. Every sensible printer finds his advantage, not in getting together all the orders he can, but in getting only the work that he can do to a profit—work that he has facilities for and that he knows how to manage. The tendency of the trade is to specialties. There are offices that do books only; others that do posters only, or labels only, or job work only, or music only. It is well that there should be such divisions of work. The materials and machinery for these and other branches of the art are expensive and require special expertness. It is unwise for the average master-printer to meddle with the work of experts.

Many printers take in work which they cannot do, with the hope that they will get a commission for the order from the office that accepts it. This wretched business of commissions should be discouraged. It has done more to make enmities in the trade and to bring down fair prices than all other causes combined. When a printer is offered work that he cannot do, his rule should be to decline it, and to refer the customer to the office that can do it. If the customer insists on having the printer take charge of the work, accept it with the understanding that the work done shall be priced by the office that does it. Never accept it at his price or at your own.

Estimates asked by any customer on work done by another printer, with plain intent to find a cause for an alleged unfairness of price, should be declined. If such a request is pressed, the customer should be told that his request may be laid before the local Typothetæ, but only after the person who has done the work has had an opportunity to name and defend his price. It is not safe to criticise any price uutil one is in possession of all the facts. These facts the customer cannot fully know. The work itself, when done, does not say whether it was done by night or day, with little or with great alterations. But these and other conditions have controlled the price.

Estimates calling for detailed specifications of the separate value of the paper, composition, electrotyping, press-work, ruling, binding, etc., should always be refused. When the estimate is asked only for composition and plates, or only for press-work, or only for binding, the customer himself furnishing the deficiencies, the request should be granted. But an invitation to estimate on a book or pamphlet, and to give the value of each item, is unreasonable, and should always be refused These details the customer has no right to. One might as well ask of a press-builder specifications of the metal and labor in a machine. To be swift in giving away these details to a customer, is the surest way to provoke unfair competition. It often happens in competitive detailed work that a certain complete price is lowest of three or more bidders, but if this lowest bid gives the items, and if it contains one higher item, the printer will be asked to reduce the price of that item.

Requests for estimates on printing known to have been done by a brother in the trade, should be entertained with caution. Attempt should be made to discover why a change in the printer is desired. · A consultation with this brother, or at least a notification to him that a change is to be made, is a fair and open procedure which will in nearly every case remove any cause for dissatisfaction at the result, whatever that result may be.

Requests for estimates from unknown persons that call for tedious calculations, and that seem to be made to gratify vague curiosity, should be regarded as professional work to be paid for. The same remark will apply to many printers. It is not considerate, to say the least, to ask a brother printer to review an estimate, or to make a new estimate, when the work called for will take one hour or more of close calculation.

Estimates asked by corporations for large amounts of work should be made on printed specifications, which should be furnished to every bidder. If the specifications are loosely stated, attempt should be made to have them corrected, not for one, but for all bidders. The request for estimate should state the names of the bidders invited. A glance at the names is often enough to show the inquirer whether it is worth the trouble to make any calculations. There should always be a consent on the part of the corporation that every bidder shall be furnished, after the award has been made, with the bids furnished by each bidder.

In making estimates we are shooting arrows in the dark. It must be that some of the arrows will hit where we did not intend they should hit. We may unwittingly wound some of our best friends. What then? If the aggrieved person thinks that he has been injured by an estimate which has taken away a valued customer, his proper course is to seek an explanation, if he thinks the matter of sufficient importance. He may properly begin this remonstrance with the assumption that the injurious estimate has been made in ignorance of all the facts, or in thoughtlessness, or by mistake. In most cases he can come to an amicable agreement with his adversary, which, even if it does not succeed in bringing the lost work back, will succeed in preventing a repetition of the error. This is what our society was organized for.

There is another way of trying to right the injury, which I mention only to condemn a way which was quite common many years ago. This was the assumption that our successful competitor meant to injure us by his lower estimate, followed up by a refusal to see him or to have an explanation, and by his general defamation. I know of no surer way than this to increase the evils of competitive bidding.

COMPETITIVE BIDDING, WITH ITS RESULTANT EVILS.

A PAPER READ BY THOMAS TODD BEFORE THE MASTER-PRINTERS' CLUB, BOSTON, MASS., JUNE 18, 1891.

Fellow Craftsmen:

Your very kind and complimentary vote, nominating me to present a paper on the "Evils which result from Competitive Bidding, and prepare such a Code of Ethics as will tend to Elevate the Dignity of the Trade," was *very* kind and complimentary, and should have ended by my declining the honor or dying, so that a successor could have been appointed at once; but, unfortunately, the golden moment passed, the session was closed, and I am left to exhaust your patience.

Were I to confine myself strictly to the letter of the first half of the subject, "The Evils which result from Competitive Bidding," I should be necessarily very brief (as I indeed expect to be in any case), and simply, parrot-like, enumerate a few words— bankruptcy, ruin, poor credit, blasted reputation, *et id genus omne.* But may I be pardoned if I ask your permission to go a little aside and inquire into the *causes* of the evils which result from competitive bidding, as well as to suggest some of the remedies that will ameliorate that condition, which results in a living death not only to one's own self, but drags down in its net all who are immediately connected with the master workman; who, no matter how he may struggle, and no matter how he may strive, yet feels the earth slipping from under him, his frenzied grasp loosening on all the ties that should hold him, and he gradually sinking down, down, to that unfathomable and unknown and undesired state where even the dogs loathe him. For no more pitiable object can be found than a decayed business man—one who has hoped against hope, and has fought against fearful odds; bravely, but without discretion; earnestly, but without knowledge; daringly, but without counting the cost, and at last finds himself stranded, with strength all spent, hopeless, breathless, the patience of his friends exhausted, money gone, credit vanished, and even a welcomed death standing afar off and shaking his skeleton finger at him, refusing to claim his own.

And I may say in a word, in enumerating the causes of the evils of competitive bidding, something which in my judgment is true, and yet a very unwelcome truth. The craftsmen whom we most dread to compete with are those who are, perhaps, good workmen, but who have no knowledge of business—in other words, are ignorant of business methods. How large a percentage of our master-printers can tell you how much it costs to set a thousand ems, for instance? How much they pay their compositor they can tell you readily; but how much should be charged to rent, taxes, insurance, light, fuel, wear and tear of type, and that largest item of all—proof-reading? If he pays forty cents per thousand ems for composition, does he not reason that sixty cents per thousand ems will yield him an ample profit? And will he not affirm positively that he is making money, hand over hand, when he cannot replace his plant without mortgaging his office, using all the money he can borrow from friends and relatives, assigning his life insurance policy, and so pledging his future that he is doomed? If a press-feeder costs twenty cents per hour, and the presses earn three dollars per day, will he not as positively assert that his profit is in the press-room, and that his presses are coining him a mint of money? Does he not fail to take into the account the thousand and one expenses that come into his business, and that are reckoned by every other branch of business, *simply because of his ignorance of business habits?* Does he not also fail to see that his work is in one sense not a business, but a profession, and that this necessitates the employment of skilled workmen, men with brains, education, and in all ways a higher grade of employees than the carpenter, mason, bricklayer, plumber, and in fact nearly every kind of artisan, and that the requirement of a better class of workmen involves the payment of a higher and better grade of wages? This factor is all-important, as it diminishes in like ratio the profit to be obtained in the employment of a given capital. It may be said, in justification and extenuation of his ignorance, that he has not been trained to business principles and habits for the very reason that the pursuit of his calling demands the habits of a recluse, the retirement of a hermit, and that perforce he is not qualified to grasp the problems that a stirring man of the world is so ready to see and take hold of. Granted; and if we grant this, we grant all; for the moment a man does so acknowledge it, that moment his eyes are opened, and he is prepared to take hold of the problem with a courage and a power that nothing can stay. The craft are not fools, but are woefully ignorant of business. I can and dare speak the more boldly because I have observed so many in just that position, and can therefore speak of that which I have seen, and not depend upon the vague reports that come floating through the air. Take the most of the craft as they are to-day. I do not mean the large offices, those with perfected organizations and completed business methods, but the weaker ones, the places from whose owners we fear the most competition. Look about you, fellow-craftsmen, not among your peers, but among some of the offices that we might call the smaller places—offices that have grown from small beginnings into a little larger entity, and have attained a position where they are "looking toward you."

The master workman is driven all day with work, with the calls and wants of customers and the many annoyances and troubles that inevitably follow in their train. At night he stuffs into his pockets whatever of proofs he has not been able to attend to through the day, and his patient and long-suffering family have to sit up and assist him through the small hours of the night, until at last, with eyeballs burning in their sockets and brain reeling from sheer exhaustion, he tumbles into bed to turn and toss and twist until daylight comes with inexorable call, requiring the resumption of his arduous labors. With gentle irony it might be called the "sweating," the tenement-house competition. This, followed day after day, unfits the master from grappling with the questions which so immediately concern him, and he gropes on and on, blindly and helplessly, hoping that somehow or in some way he may be able to redeem himself from the thralldom of his ignorance of business and emerge into the open light of peace, ease, prosperity and that which necessarily follows—a leisure to study the problem that lies before him of how to make his business profitable and avoid the "evils that result from competitive bidding." If he ever does attain to it he will dip his pen in gall and charge the rest of the craft with woeful ignorance!

Another cause of the evils which result from competitive bidding is the Yankee habit of *guessing*, instead of giving each contract its due and careful weight. Gentlemen, is our experience in a great degree dissimilar? Time and again this has been reported to us: "X said that if Y would print that job for $48 he would do it for $46, and take the risk." And if we would stop to inquire, we might find that Y had said: "If Z will do that job for $50 I will print it for $48," and so on down the list. This is no fancy sketch. We all have heard it over and over again. And we will continue to hear it echoed and re-echoed through the corridors of the trade until we all awake to our sober senses and see the evils that obtain in our business methods, and not only resolve to correct them, but *do* correct them! Guessing may do very well in story books, in papers and such places; but it should be banished from the hard pan of business, where paper weighs so many pounds to a ream and costs so much for a pound (and has to be paid for, too), and presses cost so much apiece, and ink is so much a pound, and a foreman has so many dollars a week, and a devil so few dollars a week, and the rent is exactly so much a month, our dear tax man will not wait, and the insurance man insists upon cash down, and the type founders (God bless them!) insist upon monthly payments, and we are not bank presidents, to *guess* we can borrow enough of the funds of the institution to tide over this time! Everything is on bed rock, and there is no room for guessing, but all should be brought sharply to the transaction of business upon business principles.

But what can be said in relation to the preparation of a Code of Ethics for our government—something that shall bind all the craft in bonds like steel, yet as light as silk; that will hold all our membership and all not our membership—that membership which is of the Craft Universal—together, as with the strong grip of a Samson, and yet sway them as gently as by the hand of a Delilah; that will not *force* men to go against their own convictions, but will make their convictions force them to do just *right?* How can this be attained in the application of our principles and our motives, and made not only to appear to be, but actually to be? The task is the task of a Hercules; but the result, if attained, will be worthy of the reward—the satisfaction that one can have in the thought that he has been a part of the mighty power that has helped to uplift the craft from the slough of despond into which it has fallen upon a higher plane, even the plane of self-support and self-emolument, not to say riches! This should be the Ultima Thule of the ambition of the National Typothetæ; and if it can be accomplished we can feel that we have demonstrated the necessity of our existence.

Let me for a moment touch the caustic upon one of our sore spots—the tribulation of estimating. It goes without saying, that we are all of us too careless in this matter; that we look at a fair-looking page of manuscript and cast it up at single measurement, when it should be charged at price-and-a-half, or price-and-a-half when it should be double, or fail to think of the amount of rule required for the piece of work more than we have in the office, or find we have not allowed for open matter, or blanks, or headings, or something of that sort! Suffer an allusion from my personal experience. A number of years ago I was inquired of by letter as to the cost of printing one hundred and fifty pamphlets, small pica type, the pages to be 4 x 7, and the book to be 6 x 9, the book not to contain more than 5,000 words, and to have a paper cover. Easy enough, you all say; any one could estimate on that. Well, when the copy came, there were two and sometimes three words on a line, the rest of the lines to be quads. Was I not careful in my estimate? I thought I was. Having purchased my experience on one job, I have been overcareful since, and have insisted upon seeing the MSS. ever afterward. Do we carefully examine the paper we are estimating upon if we are in a hurry, and carefully test for weight and quality, or, as I have said before, *guess* as to the cost of that which is often the largest item in the whole? If a piece of work is to be done in colors, do we simply add fifty cents for cleaning the rollers, or do we stop to realize that the covering power of black ink is eight times as great as red ink—in other words, that it will take eight pounds of red ink to cover a job that, if it were printed in black, would take but one pound of ink? Or some harmless piece of work comes in: we glance at it, and make a price upon it; and after our terms have been accepted we discover with horror that it is full of marks, signs and symbols which require the expenditure of several dollars; and so on to the end of the chapter. Craftsmen, we are ourselves greatly to blame in this matter, in not taking time enough and giving careful attention enough to this matter of estimating. We do not want to charge too much; in fact, none of us do! When we err, it is in charging too little—in not receiving a new dollar for an old one.

It will not answer to let this occasion pass without an allusion to a matter upon which the Typothetæ are endeavoring to obtain light, and of which we have such an illustrious example in our own Master Printers' Club. I speak now of the attempt which was made by our club, a few months ago, to procure estimates on a certain piece of work, and the craft generally have been scratching their metaphorical heads over it since, seeking to get order out of chaos, and find the reason why this or that style of figuring obtained. The difference between the highest and lowest figures was $153.26—probably more than the profit on the whole work if it were completed; but in the items there was too great a discrepancy, and a discrepancy which shows that some of our craftsmen must have guessed instead of working from solid bases. It may be retorted that all estimating is but a guess, and so it is; but a guess that has a substratum of hard fact upon which to rest is better than a guess with nothing but nebulous ether as a foundation. We all remember about the school-boy, who, when asked how he was enabled to tell the distance to the sun, replied, "Guess at one-half the distance and multiply by two. Now an estimate or guess like that, while ingenious and daring, may not *pay;* and (let me whisper it gently in your ear) money is what we are after in this business of ours. Fame in a way is all very nice; but fame without money is like ashes to our taste, or vinegar to our sweet tooth.

And with all our care, there is one danger we are all liable to fall into, and which we should endeavor to discourage as much as possible. Put this down as a fixed principle: *Do not estimate whenever you can avoid it.* I dare affirm that at least one-half of our estimating can be avoided if we choose to look the matter boldly in the face and make it unnecessary. A great deal of our estimating is that which is sent in for the sole purpose of ascertaining if the inquirer has been cheated by his printer—a matter which I might call the "estimate of curiosity." And certainly one does not wish to estimate after a man has told you he has been to one cheap John and another, and that the lowest bid will take the work. A little cross-examination will often bring these facts out; and then it is well to very politely, but firmly and good-naturedly, decline. A good-naturedly obstinate man is hard to handle. And perhaps now it will be a good time to say that nothing should ever be estimated at cost; that a wholesome percentage ought to be added to all items—paper, ruling, binding, blocking, numbering, perforating, extra sorts, and all those necessary concomitants that appertain to a completed whole. It would seem as if it were needless to advance such an idea, and yet we all have seen competitors estimating at cost for net cash, the parties evidently reasoning that quick cash would be equivalent to a percentage of profit, from the fact that "time is money." Do not we take all the risk, and can we afford to do so for nothing? The question admits of but one answer.

Another tribulation for us to cauterize is in the difference in measuring work—a matter of considerable importance to some of us. And it remotely touches this matter of estimating, while at the same time it is a powerful factor in our charges where no estimating is required. There are certain rules of measuring that all do not understand, but about which all would like to be informed. When a man has become a craftsman he naturally becomes desirous of obtaining the secrets that pertain to his business, and he is too often met with a flat refusal to impart those secrets; and he is left to grope along in a blind way, striving all the time, occasionally getting a little lift, but still not permitted to come into the fullness of knowledge, and the power that comes from knowledge. Master workmen should by all means be willing to give all the information in their power to those just emerging into the light of business. I heard a master printer say the other day: "Had some kind friend told me what I have since gladly told other younger craftsmen, I should have been saved much hard labor and much exasperating annoyance, as well as have made money, instead of appearing before you clothed in rags and humility." And his experience, I am quite sure, is only one of many. And it seems to me that, at the meetings of the different Typothetæ, instead of writing essays upon the "Possibilities of the Infinite," and "How to Yearn for that which is worth Yearning for," we should dismount from our Pegasus, and talk with one another about the commonplaces of our business, and how best to so conduct our affairs as to make us all successful and prosperous. Kindly remember that imparted knowledge makes a business friend of one who would otherwise be a business foe; for without the knowledge you could easily communicate, your neighbor is not by any means an intelligent competitor, but becomes one of a class that are too largely prevalent in the trade, viz.: an ignorant and narrow, because ignorant, rival.

But I have already wearied you. Suffer with me for a brief moment longer. Our business, I firmly believe, while not the best paying, is the best business to be found upon the footstool of God, and ought to be elevated to the high standard upon which it used to be; and, fellow craftsmen, it will be! I look upon this National Typothetæ as the best instrument for producing that important result that has ever been invented or discovered or evolved. Not intended for that object, but organized for another and not so noble a purpose, it has grown and developed until we see it stretching from Maine to California, from Texas almost to Alaska! And it is still a weakling, puny baby; but soon destined to be a giant. May the Typothetæ go on in its high mission—that of strengthening and encouraging and helping one another over the hard places, diffusing light and information among the craft, cultivating a proper *esprit de corps* with us all, seeking to make all believe in the motto, "Live and let live," until all the fraternity, instead of believing themselves to be common enemies, shall clasp hands across the bloody chasm of business, and shall say from the heart, and carry it out in their daily lives, "We be all brethren!"

COMPETITION: ITS POSSIBLE REGULATION.

A PAPER READ BEFORE THE SAN FRANCISCO TYPOTHETÆ, MAY 13, 1891, BY CHAS. A. MURDOCK.

Competition, as a principle, is imbedded so deeply in the very nature of man that it is safe to say it will stay by him "to the crack of doom." It is a continuation of that struggle for supremacy and survival that has lifted us from lower forms of animal life and made us men. It strongly develops the individual, and is the direct cause of most of the inventions that have made all nature man's servant, and so multiplied the comforts of life. But of competition in general I have not to do. The practice of competition to-day, in this business of printing, is what I am to consider.

We are all competing for something—we will continue to do so; the problem is, how to compete without wronging others, and without demoralizing the business in which we are engaged. Business cannot but be a sort of warfare. It is necessarily each man for himself, and we can only succeed through sharp struggle. The tendency is to utter selfishness, and a total disregard of the rights of others; but this will not do. It commonly defeats itself, and when it succeeds it is a dearly bought victory. No man can afford to gain a success that is purchased at the loss of self-respect, and failure with honor is better than success with dishonor.

Business is a warfare, but even in war there are recognized standards, and guerrillas, cut-throats and free-booters are execrated by all civilized people. And in this necessary war what is most needed to-day is a recognized standard of honor that will hold us to a fair fight, and keep us from stabbing one another in the back, or plying the deadly sand-bag in the dark. We need to be firmly convinced that there are some things we have no right to do. We need to learn that there are distinctions in our methods of conducting business equally as clear as in war; and that there are practices to which we are in danger of descending as dishonorable and dastardly as poisoning an enemy's coffee, or employing small-pox to decimate his ranks. We want to learn what is the false and what is the true competition. We want to know how far we may go and when we must stop. We want to study our duty with our rights.

We are all in business to make at least a living, and as much more, as we decently can. There is a given amount of printing to be done in a given community, and for this we compete. What is the legitimate way to do it? In the first place we may feel perfectly safe in aiming at excellence of product. The better the article we have to offer the better our chance of selling it. It is certainly legitimate to strive our utmost to do the best work. We thus promote our own interest, stimulate our fellows and elevate our craft to its true place. Printing is an art as well as a business; and although we should all starve if we relied on the appreciation of what is called art-printing, we may still mingle a good deal of art in doing every-day work of any description. We can at least do good, clean printing, that is what it pretends to be, and of course give full count; for I take it for granted that petty larceny is not one of the crimes of which we are in danger. We can also aim at being prompt and obliging, and chary of making promises we cannot keep. We can strive to establish a reputation for being reliable and honest, so that after twenty years or more we can be trusted to do a five-dollar job without giving an estimate.

These are all legitimate ways of competition. There are others still legitimate that are less admirable. We naturally expect to get work from friends who believe in us; and if a man thinks it worth while, he may join all the secret societies and social organizations recorded in the blue-book, for the express purpose of working its members by making them friends and patrons. Again, we may extend our business through employing fascinating solicitors, or by importuning, vicarious or otherwise.

One method I claim is not legitimate—the paying of commissions to book-keepers, secretaries, supervisors or others who have printing to give out. It is demoralizing to the giver and the taker. Money is passed without a proper equivalent rendered. The agent is selling something that he has really no right to sell, and unless the printer has a better conscience than commonly gets into any business, the percentage, or a large part of it, goes onto the bill, and the principal pays more than he should.

And now I come to the kernel of the nut—the most difficult thing in the printing business—how much to charge! This is the point where we break down, or fly the track. Here is where we are ugly and use the stiletto. In this fierce competition we find that, all other things being equal, the man who does any given job for the least money gets it. Quite often he gets it regardless of "all other things being equal." The end and aim in life of many of our customers would seem to be to get work done as nearly to its cost as possible, and if below it so much the better.

Now this natural tendency we encourage and feed by our ready bidding. We are anxious—too anxious—to do work. We consequently figure closely—too closely—and constantly lower the margin for profit. To be sure, our dilemma is dire. The estimate fiend is upon us—if we give him a reasonable figure we do not get the job; if we give him too low a figure we make nothing on it—so we are unhappy either way. Such is life—in the printing office; and herein is the necessity for those standards of action before referred to.

We are not in business for the fun of it. No one wants to do work without making something on it, and no one ought to do it without making that fair, legitimate profit that the business should pay. Why do we work so cheaply? and how can we stop it? It is not to be denied that much printing is done at too low a figure —often at less than cost. What justifies it? Nothing whatever. A man has absolutely no right to take a job of printing at a price that will not pay a profit. Of course we may make a blunder in our estimate—allow for only half the paper, or forget the presswork, or something—that we cannot be very severe about; there is no law against a man being a fool, and such stupidity brings its own punishment; but when a printer deliberately takes work below cost, for some ulterior purpose—to keep it from his rival, or hoping that those mythical jobs that " go with it " will give him a chance to get even in the sweet by-and-by—he is simply a pickpocket or a sneak thief, and deserves the ignominy that such professionals receive.

The provocation is often great. Perhaps some new firm, with an idle plant and great necessity for orders, will throw out a tempting bait in the form of half-rate prices. It is hard to stand by and see our customers leave us, feeling that we have been robbing them before, and we are tempted to meet all quotations, at any loss. But it is better not to do so. Such things are commonly seen through, and very soon an end will come, in some way. It may be through bankruptcy—it *must* be so unless such prices give way, and then we have our opportunity. Any business is easily demoralized, and the law of gravitation in prices is almost resistless; they go down so easily and are raised with such great difficulty.

There is a disposition to shift the blame for the demoralized condition of our trade to the middlemen. Some printers find " the stationer " the cause of their unhappiness, and consider that any one who works for him loses caste. Now, the trouble is back of this: it is not in doing work for a stationer, but in *doing it too cheaply*. If a living price is charged, his competition cannot hurt us. The cause of the difficulty is, that too much printing is done at a price too low to afford any legitimate profit. Why it is thus is not hard to see. Some printers are ignorant, some are foolish, some are unprincipled, and *all* are too greedy. We must expect that stationers, customers and the whole world of business will take advantage of our folly, and if we are not babies we will not blame them. What we need to do is to show better sense, and not invite their ravages. We should charge for every job we do what it is fairly worth—no more and no less; and there ought to be a way of getting at it that every intelligent printer could master, so that our estimatss would not present such wild variations. There is no reason under the sun why one printer should offer to do a given piece of work for half the money that another will, when each has equal facilities; yet this difference is not uncommon. One or the other is wrong—probably both are. We need to be much more careful and much more rational in giving estimates, and when given, to be quite calm and indifferent as to the result.

So long as we scatter so, estimating is a necessary evil. If our prices did not so widely and wildly differ, we would not be subjected to this constant annoyance. First-class offices in the East, I am told, decline to give competitive estimates on general work. It is my hope and ambition, before I die, to hang in a conspicuous place this notice: "No estimates given." Not that I am unwilling to tell a customer what any piece of work will probably be worth, but I do detest to enter any bidding-down contest where I must see how little I can do the job for, hoping to get ahead of some other printer who equally needs to live, and trembling when I win for fear I have gained the victory through making a blunder, and dejectedly wondering how much I shall lose.

Ignorance is probably responsible for more of this folly than anything else. Too many of us do not know what we ought to charge in order to make a profit. We know that we pay forty cents a thousand for composition, and then we get what we can above that. We do not know the actual cost of what we have to sell, and so we fail to get a profit. The expense of doing business, the wear and tear of material, the interest on money invested, the percentage of bad debts, and many other unconsidered trifles, are just as truly expense items as the forty cents for the mere composition. This should be always in our memory, and its amount should be determined, so that never, under any circumstances, should the minimum cost, plus a fair profit, be departed from. We should feel that there is here a double restraint: in the first place, that it is *foolish* to cut to cost, and in the second, that it is *wrong*. If we can afford the loss, we have still no right to do so, for we are wronging some one else—we are depriving some one of a profit that by all rules of fair dealing he is entitled to enjoy, and injuring a business that it is our interest, and ought to be our pride, to sustain.

It is quite unnecessary to enumerate at any length the special disadvantages and evils resulting from this reckless or unprincipled method of conducting business. Its general demoralization is so evident that no bill of items is required; but one danger demands special consideration: in this disgraceful scramble the man who underbids must put forth every effort to keep even, and, as he is selling his wares cheaply, he must get them as cheap as he can; away he goes to reduce his cost to the absolute minimum. He uses stock as poor as he dares, running in "a job lot" if he can find one.

Then he plays book-binders against one another, and beats them out of any profit if he can. But his strong suit is cheap labor; and how he loves boys and girls and helpless apprentices! He gloats over his smartness in getting the largest possible amount of labor for the least possible sum of money. He skins everybody and everything, and makes every one he has anything to do with uncomfortable, dissatisfied and unfriendly; and all for what? To do a large business, to get ahead of somebody else, to satisfy his greed. Does it pay? Is it right?

I think there must be in the heart of any man who is still a man, and not a mere machine for making money, a feeling that there ought to be some restraint on competition—that our business would be more satisfactory and our life more comfortable if we could in some way manage to get along without such a fierce, unfeeling, selfish scramble—if we could, in some friendly way, "live and let live."

How can we do it? It is too much to expect that the average business man will be restrained through any high moral grounds or consideration of absolute right, and the worst of it is, that all seem compelled to do business in this cut-throat way—even those who disapprove of it. We are obliged, in a great degree, to accommodate ourselves to the business methods in vogue, and cannot expect to be successful unless we use more or less of this questionable enterprise.

In this general demoralization we have cause for congratulation that there is some check on our downward progress; but it is somewhat humiliating to confess that the measure of stability we enjoy we must place to the credit of our employees, and cannot in any manner claim it as the result of our own effort. I wish to express my conviction that we owe the Typographical Union more than we are accustomed to acknowledge. In preserving equality of opportunity and checking the demoralization that follows the forcing of labor to its lowest price, they have done much more for us than we have for ourselves. I believe the advantages of an equal standard of pay are so great that we can afford to be patient, even when they are unreasonable and arbitrary. And, in the matter of apprentices some strong control is necessary, or a fair office is at a tremendous disadvantage. I believe that it is our best policy to be friendly to our employees and to their organization whenever we can; to do all in our power to influence them to wise and judicious action; and to resist them only when they are clearly wrong and impose upon us restrictions they have no right to make, and to which we cannot in honor submit.

At some other time I hope the Typothetæ may carefully consider the advantages of the system of profit-sharing. This plan of interesting employees, making their reward dependent on their exertions, has been, so far as I can learn, uniformly successful where fairly tried. DeVinne & Co., of New York, have just introduced it into their office, and, as a measure of substantial justice and mutual advantage, it is likely to extend. But to-day we are considering competition simply, and I will not digress.

To elevate the standard of business is not an easy thing. Nothing is easy that is good for anything. But certainly the organization of employers, now so happily established, gives us an opportunity to do much, in this direction, and if we do not improve the opportunity, we show ourselves to be lacking in intelligence and blind to possibilities of advancement.

The Typothetæ should be helpful, in a general way, in promoting the friendly acquaintance and good feeling of its members, and in a special way by educating through a free interchange of experience and information as to the true value of work. And this acquired knowledge should be acted upon for our own mutual advantage and the elevation of our trade.

I would not favor any effort to make a corner or a ring to inflate prices, but I cannot see why a general standard may not be established and lived up to. I mean a minimum price for composition, press-work, etc., that every member shall in honor adhere to. Let this basis be reached through careful consideration, comparison and discussion. Let each Typothetæ in the country take up in turn each branch of the business. Let a committee, for instance, report on the legitimate price to charge for plain composition, let the report be discussed at a meeting, or at as many meetings as may be necessary to a thorough understanding of all the elements of cost that should be considered in arriving at a price that would cover everything, and leave a fair, living profit. Then let a vote be taken and a price established, that shall hold for a year or till further action. Let this price be a minimum for a good-sized job of ordinary grade. Then let each member in estimating never go under it, but add to it for any special reason—the smallness of the job, any unusual care, unreasonable speed, excessive italic, or anything else that adds to its cost and ought to be paid for. And so for time-work: let it be determined what is a fair advance, and what one ought to charge a customer to cover thirty cents per hour paid to the compositor, and all expenses of conducting the business, and leave a legitimate margin of profit. So for press-work, so for percentage on paper, on binding, etc. Let this recognized standard be strictly conformed to as a minimum rate. The result would be, not a rigid uniformity of prices, as by an established scale, where no account is made of quality, but a rational agreement, sufficiently flexible to accommodate any conditions.

No scale of prices can stand, but a limit on the items of cost that determine the price seems to me to be entirely practicable, and altogether necessary to sound business conditions. When this standard is established it ought to be easy to convince printers not now members of the Typothetæ that it is for their interest to join the organization. The element of ruinous rivalry would in any event be largely eliminated. The small offices outside of the Typothetæ might profit for a time, but they would prefer getting a good price to a poor one, and would be likely to grow conservative with success; and when they found they could as well get better prices, would charge them, and their competition would grow less severe.

A special committee might be appointed to grant permission for a lower competitive rate in any special case where there was manifest reason for it. This power, sparingly exercised, would enable members of the Typothetæ to defend themselves against outside offices who may try to take advantage of them, through knowing the limit below which they could not bid.

Let us in good faith put in practice an honest, determined effort to regulate competition. Let our effort be, not to see how little a given job can be done for, but how well we can do a given job for a given sum. And when work presses, advance prices slightly, gaining thereby the recompense that merit deserves, and establishing a higher value for a higher class of work. This is better than buying many presses, for it gives others a chance, and does not unreasonably increase facilities for turning out work, which naturally are always in advance of demand. If the minimum price for press-work is based on the lowest return for ordinary work, let the printer who does finer work charge more than the schedule price. His work costs more and will command more. Let the scale above be open and free, but fixed on its downward course; then prices will follow cost and value, and all will be on an equality. The printer whose specialty is rushing out work that must be cheap will get that sort of work, and do it at a living rate; the printer whose specialty is high-class work will get that to do, and be paid for it proportionately, and there will be only that competition and emulation that is healthful and advantageous.

Let any member who has a grievance against a fellow-member, or has reason to suspect an infringement of the scale, bring his case before a committee, who shall investigate the matter, reporting to the Typothetæ if they find it necessary. Let each Typothetæ take such measures to hold its members to the agreement as they deem necessary. Pride in a good name and in standing well with one's fellows ought to be sufficient motive, but if reprimand and fines be found necessary, let them be used.

Too much must not be expected of this plan, or any plan, either in the way of immediate relief or in complete solution of the difficulties that beset us. They are of long standing and will not disappear at once. Patience will be required in any effort to overcome them, but surely it is worth while to make an effort that is based on common sense, and which ought to succeed.

My firm conviction is, that any permanent improvement must rest on the hope of better knowledge and better feeling, taking shape in better methods. No arrangement or scheme can deliver us; we must be educated, technically and morally. We must moderate our greed, raise our standard of business honor, and treat our employees, our customers, and one another with fairness. Only so can we get out of the wilderness, and gain that self-respect which, if not success, is better than success.

EVIL RESULTS OF COMPETITIVE BIDDING.

L. G. REYNOLDS, OF DAYTON TYPOTHETÆ.

This subject, like a great many others of its kind, has its practical points dulled by those of theory.

There are scores of plans and schemes for removing certain evils from the business and social world that are beautiful in theory, but almost impossible in practice, and all on account of the same ruling passion of human nature to look out for number one at all hazards. And we must bear in mind the fact that there are just as many " number ones " in a community as there are inhabitants thereof; and when the affairs of this world are managed in a way that is altogether *just* to *everybody*, and advantage sought to be taken of nobody, it will be when the whole number of inhabitants is less than two.

This is rather a pessimistic way of looking at things, perhaps but we must all admit the stubborn fact. Of course it is neither the purpose nor the hope of the National Committee having this subject in charge, to absolutely remove the evils resulting from competitive bidding, only to lessen them if possible, and to establish a Code of Ethics that will elevate the trade and increase the value of the business.

I suppose there is no trade in the world which is more seriously affected by the evils resulting from the same competitive bidding than ours. It is getting to be a serious question—one which has been the subject of much informal discussion at our frequent meetings, and the fact that the national association deemed it of sufficient importance to appoint a special committee to take the matter up, shows that we are not alone in the enjoyment of these evils. It is an every day question, and the trade has reached such a point that the most insignificant jobs are put up at auction, to go to the lowest bidder; and while it is hardly within the range of possibility to educate the trade to any other plan, it is possible to so educate ourselves that the evil results will be reduced to the minimum, and it is possible to devise plans that are perfectly practical, and would affect each man alike, which will put the business upon a more satisfactory basis all around.

To my mind the most serious cause, and one whose evil results affect both the successful and unsuccessful bidder, is the inability of certain estimators to figure intelligently upon the work submitted to them. How often we have found, in our informal discussions in these meetings, that work has gone to the lowest bidder at prices so near to the actual cost of production as to indicate either that he did not know how to estimate the cost of the job or had made some flagrant error in his calculations, and, in either case, whether it be that he was incompetent to make the estimate or that he had made an arithmetical error, the successful bidder is really the unsuccessful bidder. The fact of his getting the work is detrimental to him and to his business, because it is fair to presume that his intentions were to take the work at a profit, and that he thought his figures were correct. The real beneficiary in cases of this kind is the party who gives the order, and at the same time it spoils him for future business.

One low price establishes a precedent that it is hard to remove, and the customer cannot understand, when he has another similar, if not identical, job, why there should be such a difference in price. It sets him to asking prices here and there, and he keeps on until he strikes somebody else who makes a mistake in his calculations and he gets the job.

It is plain, therefore, that one long step may be made in the right direction by educating ourselves and each other up to a high state of proficiency in the art of estimating the cost of production. And these estimates should be made with as little guesswork as possible. The best way to judge the present and the future is by the past. If you know what it has actually cost you to do a certain job once, you can figure pretty closely as to what you can afford to do similar or identical work now; but unless you have some trustworthy data to start with, some records that you know to a dead moral certainty are correct, you are making your estimate in the dark, and the chances are that you are going to make a beneficiary of the party who asked for the bid.

System is a great bugbear to many business men, and they look upon "red tape" as a valueless nuisance. They are satisfied to jumble their whole business together, getting the most they can for all that they do, and trust to luck for the general result at the end of the year. In some cases this is prompted by laziness, in others by carelessness, but more generally, I think, it is traceable to the inferior development of the bump of order.

There is, of course, such a thing as too much system, and too much red tape, but too much is better than too little, and there is no system which can be attached to a business where the results are more direct, and where the real value is so apparent, as a system which will enable the proprietor or manager to know to a certainty precisely what it is costing him to turn out his work.

There is a large concern in this city, not in the printing business, however, who determined several years ago to ascertain this fact to a nicety. The proprietor told me that it cost them more than $10,000 in eighteen months, actual outlay, but that the information it furnished them was priceless. On many things their guess estimates had been too high, on others too low, but that now they are able to put in a competitive bid on any contract, or parts of a contract, with an absolute certainty that they will make a profit on the job if they get it, and can furnish everything according to specifications, with no desire or occasion to try and work in any inferior stock or cheap work in order to make both ends meet.

How strong a man feels when, in doing a thing, he knows that he is doing it just right.

Any office, large or small, can gather sufficient data in six months to enable their estimator to figure the exact cost to them of almost any job that is presented.

Every establishment should have a perfect system for ascertaining the actual labor cost of every job that goes through, be it large or small. Even if they only run such a system for six months or a year, it would be better than nothing, and would enable them to make up a record of the exact cost to them of such a variety of work as would make them perfectly competent to give trustworthy figures on almost any sort of a job that might be submitted to them.

Besides having the exact labor cost, the estimator for each concern should also be capable of accurately judging the quality of paper. There should be no guess-work whatever about *that* part of an estimate.

The weight of paper should be ascertained from the scales, not on feeling a small sample between thumb and finger. A variation of five pounds to the ream cannot be detected by the touch of a finger. An accurate paper scale can be procured for a few dollars, and it is as much a part of a printing office as is a proof-press.

Besides enabling the estimator to correctly ascertain the weight per ream of a proposed sheet of certain size, it will also enable the office to know whether the mill or jobber has furnished stock fully up to the required weight, which is a matter of considerable importance to every buyer; whether his purchases be large or small, it is a satisfaction to know that he is getting what he pays for.

It is plain, therefore, that a change for the better will be reached when every office has placed itself in such shape that it can correctly estimate, without guess-work, the cost to it of all competitive work.

It is probable that all of you are using more or less system in the management of your work, but the question is: are you doing it properly, are you really ascertaining the true facts, and are you making your record in such a way that you can refer to it understandingly and ascertain what you want to know after you have referred to the record?

It is not my purpose in this paper to discuss the subject of system in its details; that is a question by itself, and it would not be a bad plan to take it up separately, have plans prepared, papers read and discussed, if for no other reason than that the use of some good system for ascertaining cost accurately will have a very decided bearing, and will play no inconsiderable part in removing some of the evils resulting from competitive bidding.

Other causes bearing on this subject are not so easily handled, but the organization that has been effected through the agency of the local associations of the National Typothetæ, makes it possible to manage the question in a way that would have been all but impossible five years ago. The local associations have been the means of bringing members of the trade into closer relations with each other, and have given each one more confidence in the other. It has given us the idea that our competitors are not nearly so bad as we had supposed them to be, and it is possible to have concerted action in the management of certain questions, where without such organization it would be almost out of the question.

The success of any plan for removing the evils resulting from competitive bidding depends entirely upon the strength of your local organization. It must be a plan that will, as near as possible, affect every man alike, and if there be any chance for occasional advantage, it should be of such a nature that, in the ordinary course of business, the advantage will be distributed, that is to say, one firm may have it this time, another one the next.

There are certain times in every printing and publishing establishment, be it large or small, when work is slack. At such times the proprietor or manager is willing to take some large contracts at little or no profit in order to keep machinery running and old hands employed, and we are bound to say that there are good business reasons for his doing so. It is a hard matter to regulate circumstances of that kind, but, as mentioned above, it is one of the occasional advantages that will regulate itself. Sometimes it is one office that is slack and sometimes another, and if an office is never slack it has no occasion to object to any such advantage held by another concern. Then, too, there are instances where one of a lot of competitive bidders has a lot of stock which has been purchased at a bargain, and it is just the proper material to enter into a competitive job. He has an undoubted advantage over the others, but who can say that he has not a right to that advantage and ought not to have the job if he can do the work as cheaply? These are questions that will be found to be difficult to handle, and yet they cut quite figure in competitive bidding.

Suggestions have been made, both in our own city and elsewhere, that an agreement be entered into by all bidders to add a certain specified per cent. to the estimate, over and above their own profit, which amount shall go into a pool, to be shared in by all parties interested in the pool; but it strikes me that *that* is hardly right, even if it could be successfully engineered. It would necessitate asking the party who has the giving of the order to pay more for the work than it is actually worth, and if it became known to the general trade that an agreement of that sort existed among the local printers, they would soon be sending their business to some other city; besides, an arrangement of that kind would involve too much personal integrity. Except on public contracts, nobody except the successful bidder and his customer would know what figure the job was taken at. Of course, the other bidders would have an approximate idea, but no positive knowledge; nor would any of you agree to impart such information as would enable your competitors to know the exact figure. There would, I think, be more scheming and more evils resulting than from the present plan, unless it could be made almost national in its scope and backed up by each establishment with a good-sized money guarantee.

I think, therefore, that an amelioration of the evils resulting from competitive bidding is to be found in the education of estimators up to the highest state of proficiency in the art of figuring, and a determination on the part of every office to do work at a profit; to hold up to ourselves and to our competitors that the dead expense of an office is too often lost sight of, and that there is a big difference between the estimated profit and the *real* profit; that the education of the estimator of a printing establishment does not end with his knowing the cost of labor, but that of material enters largely into it.

The man who asks for a bid and shows the figures made by one bidder to another should be *marked*. You can depend upon it that if he will show to you some previous bid he will just as surely show your bid to a third party. You need not flatter yourself that he wants to favor *you*. He wants you to do the job if you will do it for the least money, not otherwise; and if an honorable business man has any favoritism to show you on account of the superiority of your work he is always ready to pay a little more for it.

The general trade has been spoiled by the printers themselves in this matter of putting every little job up at auction, and unless they can be educated to a plan more satisfactory to the printing craft, the evils resulting from competitive bidding must find their remedy within the craft itself, and it is a matter which should be given constant study. The fact that the evil exists should never be lost sight of. The effort of one bidder to beat his competitor, merely for the satisfaction of doing so, should be tabooed. If such a bidder would reflect but a moment, he would see that his satisfaction is but temporary. He is sure to be gotten back at sooner or later, and nobody has any advantage at the end. The National Typothetæ, by means of the strong organization it is effecting all over the country, will, unconsciously, do much toward removing the evils themselves, and I would not favor any radical steps in the matter. The general trade has been educated to the present plan, and while it may not be the right one, it would be necessary to re-educate them, or have an organization so strong that you could say to your customers, we will do thus and so, and you must abide by it.

There is no occasion, of course, to make the situation worse than it is, and the existing circumstances do not warrant the belief that it will grow worse, but that it is entirely within the power of our craft, through our strong organization, to gradually educate the buyer, and speedily educate ourselves, so that competitive bidding, which will last as long as we live, will be raised to a higher plane and be shorn of many of its evil results.

THE EVILS OF COMPETITIVE BIDDING.

PAPER BY SAMUEL REES, READ BEFORE THE OMAHA TYPOTHETÆ, TUESDAY EVENING, JUNE 30, 1891.

The evils of competition and how to overcome them, is a question well worthy the thoughtful consideration of every one engaged not only in our line, but in every branch of business. The close communication now made between communities of such great differences in regard to the expense of production, by reason of the disparity in wages, rents, fuel, etc., has brought competition that is hard for those in progressive and high-priced communities to meet and still have a profit on their work. There is, however, in the printing business, especially as we find it in our city, a large amount of work, local in its character, which of necessity must be done here; so that it will not be necessary to take time in the discussion of this outside competition, which is felt and met with only in the larger orders.

What are the causes of much of the competition in our trade? Why should a person, who will go into almost any other business house, ask the price of an article and purchase it, visit half a dozen or more printing offices and obtain prices on a small job of work of less than one-tenth the amount in money before he will leave the order? It is clear to me that the employing printers are almost wholly to blame for this state of facts. Out of ten printers estimating on a job, there will hardly be any two of them within five per cent. of each other, and the prices of some will be more than double those of some of the others. There is no use of attempting to deny this fact; it is made patent every day to any one who attempts to estimate on work. In fact, so well known is this to those who get large amounts of printing done, that I have been frequently asked if there was any basis for figuring on work, or did we just guess at it. Now there must be some cause for this state of affairs. I think there are several.

1. The printing business is peculiar in this: it is seldom that any one engages in it who has had any previous practical business experience. It is right and proper that an ambitious young man should start in business for himself, but it is unfortunate for the trade that he should not give sufficient study to the one im-

portant point, namely: the cost of running the business. It is fortunate that he will learn before many years that the wear and tear of material and machinery, the losses by bad debts and dull times, the rent, and all the thousand and one other expenses, must be paid, not out of the amount of business which he does, but out of the profits on that business. He must learn this or drop out of the ranks. It is unfortunate again, that by the time he has learned this lesson there are others to follow in his footsteps, and who will have to learn the same lesson by experience. So we can put down as the first cause of customers running around and distrusting printers, ignorance of cost and a lack of business experience or business sense of those engaged in printing.

2. The second cause is a lack of common honesty on the part of many engaged in our business. There are too many of our offices run on the principle of "Get all you can. When you bid, bid low; and when you get a chance, 'stick it to 'em.'" In other words, if Brown, a sharp, shrewd man, comes into your office, after having been the rounds of other offices, and says to you: "Smith, Jones will do this job for me for $10," and you say to him: "Well, I will do it for $9" (as many do, even though the work be worth $12 or $15), you will be compelled, in order to even things up, to charge White, who may leave you a job without questioning the price, trusting to your fairness and honesty, $12 or $15 for a job worth $9. The probabilities are that White will know that he has been overcharged, and the next time that he wants any work he will follow Brown's example. Brown has also learned that he can "work you," as the slang expression goes, so there will be two customers spoiled.

I have here mentioned two of the worst causes of the competition which we meet in this section, and the latter cause is the one which brings more disrepute on our business and is responsible for more of the competitive bidding than anything else.

Another is over-anxiety to do all the printing of the country in your own office.

Another is in allowing jealousy of your competitors to overcome business judgment and sense. There are too many printers who feel better over beating a competitor out of a job than they do over the making of a fair profit themselves.

These are some of the causes—I will not say of competition, but of the "shinning" around of customers.

When we approach the other branch of the subject, "How to overcome the evils," it is something that I am not able to solve. All I can do is to give my ideas. I do not suppose that any one lives who can tell a young and inexperienced printer anything as to how a business should be run; nor do I suppose that it is possible to convince any of those who are not printers, but who have solicited a little and then started in the business for themselves, that it costs money to produce printing. I shall not attempt either of these tasks, but shall proceed at once, as stated before, to give my ideas.

In the first place, there is no reason why a business requiring such a large expenditure of money and brain for so small a production should not be legitimately and honestly conducted, and yield a fair profit. Now the question naturally arises, "What is a fair profit?" This must be answered each for himself. My views on this subject might not coincide with those of any one present to-night, but I will state my means of arriving at it.

In the beginning, have a complete inventory of the office, including the stock of paper, etc., on hand. Go through it carefully and make an estimate on the wear and tear, bearing in mind that in this item there are many styles of type that must be purchased because they are new, and you must keep up with the times in styles, even though you may have plenty that is not worn out, and never will be; also, that some of your machinery may be superseded by later inventions. Then estimate a reasonable interest on the amount invested in the business; now figure up the rent, water, gas, power, and other expenses, including collecting, book-keeping, office expenses, and also the non-productive help, such as foremen, distributors, errand boys, stockmen, etc.; then you will have:

  Wear and tear,
  Interest,
  General expenses,
  Expenses of non-productive help,
  And you should add, percentage for bad debts.

The sum of these items I should divide among the productive help pro rata, and add to each class its just proportion, thus learning, as nearly as possible, what percentage is necessary to be added to each to get the cost per hour or per day. In different offices the amount will vary somewhat, and those of us who are fortunate enough to turn out a large amount of work with a small plant, and the other expenses at a minimum, will be able to give a little closer price on work than will our less fortunate neighbors who may have these items as a maximum. To this list then add what is a fair and reasonable profit. Make up your mind what is just, and insist upon receiving it. You will find many persons who have much printing to do will be willing to give a fair price for good work after they learn that you are asking only what is reasonable and just.

Another thing, do not be too greedy. Do not go on the principle that you will cut all the profit out of a job rather than let it go to a competitor. Remember that any number can play at that game, and if you cut the price on some job to-day, your neighbor may to-morrow cut the price on one that would naturally have come to you; and if all should indulge in this foolish procedure, it would be a question of a very short time until the profit will be completely cut off on every class of work.

Once more, never lose sight of the fact that you are working for the profit and not for the business. I should rather do a business of $10,000 a year with a profit, than one of $100,000 without a profit.

I have for years made it a point not to bid on anything but public work. In our office we give an estimate on what a job is worth, and state it to our customer, no matter whether we are the only ones estimating on the work or not, feeling that no one can do it at a less price without wronging himself; and, while it has sometimes seemed hard to lose work when we knew we were better prepared to do it than the house that secured it, we have felt that we were right; and you all know what has become of the houses that have made a practice of cutting prices. In my experience I have never known of one to succeed in the long run.

Never lose sight of the fact that you are interested in keeping the business so that it will be at least as profitable as other lines of legitimate trade, and that the surest way to break it down, so that neither you nor your neighbors can make a living at it, is by the indiscriminate slashing of prices. Many of us have been members of the Typographical Union; and, as workingmen, we understood this fact better than we do as employers. We never hear of job printers—members of the Union—coming into our offices and asking for work at a price below the scale, but how often do they want more, and herein is a suggestion to us. Let us by observation, by discussion, by the appointment of committees, or in any other way that may seem feasible, arrive at and establish a minimum scale on composition, on press-work, and for a percentage on stock, and on the various items that go into the work, and then resolve never to go under it, but to add to it for any special reason that may seem necessary. In this way our prices would be apt to vary somewhat, but not sufficiently to pay any one to run around to every office for prices on small jobs. I know it is hard to have your machinery idle and no work in to keep it moving, but it is as well for it to remain idle as to run it at a loss.

I have had hopes in connection with the Typothetæ, that it would some day be strong enough to shut down on all forms of illegitimate competition, and I am still hopeful. By illegitimate competition, I mean the indiscriminate starting of printing offices by type-founders, press builders, and machinery men, without money and without price, except on paper. We may take any measures we see fit, but they will come to naught so long as these parties sell offices with nothing down and the rest promises to pay—in other words, so long as the type-founders and press builders establish a business and assume no liability for its debts. It is true that some of the offices so started succeed; but in a majority of cases they succeed only in cutting prices, and beating paper houses and other creditors. I do not believe that any one who pays for his type, machinery and paper can turn out work as cheaply as can one who does not. Just here is where I believe the Typothetæ might take some action. I believe, if a vigorous protest is sent to these parties, backed up by a sufficient number of offices, that much can be done to stop this evil practice.

My time is so much occupied that I have not taken as much care in the preparation of this paper as the subject deserves; but since writing it I have had handed me an excellent paper on this subject by Mr. Chas. A. Murdock, of San Francisco, which embraces so many thoughts that coincide with mine, that it is with pleasure I refer to it and ask each of you to read it.

Now, in conclusion, I will repeat that the only thing I can see that will be of any service in curing the evils of competitive bidding is for each one to thoroughly educate himself as to the cost of his production, and then to insist upon having a profit on his labor and investment; to hold himself in as high esteem as an employer as he did as an employee; and to take pains to educate not only himself, but his neighbors.

THE EVIL OF COMPETITIVE BIDDING.
COMMITTEE FROM CINCINNATI TYPOTHETÆ.

The principle of competition is one of expansion or contraction as conditions obtain. If several elements that enter into this principle—as, for instance, *ignorance, dishonesty, cupidity, venality*—could be eliminated, the course of the bidder would be comparatively plain sailing. Competitive bidding, under the most favorable circumstances, is a bugaboo to the bidder, who sees in every competitor an enemy that should be annihilated without benefit of clergy.

We cannot blame the layman—by which is meant the party seeking the work—for protecting himself against imposition by taking estimates. He knows nothing of the value of the commodity he seeks except by comparison of bids, and consequently pits one craftsman against another in self-defence. If craftsmen were half as eager to protect themselves as is he who dickers for their product, there would be less poverty and fewer assignments to protect creditors.

A species of competition is that where every energy is bent toward deflecting work from a channel which it has followed for years, presupposing that there is large profit in what has been the study of years to keep and husband. This manner of competitor is prone to argue that he can do the work for less money simply because his expenses are lighter, and because *he* performs a great portion of the work himself, as though an employer's time was worth less than that of an employee.

Another class—comparatively small, it is true, yet sufficiently powerful to merit mention—is composed of those nondescripts who will do any meanness so they can work an opponent harm. They are the personification of *evil*, in that they play the devil with all honorable rivalry, and whose policy has neither rhyme nor reason to commend it. This sort of competitor can be most readily disciplined with a club.

How many of us, after years of toil and fretting, no sooner become possessed of a factor than we give the customer the advantage of it? One buys a press that costs him largely more than the one he has been using, but which accomplishes its work in a shorter time, and immediately the price of the product is reduced; another has a smart apprentice, who costs but half the wages of a journeyman, and immediately the buyer gets the benefit. One will argue that because he has a two-color press, which has cost him twice as much as one that works but a single color, he can cut the price of press-work in two; another holds that because he hires neither foreman nor proof-reader his product costs him the foreman's and proof-reader's salaries less, all the time forgetting that these worthies frequently earn their week's salaries in a single day by the exercise of their art.

The short-sighted, narrow-minded policy pursued by many of the older craftsmen to refuse to impart knowledge gained by experience to younger competitors, is much to be deplored. Mr. Thomas Todd, of Boston, in his paper on "Competitive Bidding, and its Resultant Evils," aptly says:

"When a man has become a craftsman he naturally becomes desirous of obtaining the secrets that pertain to his business, and he is too often met with a flat refusal to impart those secrets, and he is left to grope along in a blind way, striving all the time, occasionally getting a lift, but still not permitted to come into the fullness of knowledge and the power of knowledge."

Our duty and pleasure should be to impart to our less experienced competitor all the knowledge we possess, so long as it does not give him an instrument with which to brain us, and thus reduce that element of ignorance which so largely enters into this principle of competition.

Let us all seek to strengthen the hands of our organization in its aim to protect, educate, and advance the position of master-printers by—

(1) Reducing the element of ignorance, by freely imparting knowledge to all who are less favored.

(2) Discountenancing every species of dishonesty, by setting examples of integrity in every avenue of our business.

(3) Combating that inordinate greed for gain so often found among us.

(4) Discouraging the purchasable feature frequently met with in dealing with agents.

CHARLES BUSS,
J. E. RICHARDSON,
R. J. MORGAN,
W. B. CARPENTER,
WILLIAM A. WEBB,
Committee.

THE FINANCIAL ELEMENT IN THE PRINTING BUSINESS.

RICHARD ENNIS, ST. LOUIS TYPOTHETÆ.

In consequence of the increase in press facilities and labor-saving devices, and our continued growth in population and intelligence, book and job printing has become a prominent feature of commercial life. Leaving out of consideration the time and money expended in acquiring practical knowledge and special fitness, without which no one can reasonably look for success in the printing business, in proportion to the volume of trade there is more actual capital invested in its successful prosecution than almost any other line of manufacture. Although specialists, through combination and peculiar adaptability, may have a comparative monopoly in certain kinds of work, yet the aggregate business of the printing offices of the country is made up of a multitude of transactions varying materially in character and conditions. For this reason it is necessary to have a well-appointed establishment in order to do even an ordinary line of commercial printing, and it frequently occurs that the annual "output" is not more than the actual capital invested in the business. Besides, the patronage of the printer is essentially fluctuating and uncertain. He has to compete with men of ambition and intelligence, and is obliged to contend with innumerable experimentalists and tricksters, who have neither money to lose nor reputation to gain.

THE MONEY ELEMENT.

Of all other considerations it should be borne in mind that it requires a certain amount of money every working day to meet the expenses of a printing office, and it must necessarily be obtained from legitimate sources. On leaving his establishment at night and when he awakes in the morning the proprietor has to consider that a certain amount of bills payable have to be met at a given date. This duty cannot be relegated to another; he is the only one that can carry the load. He knows that he cannot claim one cent of profit until notes are met, salaries, rent, light, fuel, insurance, taxes, and all other expenses are paid in full.

If he has borrowed money to start business, or paid a percentage of cash and given a mortgage for the unpaid balance, the interest must be paid promptly or else a foreclosure will eventually sweep away all previous payments. This is inevitable, whether we borrow from friend or any one else.

Money has no heart; it bears no relation to anything else in the world. The interest, like a perpetual stream, is always flowing onward and compounding until it eats up the principal.

If the property has been purchased for cash, the investment should yield at least legal interest, after paying a liberal salary to those giving their whole time and attention to the management of the business, and allowing a reasonable margin for wear and tear and purchasing a limited amount of new material. Otherwise the running of a printing office or any other kind of establishment could not be considered a paying business, because money can be profitably invested at any time in securities that will pay fixed rates of interest.

EXPENSES GO ON CONTINUALLY.

Many of the employees of a printing office cannot be discharged or suspended at pleasure. Independent of legal and civic holidays, there is a great deal of slack time for which no one pays the employing printer. Every moment the establishment is open should yield a certain amount of profit. Neither time-servers nor periodical absentees can be tolerated. Honest work for fair remuneration should be the rule. Every inch of space in the establishment is worth just so much money. Tardiness in beginning work, time spent in gossip or receiving visitors, involves not only loss to the proprietor, but lessens his chance for paying indebtedness. During business hours all are equally obligated to produce profitable results, and the person who neglects this part of the contract does injustice to the other contracting party. In case of failure he is incidentally responsible for the calamity. Proprietors and heads of departments should do their full duty, and be promptly at their posts to see that others do likewise. Through the want of constant supervision by some one who has a financial interest in the welfare of the establishment, it often occurs that printing offices become wasteful and unmanageable. Many an industrious hand has degenerated into a time-server through not feeling that the eye of the proprietor was on him. After the closest scrutiny of all expenditures, including the pay-roll, the most rigid economy in purchasing goods and materials should be practiced. No man should be unnecessarily tempted.

All orders for supplies ought to pass through the proprietor's hands for approval. As little communication as possible should be permitted between the vendor of goods and the workmen, and bribe-giving or percentage payments should be promptly checked and punished.

Notwithstanding the pressure of work, or the clamor of enthusiastic employer, the increase of material and presses should be subordinated to the profits and income. Any departure from this should be promptly adjusted, or else an officer of the law will eventually insist upon its enforcement. A man may be a good printer, an excellent solicitor of work and manager of a printing establishment; if he is a poor financier all these qualities count for little in the battle of life.

FREE-LIST PRINTING.

Printing either for glory or gratitude may be a time-honored custom, but it is done in direct opposition to the financial element of the business. Not excepting the physician or druggist, there is no line of trade in which so much is asked and nothing but thanks is paid in return. The average citizen acts as if a printing office costs but little money, and that running expenses are insignificant; that proprietors should be willing to do free printing from their most expensive material and stock for the glory of having their imprint attached to the work. As a rule the printer is the first man in the community selected to furnish, without pay, the necessary advertising matter for every conceivable charity or enterprise, and if he hints at getting half price for the work he is considered a very mean citizen. Such cases are of daily occurrence; there seems to be no limit to the number of people who ask for favors they would not grant if cases were reversed. The wealthiest ask more than the humblest citizen. While printers are generally charitable and enterprising, yet the custom of taxing their business to swell contributions which the individual should give is radically wrong. In dealing with a customer the profit problem should be paramount, and some plan should be formulated by which this great drain on the printer may be checked, if not abated. Newspapers have fixed rules in such matters; why should job printers not do likewise? It is at present a most unpleasant feature in an employing printer's life.

FAIR PRICES A NECESSITY.

In competitive bidding the safest rule to follow is to decline work that will not pay reasonable compensation. It is invariably the printing offices that are overcrowded with work that make the least profit. You cannot afford to wear out your material without having the money in sight to have it replaced. Within the past few years one of the oldest and largest printing offices in Boston, a handsomely equipped establishment in St. Louis, and a very extensive plant in Kansas City had to be dismantled and sold, not for want of plenty of work, but in consequence of inadequate profit. No one could be found to purchase them. During the first meeting of the United Typothetæ of America, in Chicago, a large pressroom that was kept running night and day with an over-rush of work had to close its doors and stop business for want of adequate profits on their out-put. To my certain knowledge there is more than one large establishment in St. Louis running without a profit although overcrowded with work, and no doubt the same can be said of every other large city in the country.

CONSEQUENCES OF TAKING UNPROFITABLE WORK.

Several years ago a now defunct printing firm of medium capacity became the successful bidder for the catalogue of a large St. Louis manufacturing establishment. Their bid was several hundred dollars below the next lowest bidder. The job was executed in acceptable shape, and very soon thereafter the said printing firm went out of business, insolvent. Two or three years later this same manufacturing establishment invited bids for printing another and rather larger catalogue. The successful bidder took it in, as in the former case, much below the average bids of competitors. The job was turned out satisfactorily, and in a few days afterwards the red flag waved in front of the office of the printer. Still later another printer, who was struggling to build up a business, thought he saw a big chance for prosperity in printing this same catalogue. He distanced all competitors in his bid and got it. As he progressed with the work, he saw he had made a mistake, and on completing the job yielded up his outfit for the benefit of creditors. Less than two years ago, the aforesaid manufacturers again invited proposals for printing their catalogue. It was taken in at a knock-down figure by a Third-street printer, who, when the job was completed, made an assignment, and his place was sold out under the hammer. In the past few months, the same job, for the same house, was secured by a Pine-street office at a price no wide-awake printer would accept. The job was completed in good shape, and for the fifth time its printer succumbed to the inevitable immediately after completing the work. All these printing firms were managed by apparently sensible people, whose object in business was to make money. That they did not do so, no doubt, was because they did not have a comprehensive idea of the cost of doing business. Their offices were full of work, but the prices were below the remunerative point. These are no fanciful cases. The names of the unfortunate printers will be given on application to the St. Louis Typothetæ.

CAUSE OF FREQUENT FAILURES.

We give only a few illustrations of the consequence of doing unprofitable printing. It is universally conceded that the majority of printing houses doing cheap work invariably end in bankruptcy and failure. They come and go every day in the year. It is only the establishments that do good work at fair prices that live any length of time. In the cause of humanity the Typothetæ should take action in this direction, and point out some way to stop the frequent failures occurring in the printing business. One way suggests the propriety of every Typothetæ keeping a record of failures occurring within their jurisdiction, with the causes that have led up to them. By omitting names, the report could be read at Typothetæ meetings and published in trade journals, and thus the younger members of the craft could come into possession of valuable information, which might prevent them from drifting into the same maelstrom which engulfed their former competitors.

KEEP OUT OF DEBT.

Nothing makes a person so conservative and economical as the investment of his own money in business. Like a child, a printer should gain strength gradually, and only add to his plant as the income justifies. The rock on which most printers founder is going into debt. A good line of credit is a great temptation to take work at non-paying figures. Many a brilliant and competent man has met with financial disaster by being tempted to discount the future, and giving a blanket mortgage, "not to be placed on record" until danger is in sight. Recently there has been much discussion on this point, and the St. Louis Typothetæ, at its meeting September 12, took steps to check this growing evil. By resolution it deplored the practice prevailing on the part of dealers in printing material, machinery, paper, and ink, of selling goods to parties secured by lien on their plant, and withholding the same from the public records. To make more effective their sense of the injury which such practices are calculated to work, they consider that members would be justified in withdrawing patronage from all parties engaged in such practices.

MORE NERVE AND DISCRIMINATION.

Of all classes, the average employing printer lacks nerve and discrimination in asking a good price for his work and editorial labors. Both have a market value. In making a bargain there is generally an emotional man, of literary ability and artistic instincts, at one end, who is thinking how good a job of printing he can give for the smallest amount of money. He feels that the customer has consulted all his competitors, and has in his possession some very low bids; if he asks too high a price he will be ridiculed and humiliated, and if too low a figure is quoted the offer will be accepted with the remark, " Cannot you do the job for less money?" This emotional printer finds at the other end of the bargain a cold, stern financier, who, although " wanting the best work," has taken good care to purchase it for the least amount of money. After the bargain is made, most customers think it no trouble or expense to have the printer edit his copy and supply all deficiencies in its construction, which often is worth more than the price charged for the work. When a proof is furnished, the customer feels at liberty to keep you waiting its return until it suits his convenience; he alters display lines and body type, changes the make-up and blank spaces for which rules and leads have been cut, strikes out or adds to matter, and makes such other changes as suit his fancy. Afterwards he will call for a revise and insist that the work must be done at once to the detriment of everything else. Notwithstanding that all these changes involve both time and money, yet when a bill of extras is presented the customer declines to pay more than the first figures mentioned. On the points herein outlined it is hoped some plan will be formulated which may result in lasting benefit to the trade.

IN ORDER TO MAKE MONEY

in the printing business, sentiment and artistic considerations must be subordinated to the financial element. Affairs should be conducted on the same basis as the builder or merchant—give nothing for which customers are not willing to pay. The person who figures on competitive printing ought to be a good judge of human nature, and, like a physician, diagnose each case according to its bearings. Take plenty of time to do the figuring, and do not give an opinion without consulting the authorities and looking at the transaction from every possible standpoint. Look the matter through and through. No two customers deserve the same treatment unless conditions are alike; neither are all printers possessed of the same taste and skill. Lose sight of the artistic side of a bargain until the financial element has been adjusted. Terms and time of payment should be clearly understood, and where there is question of responsibility give yourself the benefit of the doubt.

The Code of Ethics best calculated to elevate the

STATUS OF EMPLOYING PRINTERS

must necessarily be evolved from the development of moral and intellectual manhood, and a study of the printing business from a financial point of view. Nothing else will elevate the dignity of the trade and mitigate the evils of competitive bidding. A set of books, systematically kept, is an excellent labor-saving device. Check off your work in person, or have it done by your most conscientious assistant. Look up and prove all charges before work is sent home. While not allowing any one to get more than a fair share of a bargain, never permit a charge to be entered on your books that cannot be proved by competent evidence in a court of justice as a fair, competitive price. Take advantage of no man's ignorance; be truthful and straightforward, and see that employees do not deceive nor misrepresent. Your own character and self-respect should never be for sale. Be prepared at any moment to close your books and go home at night as if it was probable you might not be able to return to duty in the morning. Feel that the secrets of a printing office will eventually leak out, and the just criticism of an employee may destroy a good name, which, once tarnished, can never be restored. Mix freely with the honorable members of your craft, and study their ways and methods. Gain a reputation in the community as an intelligent, honest, first-class printer, whom people are willing to trust with their work without competitive bidding. Be a man among honorable men, and of value to the community in which you live. Look at every job of printing coming into your hands through a financial microscope. The profit and loss can then be ascertained before it is too late for reform.

THE EVILS OF COMPETITIVE BIDDING: HOW CONTROLLED.

J. E. C. FARNHAM, MASTER-PRINTERS' ASSOCIATION OF RHODE ISLAND.

The days in which we live are periods of ever increasing activity. Ever and anon we are confronted with something "new under the sun," born of persistent endeavor, at which we are startled, marvel for a brief period, and then accept the "new idea" as inexplainable, yet find it to be practical, so introduce it into daily use, and eagerly await the next development. Each succeeding change, brought about by ingenious invention, broadens the field of business enterprise, and constantly adds to commercial capacity. Thus artisan, mechanic and manufacturer are devotedly and persistently vieing with co-laborers in each of their chosen pursuits for supremacy. And so on, throughout the years past, there has been a progress commanding admiration as a result of inventional business strife. Man, by the cunning and craftiness of his own brain, is furnishing to the world, in amplified form, the needs of the hour.

As population grows, demands increase, and devices equal to the emergency must be certainly forthcoming, or suffering for lack of actual necessities would be the direful result. What was good enough for our fathers is not good enough, in fact, for us; or, at least, to change the phrase, what was sufficient for the use of our fathers is inadequate to our needs to-day. Push, determination, strife, energy, activity, ambition to excel, are simply terms which, upon close analysis, mean competition. This crowding for the ascendancy, which must inevitably be accepted, is nevertheless commendable, and receives and must continue to receive honorable recognition. The old adage, that "competition is the life of trade," is an ever new practical declaration, repeating itself over and over in every-day business life. Competition is stimulation, and without this quality inherent in mankind there would be to-day dearth, indolence, inactivity and desolation instead of the business integrity and progress which we everywhere see and admire.

It is said of Horace Greeley, the late learned sage, and one of the honored in our own profession, that, when he projected the idea of the establishment of his newspaper in New York, he was confronted with the remark that there were newspapers sufficient then in existence in that city. Undaunted, Mr. Greeley rejoined with the declaration that there was room at the top. His first edition of six hundred copies of *The Tribune* he found difficulty in giving away; yet he persevered in his aim to make a good newspaper, which should win commendation and support, and was signally successful in establishing one of the strongest newspaper enterprises of the day. This spirit, dominant with Mr. Greeley in the founding of his newspaper, is the spirit of the age, and must necessarily continue to be the ruling order of the hour until the crack of doom. Competition, then, is inevitable; it is with us to stay, and we might as well attempt to dam the falling waters of the graceful and majestic Niagara with an ordinary cedar shingle of diminutive size, as to attempt to stem the tide of competition. Honest, fair competition is stimulating and healthful to business development and success.

Accepting then, as we must, as both logical and conclusive, that competition in trade is as honorable as it is unyielding, the question, perforce, at once arises: How can we successfully compete and give all a fair business show? Labor has long since learned the full force of the law of competition, and to prevent calamity, which might befall them, men organize for mutual protection and the upbuilding of their interests in all respects. So, too, must invested business capital, in view of this same law of competition, unite for mutual helpfulness, co-operative protection and wider advancement of business.

It has been successfully demonstrated that business men, although in competition, the one with the other, in the same lines of operation, can unite for the development and complete helpfulness of their calling. The National Typothetæ, composed of delegates of local Typothetæ scattered over this broad fair land of ours, stands typical of united business enterprises which have been, in the broadest sense, subserved.

With labor organized for mutual protection, with invested business capital united for co-operative help, we further question as to the way to honest and successful competition in trade. The marts of commerce are active; business demands are urgent, increasing, and will continue to grow with the ever-swelling population. All business successfully pursued rests on the simple basis of cost, and is maintained with a percentage of profit added. A principal object of the association of labor is to establish a price for services rendered, and a determinate and unyielding effort is made to secure the end designed—a result most frequently secured. Business in association means the same thing. While conference in matters of business concern is stimulating; while interchange of business views are helpful; while social intimacy in trade by way of stated or occasional gatherings and meetings proves pleasing, yet the fact remains that success, true and complete, born of organized business endeavor, rests on the same basis of an established price, rigidly and faithfully adhered to. A scale of prices based on cost, with a fair percentage of profit added, is an absolute necessity to business integrity, and is unquestionably essential to commercial progress. This is feasible, possible, yea, is in fact inevitable to ultimate success in trade.

Competition under such an order is equally pushing and determinate, nevertheless brings to the business man far better returns. It prevents, too, where the trade honestly abides by the adopted scale, a vast amount of " beating " about from one place to another on the part of those who are close and parsimonious, in the hope of saving fifty cents or a dollar on their work. Better than this, it establishes a uniformity in trade, and guarantees a regular and abiding line of customers.

Merit in execution of the work intrusted to an office should be the sole competitive test. That is, with a reasonable scale of prices to which all have subscribed, there should be a constant aim to excel, and an ever-vigilant strife to produce the best work possible. It should be, in the truest sense, an honest endeavor for supremacy strictly on the line of doing well and yet striving to do better with every succeeding piece of work.

Ours is an artistic business. It is high removed, on account of its educating and developing influences upon the mental capacity of man, from the ordinary level of business. It has well been called the " art preservative," and is indeed the art of all arts.

The advance made in fine printing has been marvelous, as demonstrated by retrospective comparison. Place work of to-day alongside of productions of fifteen, ten, or even five years ago, and we ourselves, as craftsmen, are admiringly impressed with the progress and improvement made.

Competition is ever with us. Laudable is the ambition which impels us to unceasing business activity. We can, however, most successfully compete when we learn to regard the rights of those who are fellow-tradesmen. And this success is due, beyond question, on account of the organized forces of labor and the environment of trade, to rigidly following a carefully arranged scale of prices, resulting from mutual consultation of local competitors. Under this arrangement there should be an earnest, constant endeavor to elevate the trade, ever remembering that merit in production is the only just criterion for the customer. The best results in press-work upon a form which has had careful and painstaking skill towards typographical symmetry and beauty, will inure to the reputation and credit of the office producing it. Good printing is appreciated, commands a fair price, and will be rewarded. "Cheap Johns," who are looking for the most for their money, will always exist, but the average merchant and business man will patronize where the best is produced.

In conclusion, then, my opinion is, and it has already been substantiated in fact, that under the conditions herein set forth, competition becomes a matter of honorable and faithful adjustment, and none may lack for business, as there will necessarily be sufficient for all. Best of all, in this way, and this way only, the profits will be commensurate with the capital invested, and a proper reward will be secured for the brain, thought and effort devoted to this hitherto much-abused, but honorable, occupation. The printing business is an enviable business, it has been the educator of many who have achieved prominence in life, notwithstanding poverty deprived them of scholastic and academical training. Let us, then, as we preserve in permanent form the "records of the times," see to it that we do our work well, and ever be on the alert to compete for the supremacy.

PROVIDENCE, July 16, 1891.

EVILS OF COMPETITIVE BIDDING.

EDWIN FREEGARD.

Not the least serious of the " Evils of Competition " is the demoralization of the individual. Any printer who, in the endeavor to "get even," in consequence of having made too low a price for work undertaken, resorts to dishonest practices—such as giving short count, the substitution of an inferior or lighter weight paper than that agreed upon, furnishing inferior press-work, and scrimping the job in every other direction—undermines his own character as well as defrauds his customer and his fellow-printer. That this is not an uncommon occurrence among printers is too well known, and not a few of the disputes arising upon the endeavor to obtain settlements of accounts are a consequence of this practice. In the long run "honesty will be found the best policy" in this as in other things; for the man who fails to adopt honest principles is ultimately sure of being shunned. The remedy for the evil is courage to ask enough for work offered, assured that it will be quite as profitable to be without a job as to secure one in which it is necessary to resort to disreputable methods in order to avoid financial loss.

Another evil of the business is that printers make themselves "too cheap" by inordinate solicitation. It may be true to some extent that business must be "gone for"—that it will not come unless sought; but it is also true that it can be sought too much. Persistent canvassing day after day of the same people, and by different firms, reveals to those solicited the weakness of the printing trade; and it is so common for advantage to be taken of this fact, and figures submitted played one against another (sometimes untruthfully), that in the intense effort to get a job there is often no margin of profit whatever in the price for which it is done.

The business of some houses we know of is now not worth having, and this because they have learned how to get printers by "the nose" as it were; indeed, there are those in the trade who refuse to furnish them figures when asked to do so. Therefore, the advice often given young ladies not to hold themselves "too cheap" applies right here; and a little less enthusiasm in running after customers would result in customers coming to us. Probably there is no more work given out in consequence of this endless solicitation than there would be if it were not so prevalent; but there would be better prices, and all would get their share. Printers are great cowards—they have not moral courage to ask what is fair for their product for fear of losing a customer; whereas, if they persistently asked more they would be sure to get it after awhile, and probably do as much work as before.

Again, there is the evil of "brokers" or "middle-men"—men who have no "fortune" but that of their "face"; but who solicit work and then get figures from a number of printers (if they can), and, adding a commission to the lowest price, compete to get the work.

There are quite a number of such in the city, some of whom we know well; and these we permit to use our capital to take away the profits of our business.

No one of us can be in so favorable a position to compete as they, for none of us can know another's figures, whereas they sometimes get figures from as many as a half-dozen houses. The remedy for this evil is to let all "middle-men" severely alone.

One other evil sometimes is met with, and that is the one of book-keepers or clerks, or whoever has the printing to give out for a house, expecting a commission or gratuity of some kind for the favor of securing their trade. This is such flagrant dishonesty towards employers that no person having respect for his character would do it. This is bribery; and yet there are some men guilty of it, and, worse still, there are some printers very willing to suggest such a thing when they think it can be safely done. In the *American Bookmaker* for September, 1890, there was an article on this subject by Mr. H. G. Bishop, from which the following extract is made:

"The following advertisement, taken from a daily paper, shows that the printing business is not free from this class of persons, though it only shows one form of the illegitimate practices which such an advertiser would doubtless indulge in:

> **PRINTING.**
>
> TO book-keepers—Profits divided on all orders for printing, lithographing, account books, &c., by old established house. Address G. J., Press office.

"Now what shall be said of a firm which stoops to advertise for trade in this dishonest fashion? Such firms are a disgrace to any business and to any community. Is it not strange that a respectable newspaper should receive such advertisements? Here is a distinct invitation for a book-keeper to be dishonest to his employer. It is a flagrant case of bribery, and is therefore an unlawful act. The firm or person that will be guilty of such methods is dishonest, and is an inciter to dishonesty on the part of others."

EVILS OF COMPETITIVE BIDDING.

SAM. SLAWSON, ST. LOUIS TYPOTHETÆ.

There are many remedies that might be suggested to correct the evils which all acknowledge do now exist in the printing business, and which, as a Code of Ethics, would go far to accomplish the end in view; provided there were no *ifs* and *buts* in the way.

Perhaps the most simple and effective scheme is the one often heretofore mentioned—to-wit: make a fair and honorable scale of prices to be charged for our work, and then *stick to it*. And just here come in the *ifs* and *buts*. St. Louis Typothetæ tried it. Our best men, after careful consideration and many revisions, reported a price-list, which the Typothetæ adopted after much discussion. It covered a general range of commercial work, composition, both piece and time work, and the various kinds of cylinder press-work. The schedule proved a failure, simply for the reason that so many of our members found, or thought they found, that they could not hold their customers and adhere to the scale. They must withdraw from the Typothetæ or the scale must go. The scale went. Now, *if* we had *stuck to the scale*, there can be no reasonable doubt that, however it might have operated for a time in individual cases, there would now be a better-paying state of the trade, and each man would have been able to secure his fair proportion of it; and it may well be doubted if any other so efficient remedy can be devised, *provided* some way can be pointed out to supply the backbone necessary to its strict observance.

Other devices may be suggested, and might prove more or less remedial, but the scale of prices *adhered to* will prove a radical cure.

We might refuse to do work for middle men—that is, for parties who do not control and operate a printing plant. We might agree not to bid on a job we know is being hawked about the streets for estimates. We might agree to withdraw all solicitors from the street. We might jointly refuse to patronize type-founders or press builders who sell their wares to amateurs, or who extend credit to impecunious adventurers and afterwards carry them under mortgages in violation of sound business principles. All these might, if carried out, be of some benefit to the trade. But would there not be the same difficulty in securing such general acceptance of them as to work any benefit, as there would be in securing a strict adoption of a uniform scale of prices?

It is fair to presume that no sane business man would offer to do work at less than cost, and that no prudent man would offer to do it at less than a living profit; yet we all know that jobs are sometimes taken in St. Louis and elsewhere at less than the actual cost of production, and that work is frequently taken at less than a living profit. When we look for a reason for this condition of things, it can only be accounted for on the theory that the parties are simply mistaken in supposing that their low figures will pay a profit; and so we are warranted in saying that it is through *ignorance* that the present unremunerative prices prevail. Hence we may conclude that if the radical remedy of a fair *price-list* rigidly adhered to cannot be made to work, then there can be no remedy except in replacing trade ignorance with an enlightened understanding of the commercial side of the printing business.

LIST OF MEMBERS

OF THE

LOCAL TYPOTHETÆ

COMPRISING

The United Typothetæ of America.

OCTOBER, 1891.

ALBANY TYPOTHETÆ.
ALBANY, N. Y.
A. S. BRANDOW, *President.*
C. F. WILLIAMS, *Secretary.*

Evening Times.
The Press Co.
Evening Journal.
Argus Co.
Brandow Printing Co.
Charles H. Luck.

Riggs Printing Co.
C. F. Williams Printing Co.
Burdick & Taylor.
Evening Union.
Weed, Parsons & Co.
G. E. Reynolds.

MASTER-PRINTERS' CLUB.
BOSTON, MASS.
FRANK H. MUDGE, *President.*
L. A. WYMAN, *Secretary.*

J. J. Arakelyan.
Cyrus M. Barrows & Co.
L. Barta, (L. Barta & Co.)
Aug. N. Berry, (J. N. Allen & Berry.)
Jas. Berwick, (Berwick & Smith.)
W. S. Best, (W. S. Best & Co.)

A. P. Bicknell.
J. T. Blair.
A. T. Bliss.
Louis K. Brown, (Brown & Clark.)
C. W. Calkins, (C. W. Calkins & Co.)

F. W. Calkins, (C. W. Calkins & Co.)
G. A. Churchill, (Rockwell & Churchill.)
David Clapp.
H. G. Collins.
John J. Croke, (Croke Ptg. Co.)
Geo. E. Crosby, (Geo. E. Crosby & Co.)
J. S. Cushing, (J. S. Cushing & Co.)
W. H. Daniels, (Winship & Daniels.)
H. B. Dennison, (Dennison Mfg. Co.)
George H. Ellis.
W. H. Forbes, (W. H. Forbes Lith. Co.)
F. C. Fairbanks, (T. R. Marvin & Co.)
P. H. Foster, (Parker H. Foster & Co.)
R. S. Gardner, (Rand-Avery Supply Co.)
F. H. Gilson.
A. Hallett.
C. H. Heintzemann.
J. C. Heymer.
J. Edw. Heymer.
H. O. Houghton, (Riverside Press.)
H. O. Houghton, Jr., (Riverside Press.)
W. N. Hughes.
M. J. Kiley.
C. H. Knight, (Mills, Knight & Co.)
T. W. Lawson, (Lawson Mfg. Co.)
H. E. Lombard.

John A. Lowell.
H. A. Maley, (Ginn & Co.)
W. T. R. Marvin.
C. D. W. Marcy, (Sampson, Murdock & Co.)
James W. McIndoe, (McIndoe Bros.)
Frederick Mills, (Mills, Knight & Co.)
J. L. McIntosh.
F. H. Mudge, (A. Mudge & Son.)
W. E. Murdock, (Sampson, Murdock & Co.)
Frank H. Nichols.
Fred H. Nichols.
T. P. Nichols.
J. H. O'Donnell, (Wright & Potter Printing Co.)
Cyrus A. Page, (Treas. Beacon Pub. Co.)
C. L. D. Parkhill, (S. J. Parkhill & Co.
S. J. Parkhill, (S. J. Parkhill & Co.)
C. J. Peters, (C. J. Peters & Son.)
Geo. E. Peters, (C. J. Peters & Son.)
J. W. Phinney, (Dickinson Type Foundry.)
C. A. Pinkham, (C. A. Pinkham & Co.)
A. L. Rand.
T. W. Ripley.
W. J. Robinson, (Robinson & Stephenson.)
H. T. Rockwell, (Rockwell & Churchill.)
L. W. Rogers, (Bay State Electro. Foundry.)

Henry N. Sawyer, (Nathan Sawyer & Son.)
Josiah B. Scott, (Geo. C. Scott & Co.)
Geo. W. Simonds, (C. H. Simonds & Co.)
J. N. Smart.
G. H. Smith, (Berwick & Smith.)
Wallace Spooner.
T. C. Stephenson, (Robinson & Stephenson.)
E. B. Stillings.
Thomas Todd.
Samuel Usher.
Wm. Walker, (Walker, Young & Co.)
Jos. H. Ware, (H. C. Whitcomb & Co.)
Chas. E. Wentworth, (John Wilson & Son.)
H. C. Whitcomb, (H. C. Whitcomb & Co.)
B. Wilkins, (B. Wilkins & Co.)
John Wilson, (John Wilson & Son.)
A. L. Winship, (Winship & Daniels.)
Frank Wood.
A. J. Wright, (Wright & Potter Printing Co.)
Louis A. Wyman, (Wright & Potter Printing Co.)

CHATTANOOGA TYPOTHETÆ.

CHATTANOOGA, TENN.

FRANK MCGOWAN, *President*.
E. W. MATTSON, *Secretary*.

Bradt Printing Co.
News Publishing Co.
Times Printing Co.
Argus Publishing Co.
Republican Printing Co.
Press Publishing Co.
J. M. Deardorff & Sons.
Chattanooga Medicine Co.
L. Geistle & Co.
Keelin Printing Co.
W. I. Crandall & Co.
McGowan & Cooke.

CHICAGO TYPOTHETÆ.

CHICAGO, ILL.

C. H. BLAKELY, *President*.
THOS. KNAPP, *Secretary*.

C. H. Blakely & Co.
Blakely Printing Co.
Barnard & Gunthorpe.
Baker & Vawter Co.
A. R. Barnes & Co.
Edw. Beeke, Jr.
Cameron, Amberg & Co.
Chicago Newspaper Union.
S. D. Childs & Co.
Commercial Printing Co.
Geo. E. Cole & Co.
Chicago Journal of Commerce.

Daniels, Pitkin & Hall.
R. R. Donnelly & Sons Company.
E. J. Decker.
W. P. Dunn & Co.
Dean Brothers.
Donohue & Henneberry.
Empire Printing Co.
Fergus Printing Co.
Franz Gindele Printing Co.
Hack & Anderson.
Hornstein Bros.
J. J. Hanlon.
James T. Hair Co.
Wm. Johnson Printing Co.
W. J. Jefferson.
Jameson & Morse Co.
J. M. W. Jones Stationery and Printing Co.
Knight & Leonard Co.
A. W. Kellogg Newspaper Co.
Knapp & Johnston.
Geo. M. D. Libbey.
A. W. Landon.
H. C. Marsh & Son.
Geo. E. Marshall & Co.
R. R. McCabe & Co.
J. S. McDonald & Co.
National Journalist Publishing Company.
National Printing Co.
C. O. Owen & Co.
P. F. Pettibone & Co.
Pettibone, Wells & Co.
Pictorial Printing Co.
Poole Brothers.
E. Rubovits & Bro.
J. L. Regan.
Rand, McNally & Co.
Rubel Brothers.
Rollins Publishing Co.
Stranberg, Allen & Co.
C. M. Staiger.
H. S. Tiffany & Co.
Thayer & Jackson Stationery Co.
The Corbett & Skidmore Co.
Geo. P. Englehard & Co.
W. D. Boyce.

TYPOTHETÆ OF CINCINNATI.

CINCINNATI, O.

C. J. KREHBIEL, *President.*
ALLEN COLLIER, *Secretary.*

American Book Co.
Armstrong & Fillmore.
Braunwart and Brockhoff.
The C. F. Bradley Co.
Boake & Miller.
Bloch Publishing and Printing Company.
L. E. Casey.
Allen Collier.
Commercial-Gazette Job Printing Co.
Robert Clark & Co.
Cohen & Co.
W. B. Carpenter & Co.
Dittgen & Co.
Earhart & Richardson.
C. J. Krehbiel & Co.
Keating & Co.

McDonald & Eick.
R. T. Morris.
Newport Printing and Newspaper Co.
Ohio Valley Press.
A. H. Pugh Printing Co.
S. Rosenthal & Co.
United States Printing Co.
C. Souer & Co.
Sullivan Printing Co.
Wm. Skinner & Co.
Jos. Wachtel.
Webb Stationery and Printing Company.
Woodrow, Baldwin & Co.
Zinsle & Co.
Spencer & Craig.

COLUMBUS TYPOTHETÆ.
COLUMBUS, O.

L. D. MYERS, *President.*
J. WIGGINS, *Secretary.*

Columbus Printing Co.
Gazette Printing House.
Ham & Adair.
J. L. Granger.
J. C. McCracken & Co.
Myers Bros.
Nitschke & Co.
Ohio State Journal.
D. E. Orvis.
J. Wiggins & Co.
Fred J. Wendell.
Columbus Evening Dispatch.
Hooper & Connelly.
Westbole & Co.

DAYTON TYPOTHETÆ.
DAYTON, O.

J. W. JOHNSON, *President.*
WILL C. KETTE, *Secretary.*

J. W. Johnson.
Groneweg Printing Co.
Reform Publishing Co.
Huffman Publishing Co.
Galen C. Wise.
Reynolds & Reynolds Co.
Walker Litho. and Printing Co.
Sweetman Printing House.
The Herald Co.
Giele & Pflamm.
Troup Manufacturing Co.

DETROIT TYPOTHETÆ.
DETROIT, MICH.

JOHN F. EBY, *President.*
J. H. GOULD, *Secretary.*

John F. Eby & Co.
Raynor & Taylor.
J. W. Morrison & Co.
Schober Printing Co.
Peninsular Printing and Publishing Co.

The Wm. Graham Printing Co.
Winn & Hammond.
Wm. F. Moore.
Jos. A. Topping.
O. S. Gulley, Bornman & Co.
C. M. Rousseau.
Detroit Free Press Printing Co.

GALVESTON TYPOTHETÆ.
GALVESTON, TEXAS.
Clarke & Courts.

INDIANAPOLIS TYPOTHETÆ.
INDIANAPOLIS, IND.
WILLIAM FISH, *President*.
H. O. THUDIUM, *Secretary*.

Baker & Randolph.
W. B. Burford.
Carlon & Hollenbeck.
Willis Engle.
Hasselman Printing Co.
Guttenberg Co.
Indiana Newspaper Union.
Indianapolis Printing Co.
Journal Job Printing Co.
Levey Bros.
National Card Co.
Jos. Ratti.
Sentinel Printing Co.
Frank Smith.

KANSAS CITY TYPOTHETÆ.
KANSAS CITY, MO.
FRANK HUDSON, *President*.
Ro. W. HART, *Secretary*.

Tiernan-Havens Printing Co.
Hudson-Kimberly Pub. Co.
Lawton & Burnap.
S. F. Woody.
Tew-Lyle Printing Co.
Union Bank Note Co.
Spencer Printing Co.
J. A. France.
Robert W. Hart.

LA FAYETTE TYPOTHETÆ.
LA FAYETTE, IND.
W. BENT. WILSON, *President*.
FRED. S. WILLIAMS, *Secretary*.

Daily Call.
Daily Courier.
Daily Journal.
Sunday Times.
Sunday Leader.

LITTLE ROCK TYPOTHETÆ.

LITTLE ROCK, ARK.

A. M. WOODRUFF, *President.*
ALLEN W. CLARK, *Secretary.*

Press Printing Co.
Woodruff Printing Co.
Democrat Co.
John Covington & Co.
Gazette Publishing Co.

LOUISVILLE TYPOTHETÆ.

LOUISVILLE, KY.

L. T. DAVIDSON, *President.*
JAS. DAVIDSON, *Secretary.*

Bradley & Gilbert Co.
John P. Morton & Co.
Courier-Journal Job Printing Company.
Geo. H. Dietz & Co.
Falls City Litho. & Print'g Co.
Geo. G. Fetter Printing Co.
Morton Bros.
B. F. Converse & Co.
Courier-Journal Co.
Eugene Bell Letter Press Co.
C. T. Dearing.
Evening Post Co.
Guide Printing and Pub. Co.
Louisville Lith. and Bank Note Company.
Times Co.
J. C. Parker.
Moore & Stark.

MEMPHIS TYPOTHETÆ.

MEMPHIS, TENN.

EDWIN WHITMORE, *President.*
GEO. S. LANDIS, *Secretary.*

Edward Whitmore, J. W. Vernon, Memphis Printing Co.
A. B. Pickett, Ed. and Mgr. "Scimitar" Publishing Co.
A. J. McCallum, Mgr. A. N. Kellogg Newspaper Co.
Wm. Fitzgerald, Pres. and Mgr. Catholic Pub. Co.
Rabbi Samfield, Prop. Jewish Spectator.
S. C. Toof, Wm. H. Bates, } S. C. Toof & Co.
Dan. C. Jones, Jno. D. Huhn, } Jones, Huhn & Co.
Peter Tracy, Pres. Tracy Printing Co.
Col. J. M. Keating, Man. Editor Commercial Pub. Co.
A. J. Doolittle, Bus. Man. Commercial Pub. Co.

MONTREAL TYPOTHETÆ.

MONTREAL, CANADA.

E. G. O'CONNOR, *President.*
JOSEPH FORTIER, *Secretary.*

Burland Lithographic Co.
Benallack Lithographic Co.
A. Carmel.
David English.
Joseph Fortier.
J. H. Foisey.
Gebhardt-Berthiaume Lithographic Co.
George Bishop Engraving Co.
Higgins Bros.
J. B. Laplante.
John Lovell & Son.
True Witness Office.

FIFTH ANNUAL MEETING. 279

W. A. Collier, Pres., T. B. Hatchett, Gen. Mgr., and Thos Taylor, Bus. Mgr., Appeal-Avalanche Pub. Co.

Geo. S. Landis, Prop. Sunday Times.

J. T. Wilson, Pres. Phœnix Job and Book Printing Co.

Capt. J. H. Mathes, Pres., and Zeno T. Harris, Bus. M'r., Ledger Pub. Co.

Wirt Wills and James Crumpton, Wills & Crumpton.

A. M. Paul, Pres. Great South Pub. Co.

HONORARY MEMBERS:

A. D. Allen.
Barney Hughes.
Col. M. C. Galloway.

John S. Toof.
Jacob Henry.
O. P. Bard.

MILWAUKEE TYPOTHETÆ.

MILWAUKEE, WIS.

JOHN F. CRAMER, *President*.
H. H. ZAHN, *Secretary*.

Burdick, Armitage & Allen.
R. S. Baird.
Cramer, Aikens & Cramer.
J. M. Everly.
B. L. Hoard.
E. L. Hurlbut.
Journal Company.
King, Fowle & Co.

B. Lowenbach & Son.
Riverside Printing Co.
Swain & Tate.
Standard Printing Co.
Sentinel Company.
John Tainsch.
J. H. Yewdale & Sons Co.
H. H. Zahn & Co.

MINNEAPOLIS TYPOTHETÆ.

MINNEAPOLIS, MINN.

C. A. MITCHELL, *President*.
A. M. GEESAMAN, *Secretary*.

A. C. Bausman.
Co-Operative Printing Co.
Geesaman & Murphy.
Hall, Black & Co.
Harrison & Smith.
Kimball Printing Co.

Lumberman Pub. Co.
Leighton Bros.
Periodical Press Co.
Price Bros.
Alfred Roper.
Swinburne Printing Co.

Tribune Job Printing Co.

NASHVILLE TYPOTHETÆ.
NASHVILLE, TENN.
J. H. BRUCE, *President.*
C. H. BRANDON, *Secretary.*

Southern Methodist Pub. House.
Brandon Printing Co.
Marshall & Bruce.
Foster & Webb.
A. B. Tavel.
Haslock & Ambrose.
McClure & Rose.
Gospel Advocate Publishing Co.
Cumberland Presbyterian Publishing House.
American Pub. Co.
Evening Banner Pub. Co.

NEW HAVEN TYPOTHETÆ.
NEW HAVEN, CONN.
C. S. MOREHOUSE, *President.*
E. N. ALLING, *Secretary.*

Tuttle, Morehouse & Taylor.
O. A. Dorman.
The Price, Lee & Adkins Co.
The Stafford Printing Co.
Hoggson & Robinson.
D. S. Thomas.
A. L. Barnes.
Munson & Co.
E. N. Alling.
G. J. Moffatt.
The E. B. Sheldon Co.
The Register Pub. Co.
The Palladium Co.
The Carrington Pub. Co.
The Morning News Co.
J. M. Emerson.
Journal Publishing Co.
C. S. Haviland.
J. N. Near.
W. H. Marigold & Co.
Geo. W. Hills.
Buckingham & Brewer.
Peck & Prouty.
Sam'l Clark.

NEW ORLEANS TYPOTHETÆ.
NEW ORLEANS, LA.
T. FITZWILLIAM, *President.*
LEWIS S. GRAHAM, *Secretary.*

T. Fitzwilliam & Co.
A. W. Hyatt Stat. Mfg. Co., L'td.
Garcia Stat. Mfg. Co., Limited.
T. H. Thomason.
L. Graham & Son.
J. B. Cameron.
V. Mauberret.
F. C. Phillipe.

Malus & Hofeline.
George Muller.
S. S. Earl.
John Hopkins.

Paul Marchand.
Patterson & Ray.
McGrane & Leslie.
E. A. Brandao.
Wehrmann & Delord.

NEW YORK TYPOTHETÆ.

NEW YORK, N. Y.

THEO. L. DEVINNE, *President*.
E. PARKE COBY, *Secretary*.

D. Appleton & Co.
Argyle Press.
Wm. P. Atkin.
Henry Bessey.
L. H. Biglow & Co.
Martin B. Brown.
William L. Brown.
Ben. Franklin Press.
Burr Printing House.
The Caulon Press.
The Caxton Press.
The Clucas Publishing Co.
E. P. Coby & Co.
Peter DeBaun & Co.
Theo. L. DeVinne & Co.
John DeVries & Son.
The Hub Press.
Exchange Printing Co.
Evening Post Job Printing House.
Fless & Ridge Printing Co.
Freeman & Brother.
Gillis Bros.
Wm. Green.
Estate David H. Gildersleeve.
Harper & Brothers.
Wm. M. Halsted.
Holt Bros.
Edward O. Jenkins' Son.

Chas. C. Shelley.
Jos. B. Stilwell.
Elliott F. Shepard.
R. Harmer Smith & Sons.
Styles & Cash.
Douglas Taylor.
The Textile Publishing Co.
Thomson & Co.
B. H. Tyrrel.
Jenkins & McCowan.
Chas. H. Jones & Co.
E. L. Kellogg & Co.
Kepplar & Schwarzmann.
New York Sun.
Homer Lee.
Louis A. Lehmaier.
J. J. Little & Co.
Howard Lockwood & Co.
P. F. McBreen.
Willis McDonald & Co.
Macgowan & Slipper.
Estate William C. Martin.
Livingston Middleditch & Co.
The Mershon Co.
N. Y. Economical Printing Co.
N. Y. Eng. & Printing Co.
Nicoll & Roy.
John Polhemus Printing Co.
J. W. Pratt & Son.

Price Printing House.
G. P. Putnam's Sons.
Wm. J. Pell.
J. C. Rankin Co.
James A. Rogers.
Rogers & Sherwood.
H. A. Rost.
Thorne Type-Setting Machine Company.
Trow's Printing & Book Binding Company.
The U. S. Printing Co.
William H. VanWart.
Winthrop Press.
Wynkoop, Hallenbeck & Co.

TYPOTHETÆ OF OMAHA.

OMAHA, NEB.

CHARLES H. KLOPP, *President.*
JULIUS T. FESTNER, *Secretary.*

Burkley Printing Co.
Festner Printing Co.
Pokrok Zapadu Printing Co.
Reed Printing Co.
Rees Printing Co.
Redfield Printing Co.
Republican Printing Co.
Western Printing Co.
Henry Gibson.
F. A. Manger.
Dan C. Shelley.
John A. MacMurphy.
Isaac Sylvester.
Lew W. Raber.
Chase & Eddy.
Klopp, Bartlett & Co.
Swartz & McKelvey.
Wm. Kimmell & Co.
Sam P. Brigham.
Hammond Bros.
John Douglas.

TYPOTHETÆ OF PHILADELPHIA.

PHILADELPHIA, PA.

JOHN R. MCFETRIDGE, *President.*
JOHN W. WALLACE, *Secretary.*

The North American.
Evening Bulletin.
The Press.
The Times.
Evening Star.
The Item.
Herald Co.—Limited.
Taggart's Sunday Times.
Paper and Press.
Sherman & Co.
MacKellar, Smiths & Jordan.
Burk & McFetridge.
Wm. H. Hoskins & Co.
Lineaweaver & Wallace.
McLaughlin Bros. Co.
Edward Stern & Co.
Morrell Bros.
Wm. F. Murphy's Sons.
Wm. Mann Co.
National Publishing Co.

FIFTH ANNUAL MEETING.

George S. Ferguson & Co.
Alfred M. Slocum & Co.
James B. Rodgers Printing Co.
Franklin Printing Co.
George H. Buchanan & Co.
Review Printing House.
Dando Printing and Pub. Co.
Billstein & Sons.
Wm. F. Geddes & Son.
Dunlap & Clarke.
George F. Lasher.
Stephen Greene.
James Beale.
William F. Fell & Co.
Col. M. Richards Muckle.

R. W. Hartnett & Bros.
Irwin N. Megargee & Co.
C. R. Carver.
H. P. Feister.
John Woodruff's Sons.
Craig, Finley & Co.
A. G. Elliot & Co.
Wolf Bros.
Magargee & Green.
C. W. Edwards.
Charles Eneu Johnson.
Ferris Bros.
Wm. J. Dornan.
A. H. Sickler & Co.
Charles W. Bendernagel.

Edwin S. Stuart.

PORTLAND, ORE., TYPOTHETÆ.

PORTLAND, ORE.

H. R. LEWIS, *President*.
F. W. BALTES, *Secretary*.

The Lewis & Dryden Printing Co.
A. Anderson & Co.
F. W. Baltes & Co.

George H. Himes.
R. H. Schwab & Bro.
E. A. Swope & Co.
George W. McCoy.

TYPOTHETÆ OF PITTSBURG, ALLEGHENY AND VICINITY.

PITTSBURG, PA.

JOSEPH EICHBAUM, *President*.
A. H. HOLLIDAY, *Secretary*.

E. F. Anderson & Co., Ld.
Best & Co.
H. P. Callow & Co.
W. H. Barnes.
Ewens & Eberle.
Duquesne Printing & Pub. Co.
Jos. Eichbaum & Co.

Chas. K. Gibson.
W. T. Nicholson.
H. L. McGaw & Son.
Jas. McMillan.
Murdoch, Kerr & Co.
E. E. Kennedy & Co.
Wm. G. Johnston & Co.

Myers, Shinkle & Co.
Percy F. Smith.
Smith Bros.
Stevenson & Foster.
A. P. Supplee.

Shaw Bros.
John Ogden.
Pittsburg Label Co.
Reese Bros.
Chas. F. Foster.

MASTER PRINTERS' ASSOCIATION OF RHODE ISLAND.

PROVIDENCE, R. I.

CHAS. C. GRAY, *President.*
THOS. S. HAMMOND, *Secretary.*

R. I. Printing Co.
E. A. Johnson & Co.
Snow & Farnham.
Livermore & Knight.
T. S. Hammond.
Geo. F. Chapman.
J. A. & R. A. Reid.
Geo. A. Wilson.
Whittemore & Colburn.

Standard Printing Co.
O. A. Carleton.
Chadsey & Clarke.
F. H. Townsend.
C. W. Littell.
Chas. A. Lee.
The Adam Sutcliffe Co.
John W. Little.
Ryder & Dearth.

E. L. Freeman & Son.

RICHMOND TYPOTHETÆ.

RICHMOND, VA.

Ro. WHITTET, *President.*
EVERETT WADDEY, *Secretary.*

Wm. Ellis Jones.
Andrews & Baptist.
Everett Waddey Co.
Baughman Stationery Co.
E. B. Marquess & Co.

Juan A. Pizzini.
Patrick Keenan.
James E. Goode.
J. W. Fergusson & Son.
Whittet & Shepperson.

ROCHESTER TYPOTHETÆ.

ROCHESTER, N. Y.

E. R. ANDREWS, *President.*
ERNEST HART, *Secretary.*

Rochester Printing Co.
E. R. Andrews.
Post-Express Printing Co.

Sunday Herald Printing Co.
John P. Smith.
Union & Advertiser Co.

Andrew J. Wegman.
Rochester Herald Pub. Co.
R. M. Swinburne.
Alling & Long.

Charles Mann.
M. H. Smith.
Artistic Print. & Eng. Co.
Ernest Hart.

SAN FRANCISCO TYPOTHETÆ.

SAN FRANCISCO, CAL.

CHAS. A. MURDOCK, *President.*
AI ROLLINS, *Secretary.*

Charles A. Murdock & Co.
Filmer-Rollins Elec. Co.
Brunt & Co.
S. W. Ravely.
J. R. Brodie & Co.
Frank Eastman & Co.
W. A. Woodward & Co.
Bosqui Eng. and Ptg Co.
Joseph Winterburn & Co.
George Spaulding & Co.
The Bancroft Co.
The Hicks-Judd Co.
Schmidt Label & Lithographic Co.
William C. Brown.
Francis, Valentine & Co.
H. S. Crocker Co.
P. M. Diers & Co.
P. J. Thomas.
Upton Brothers.

W. A. Bushnell.
James H. Barry.
B. F. Sterett.
J. O. Jephson.
D. S. Stanley & Co.
Cubery & Co.
J. C. Hall Eng. & Printing Co.
Palmer & Rey.
William E. Loy.
Dickman-Jones Co.
Estate of A. J. Leary.
W. M. Langton Printing Co.
P. E. Dougherty & Co.
Valleau & Peterson.
Carleton & Kimball.
Hawks & Shattuck.
R. Munk.
McCormick Brothers.
L. Rosenthal & Co.
Roberts Printing Co.

E. C. Hughes.

SPRINGFIELD TYPOTHETÆ.

SPRINGFIELD, OHIO.

J. S. CROWELL, *President.*
J. GARVER, *Secretary.*

Crowell & Kirkpatrick.
Daily Republic.
Times.

Winters P'tg and Litho. Co.
Daily Gazette.
Sunday News.

H. S. Limbacker Job Printing Co.

ST. LOUIS TYPOTHETÆ.

ST. LOUIS, MO.

Edwin Freegard, *President.*
Walter Slawson, *Secretary.*

Geo. D. Barnard & Co.
Becktold & Co.
S. G. Burnham.
Buxton & Skinner Stat. Co.
Dennison Manufacturing Co.
David Edwards & Co.
R. & T. A. Ennis Stat. Co.
H. Feldbush.
Aug. Gast Bank Note & Lith. Company.
Graham Paper Co.
N. T. Gray.
L. C. Hesse.
Herman Heiser.
Standard Printing Co.
A. N. Kellogg News Co.
Levison & Blythe Stat. Co.
Little & Becker Printing Co.
Parker-Ritter-Nicholls Stat. Co.
Scott & Richarz Press R'm Co.
Slawson Printing Co.
Owens Printing Co.
J. W. Steele & Co.
St. Louis Paper Co.
R. P. Studley & Co.
Ev. E. Carreras.
Clayton & Son.
Commercial Printing Co.
Continental Printing Co.
C. W. Crutsinger.
St. Louis Printers' Supply Co.
Woodward & Tiernan Ptg. Co.
C. B. Woodward Ptg. & Mfg. Co.
St. Louis Bank Note Co.
Aug. Wiebush & Son Ptg. Co.
W. J. Gilbert.
Nixon-Jones Printing Co.
St. Louis Label Works.
R. J. Compton & Sons Litho. Company.
F. M. Call.
Chas. A. Drach & Co.
St. Louis Type Foundry.
Central Type Foundry.
Edgar F. Alden.
Geo. R. Dickinson Paper Co.
B. Thalmann.
Mangan & Co.
Carl Schraubstadter, Jr.
Theodore Lange.

ST. PAUL TYPOTHETÆ.

ST. PAUL, MINN.

Geo. M. Stanchfield, *President.*
W. T. Rich, *Secretary.*

Pioneer Press Co.
D. Ramaley & Son.
H. L. Collins & Co.
Kellogg Newspaper Co.
Frank Shoop.
W. L. Banning & Co.
Brown, Treasy & Co.
G. W. Cunningham & Co.

Rich & Clymer.
Stanchfield & Co.
Commercial Printing Co.
West Publishing Co.
Price, McGill & Co.
Payne, Vose & Co.
H. M. Smythe & Co.
St. Paul Dispatch.
Minnesota Type Foundry.

EMPLOYING PRINTERS ASSOCIATION OF TORONTO.

TORONTO, CANADA.

W. A. SHEPARD, *President.*
BRUCE BROUGH, *Secretary.*

The Globe Printing Co., L'td.
The Empire Printing and Publishing Co., L'td.
The Mail Printing Co.
The News Printing Co.
The Morning World.
The Evening Telegram.
James Murray & Co.
Mail Job Department.
Hunter, Rose & Co.
Kilgour Bros.
Presbyterian Printing and Publishing Co.
Methodist Book and Publishing Company.
Warrick & Sons.
S. Frank Wilson.
Central Press Agency.
Robert G. McLean.
Dudley & Burnes.
Imrie & Graham.
Trout & Todd.
Thos. Moore & Co.
A. W. Croil.
Apted Bros.
J. B. McLean.
C. H. Mortimer.
Daniel Rose.
Ph. DeGruchy.
Brough & Caswell.

TYPOTHETÆ OF TROY.

TROY, N. Y.

HENRY STOWELL, *President.*
ALEX. MEEKIN, *Secretary.*

Henry Stowell.
E. Green & Son.
J. A. Fonda.
T. J. Hurley.
J. E. Russell.
Giles Bros.
A. Meekin & Co.
Troy Press.
J. W. Gemmill.
Alex. Kirkpatrick, Jr.
E. H. Foster & Co.
J. & M. Wallace.
E. H. Lisk.
Richard S. Clark.
Joel W. Smith.
John P. Pratt.
Catholic Weekly.
G. R. Palmateer.

TOPEKA TYPOTHETÆ.

TOPEKA, KAN.

Geo. W. Crane, *President.*
W. N. Hall, *Secretary.*

Geo. W. Crane & Co.
Hamilton Printing Co.
C. W. Douglas.

Hall & O'Donald Lithographing Company.
Geo. W. Reed.

ASSOCIATED PUBLISHERS OF WASHINGTON.

WASHINGTON, D. C.

C. S. Noyes, *President.*
T. B. Kalfus, *Secretary.*

The Evening Star.
The Washington Post.
The Sunday Gazette.

The Sunday Herald.
Judd & Deitwiler.
Byron S. Adams.

Gedney & Roberts.

WORCESTER TYPOTHETÆ.

WORCESTER, MASS.

Lucius P. Goddard, *President.*
F. S. Blanchard, *Secretary.*

Gilbert G. Davis.
Charles R. Stubbs.
E. H. Tripp.
W. E. Felt.
Charles G. Marcy.

Maynard, Gough & Co.
James J. Doyle.
F. E. Kennedy.
F. S. Blanchard & Co.
Charles W. Burbank.

No reports were received from—
Fort Wayne Typothetæ, Fort Wayne, Ind.
Toledo Typothetæ, Toledo, O.

INDEX.

	PAGE.
Account of Time, How to keep	165
Address of Welcome, by President Krehbiel	5
Address by the President U. T. A	9
American Newspaper Publishers' Association	15
Amendments (Constitution)	62
American Copyright League, report of Delegates to	111
American Newspaper Publishers' Association, report of Delegates to	155
Amos, Mr., Address of on behalf of National Editorial Association	110
Annual Dues, increase of	28
Apprenticeship, form of (President's Address)	12-13
Apprentices, School for Instruction of (President's Address)	13
Approval of Action of Pittsburg Typothetæ	120
Assistance, Furnishing	39
Auditing Committee Appointed	31
report of	94
Blue Grass Excursion	202
Bureau of Information and Supply Recommended	37
report of Committee on	102
Canada, Free Admission to, of Trade Journals	127
Certificates for workmen	40, 175
Chamber of Commerce, invitation from	55
Chattanooga scale of prices	23
Change of method of nominating officers	164
Cincinnati and Suburbs	202
Cincinnati Typothetæ, vote of thanks to	198
Cincinnati Type Foundry, invitation from	97
Code of Ethics, Constitution and	213
Competition, Ignorant (President's Address)	14
Competitive Bidding, the Evils of, by Committee from Cincinnati Typothetæ	255
the evils of, by Samuel Rees	250
evil results of, by L. G. Reynolds	243
with its resultant evils, by Thomas Todd	228
Competition, its Possible Regulation, by Charles A. Murdock	235
evils of, report on	42
Constitution, notice of revision of	28
as reported by Committee on Revision	58-62
discussion of	64-94
adopted	94
and Code of Ethics	213
Corresponding Secretary, report of	21

Credentials 18
Daily Proceedings not to be printed 39
Deceased Members, report of Committee to Prepare Resolutions on 190
Distribution of Subjects, report on 63
    committees on 94
Eichbaum, Mr., of Pittsburg, address of 117
Electricity in the Press Room, paper on 129
Estimates, paper concerning, by Theo. L. DeVinne 223
Ethics, Code of and Constitution 213
Envelopes, Printing of, by the Government 23, 38, 94, 125
Evils of Competitive Bidding, report on 42
Executive Committee, expense of meetings of 15, 31, 103, 118
    report of 31
Executive Session 119
Expenses of Officers and Executive Committee, Committee on 95
Future Conventions, Place for holding, Committee on 94, 127
Government, Printing of Envelopes, by 23, 38, 125
Graded Labor (President's Address) 14
Hours of Labor, Reduction of 158, 175
How to Keep Account of Time 165
Ignorant Competition (President's Address) 14
Increasing Number of Local Typothetæ, Plan for, Committee on 95
Indianapolis Typothetæ Organized 23
Information and Supply, Bureau of, recommended 37
    Bureau of, Committee on 94
    Bureau of, report of Committee on 102
Inquiry, Circular of, by Executive Committee 32
    replies to Circular of, by Executive Committee 33
Instruction of Apprentices, School for (President's Address) 13
Interest of Employer and Employee, common (President's Address) 16
Financial Element in the Printing Business, by Richard Ennis 257
Free Admission of Trade Journals to Canada 127
Labor, Committee on 94
    Cost of (President's Address) 13
    Hours of 175
    Graded (President's Address) 14
    Report of Committee on 118
Lafayette, Ind., Typothetæ organized 23
Martin, W. C., death of, announced 17
    resolutions on 190
Macmillan Typesetting Machine 137, 148
Mergenthaler Linotype 139
Mortuary Resolutions, Committee on 94
Names, Alphabetical List of members of Local Typothetæ 372
National Copyright Law, report of Committee on 112
    Editorial Association, address of Mr. Amos on behalf of 110
    Editorial Convention, reports of Delegates to 105
    Press Association, address of Mr. Price on behalf of 109
Negligence of Officers of Local Typothetæ, Committee on 95-108
Next meeting, place of 96, 161

Nominations, Committee on.................................. 100
Nine-hour day.................................. 10–12, 35, 197
Nominations, Report on.................................. 159
Officers, List of.................................. 3
    change of method of nominating.................................. 164
    election of.................................. 194
Ohio Editorial Association, Delegates present.................................. 180
Organization of Indianapolis Typothetæ.................................. 23
    of Lafayette, Ind., Typothetæ.................................. 23
    of Pittsburg Typothetæ.................................. 23
Paige Compositor.................................. 153
Pears, Mr., Letter from, received.................................. 97
Pittsburg Delegation Invited to seats on platform.................................. 113
    Typothetæ organized.................................. 23
    Typothetæ, Greeting from.................................. 81
Proofs of Proceedings to be Furnished Trade Journals.................................. 196
Proceedings of Last Convention, Question of their Approval.................................. 98
Printing Plants, Value of (President's Address).................................. 12
    of Envelopes by the Government.................................. 23
    Business, the Financial Element In, by Richard Ennis.................................. 257
Price, Mr., Address of on Behalf of National Press Association.................................. 109
Press Room, Electricity in, Paper on.................................. 129
Place of Next Convention, Committee on.................................. 100
Pittsburg Typothetæ, Telegram from.................................. 101
Register Read.................................. 18
Report of Delegate to American Copyright League.................................. 111
    Delegates to National Editorial Convention.................................. 105
    Committee on Labor.................................. 118
    Committee on National Copyright Law.................................. 112
    Corresponding Secretary.................................. 21–27
    Recording Secretary.................................. 27
    Treasurer.................................. 29–31
    Executive Committee.................................. 31
    Committee on Evils of Competitive Bidding.................................. 42
Report on Future Meetings of the Convention.................................. 127
    on Hours of Labor, Wages and Trade Usages.................................. 176
    on Printing of Envelopes by the Government.................................. 125
Revision of Constitution, report on.................................. 57
Rogers Typograph.................................. 136
Rollers and their Proper Treatment, by R. J. Morgan.................................. 182
Russell, A. O., Treasurer, Vote of Thanks to.................................. 198
San Francisco Typothetæ, Telegram from.................................. 101
    Typothetæ, Reply to.................................. 108
Scale of Prices.................................. 35
    of Prices, Chattanooga.................................. 23
Schepker, H. G., death of announced.................................. 17
    resolutions on.................................. 193
School for Instruction of Apprentices (President's Address).................................. 13
Secret Sessions.................................. 39
Sproull, Mr., of Pittsburg, address of.................................. 113

Shepard, W. A., President, Escorted to the Chair 195
Studley, R. P., death of announced 17
    resolutions on 192
St. John Typobar 140
Technical School 13
Thanks, Vote of 196–198
Thorne Machine 141
Time of Meeting, Change of proposed 35
    and place of next meeting 161
    how to keep account of 165
Topics, Distribution of, Committee on 55
Toronto Typothetæ, Telegram from 101
Trade Journals, Proofs of Proceedings to be furnished to 196
    Journals, Free admission of to Canada 127
    Usages, Hours of Labor and Wages, Report on 176
Treasurer, report of 29
Typesetting Machines, report on 135
Value of Printing Plants (President's Address) 12
Vote of Thanks 196
Wages, Trade Usages, and Hours of Labor, report on 176
Welcome, Address of, by President Krehbiel 5
Workmen's Certificates 40, 175

www.ingramcontent.com/pod-product-compliance
Lightning Source LLC
Chambersburg PA
CBHW032053220426
43664CB00008B/980